for
and a
beetle

for love and a beetle

A Tale of Two Journeys

by

Ivan Hodge with Petronella McGovern

Published in Australia in 1999 by
New Holland Publishers (Australia) Pty Ltd
Sydney • Auckland • London • Cape Town

14 Aquatic Drive Frenchs Forest NSW 2086 Australia
218 Lake Road Northcote Auckland New Zealand
24 Nutford Place London W1H 6DQ United Kingdom
80 McKenzie Street Cape Town 8001 South Africa

First published in 1999 and reprinted in 1999

National Library of Australia
Cataloguing-in-Publication Data:

Hodge, Ivan and McGovern, Petronella.
  For love and a beetle.

ISBN 1 86436 558 7

1. Hodge family—Journeys. 2. Volkswagen automobile.
I. McGovern, Petronella. II. Title.

910.4

Publishing Manager: Anouska Good
Editor: Catherine Hammond
Project Editor: Howard Gelman
Designer: Nanette Backhouse
Typesetter: Midland Typesetters
Printer: Griffin Press

Contents

The Journeys

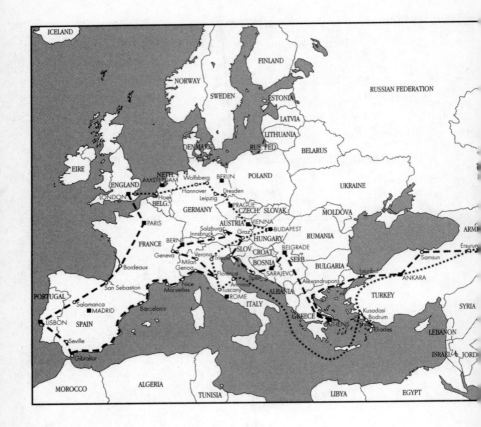

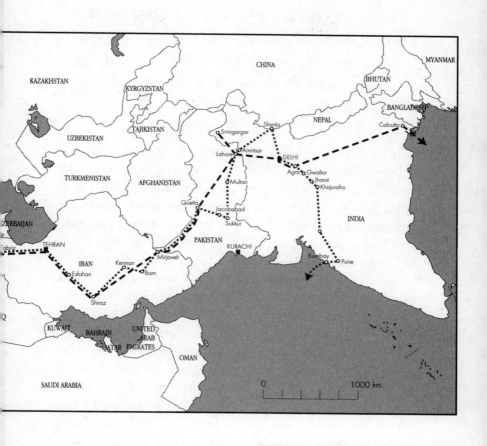

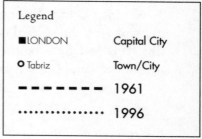

Legend

■ LONDON	Capital City
O Tabriz	Town/City
– – – – –	1961
....	1996

For our parents, Eveline and Reece and Joyce and Maurice who, like so many parents of young adults in the 1950 and 1960s, never had the chance to travel themselves, but proudly waved off their sons and daughters on overseas adventures

After the death of his mother, Ivan Hodge was reflecting on the past. Sorting through the memorabilia of 35 years, he and his wife Beth realised that their 1961 trip across Europe and Asia had been a unique adventure for them and their family. All the letters, postcards and tape recordings had been saved. It became obvious in 1996 that they should do it again. The original 1961 Beetle was back in their possession and they had the leisure and enthusiasm for travel. With the help of writer Petronella McGovern, they were able to chronicle their two momentous trips and the result is *For Love and a Beetle*.

Petronella McGovern is a Canberra based writer who has worked in marketing, advertising and journalism since she received her BA in Communications from UTS, Sydney. Like Ivan and Beth, she is an avid traveller. In 1996 she made a solo trip by bus, ferry and train from Sweden across Finland and Russia through China and down into Hong Kong. Her latest adventure was trekking in the Nepal Himalaya. She is grateful to Christina and Lyn for their introduction to the Hodges, and to her family, and Jamie for their love and support.

Chapter 1

Two Honeymoons and One Car

A year after I married Beth, I fell in love again. She was not as pretty as Beth, more of an ugly duckling, a rebellious type with a funny, unassuming personality. There was one similarity though. Beth was tiny (a nineteen-inch waist on our wedding day!), and so was she. It was an almost comical contrast to my height, and she proved to me, time and time again, that smallness and strength could go together. She had her quirks, but she was easy to look after and shared my boyish sense of adventure. Thirty-five years later, the relationship continued.

It was a love affair shared by many in the swinging sixties. The romance brought people together in a joyful camaraderie, recognising one another with a wave or a toot.

Beth fancied the unique beetle shape—she considered it smart. I loved her colour, her modern style and her loyalty, an engine which would never break down. It was the adoration of the non-mechanically-minded. Like us, she didn't quite conform to social norms. Other cars of the day were large and brash, she was petite and rounded. She made us the envy of our friends.

And we trusted her. *We could go anywhere in this car*, we thought, and we did. Our destiny was a foreign land, a continent away, driving through unknown countries in unimagined conditions. The three of us were game. The Beetle, Beth and I.

for love and a beetle

August 1996—London

Driving Down Memory Lane

We never expected the love affair to be so strong thirty-five years on—strong enough to take us from our comfortable apartment overlooking Sydney Harbour and back into the Beetle to retrace our tracks across the middle of the world.

We marvelled at the naiveté and courage we had had, as two wide-eyed Kiwis in 1961, to drive home from our fourteen-month sojourn in London. The memories of that journey are still alive in us. It was a world of daring, before the responsibilities of a family and business. A world where an aeroplane trip was out of our reach and international travel unconventional. London to Calcutta by Beetle; Calcutta to Auckland by sea.

And now we were setting off all over again. In a new time frame. London to Bombay. To see if we could. To recapture that freedom. To spend some time alone again after nearly forty years of marriage. We nicknamed ourselves 'Young Ivan and Beth'. It was to be our second honeymoon.

The old Beetle was probably in better shape than both Beth and I as we began the journey in August 1996. But the car seemed to have shrunk. We were accustomed to the length and width of our modern luxury sedans. It was not only that. My slim, fit, twenty-seven-year-old build had matured into a fuller sixty-two-year-old figure, which took up just a little more space in the car.

On the day of our departure from London, I surprised Beth. Sneaking up to Kensington High Street, I bought twelve red roses from the fruit and barrow boy, raced back to our apartment Copeland House and hid them under the stairs. After collecting

2

the last-minute items and the maps for western Europe, the first leg of our trip, Beth finally sat down inside the Beetle.

'These are for our second honeymoon,' I said, kissing her and presenting the roses. 'I hope the journey lasts longer than the flowers,' I joked, knowing that it would take a catastrophe to stop us making this trip.

Beth laughed, her blue eyes glistening, her cheeks flushed. 'You always were a smoothie, Ivan,' she quipped, as we both wondered where we would keep the roses in the overflowing back seat.

'I didn't pack a vase.' Beth was unhappy at being caught short when we were carrying items for almost every other eventuality. Unearthing the washing-up bucket, she filled it with a little water and lodged it behind her seat. The delicate scent sweetened the air inside the Beetle.

It was a jolly farewell. Waving goodbye were Caroline and Ian, Nanette and Stel, and the charming ninety-something Miss Kentish—all friends and colleagues from our London apartments. Nanette had cut some roses from the courtyard garden and placed them under the windscreen wiper. No-one would admit to the 'Just Married' sign on the back window. Red, white and blue balloons danced above the rear bumper. The years lifted from us and we felt that freedom again. Excitable as a young schoolboy on the first day of a never-ending summer, I tooted at the passing faces as we eased through the Saturday morning traffic on the streets of London. Children pointed at the balloons and people cheered at our 'Just Married' sign.

Within a few hours, our high spirits were crushed.

It had been going so smoothly. The drive down to Folkestone was pleasant on this clear day. Beth was amazed at the ease of the customs proceedings. We were treated differently this time: now that we were mature travellers setting off on a slightly eccentric

journey. As twenty-seven-year-olds in 1961, we had been inter-
rogated about the carnet, the Beetle's 'passport', before being
permitted on the ferry. On this summer day, thirty-five years later,
we simply bought our tickets for the next train on the 'Chunnel'
and then went duty-free shopping while we were waiting. The
sounds of England's latest pop sensation, Oasis, blared from the
speakers as we drank coffee.

We were back in the car, ready to drive onto the train, when
it happened. I turned the ignition. Silence. No gentle 'dak-dak-
dak' and the Beetle springing into action. Nothing. We were
about to embark on our eleven-thousand-mile journey and the
engine was dead.

Beth rested her head against the new lamb's wool seat cover, her
wavy light brown hair just below her ears (a shorter style than usual,
as this 'travel cut' had to last three months). She was pleased to be
doing the journey—that, I knew—but she wasn't so confident about
the Beetle. I had tried to convince her it was reliable. 'The Beetle
will just keep on going,' I had told her. Beth's logical reply was,
'Why should a thirty-six-year-old car survive that distance?'

As we were making our plans, she had declared, 'When the
Volkswagen factory check the car over and say it's okay, then I'll
be happy.'

But here we were, still on English soil, three countries from the
Volkswagen factory in Germany, and about to miss the next train
to Calais.

My mechanical skills, which could generously be described as
basic, were usually of little use. To Beth's astonishment, I thought
I could guess the problem: an oversight which I should have fixed
days ago. In fact, we were fortunate this hadn't occurred the day
before, when we were being filmed by TV New Zealand. At least
now only Beth would be privy to my forgetfulness.

'The battery leads mustn't be attached properly,' I muttered. 'The bloody shipping company should have done them up. We paid them enough money.' Beth glowered at me. She knew it was my fault, but as usual my reaction was to blame someone else. 'We'll have to unpack the back seat.'

In terse silence, our clothes and camping gear were piled onto the carpark tarmac for all to see. Cardboard boxes of food, pots and pans, cleaning products, toilet paper, clothes, linen, maps, tapes, books. The English watched without looking, whispering between themselves. Amused travellers stared openly.

Beth held her fury as her careful packing of the day before was destroyed. In our small car, everything had its place, the most frequently used items in quickly accessible spots to avoid partially unpacking each night.

The Beetle's wide doors made it easier to reach inside but still, we were tiring in the early afternoon heat. Thankfully, Beth was wearing trousers and could climb into the back seat without too much bother. Without a word, she passed everything out to me, handing it backwards. I knew it was an uncomfortable position and we weren't as supple as on the last trip. My joints and muscles ached with each bag I placed on the ground.

When we finally uncovered the battery, it was as I had thought. I felt pretty good that I'd solved the problem but stupid for having let it happen in the first place. The battery leads had been detached before the Beetle was shipped to London. It was raining at Tilbury Docks when I collected the car so I had quickly placed the leads on the battery, making a mental note to screw them on later at a more convenient moment—not at the entrance to the Chunnel!

Testing the battery, I turned the key again and was rewarded with a running engine. We both grunted in relief and began the task of re-packing. Little was said as we stuffed the gear back in.

Two hours later, we were ready to board the train. The incident did not bode well for a second honeymoon.

After we arrived in France, the score evened out and I had the chance to feel less stupid. As we came out of the Chunnel, now on the right-hand side of the road, Beth said to turn right. We took our roles seriously: I was the driver and she the navigator. I was not to question Beth on directions, and she would not comment on my driving skills. Half an hour after the right turn, Beth seemed agitated. She was saying little and flicking frantically through the large European road map.

Although unwilling to admit a navigational error on the first day, she finally spoke. 'I think we'd better turn around, otherwise we'll end up in Holland.'

It was ten more minutes before we could exit from the highway and double back onto the other side. I could be generous with her mistake because of mine. It was a square-off. After thirty-seven years of marriage, we recognised that in our relationship we occasionally experienced 'stress points', as we called them. In the short term, it could be tense but, in the long run, we tended to recover well and that was what mattered. There was no bearing grudges nor storming off; we dealt with the situation and then moved on.

Heading back in the right direction towards Brugge, we shared a good laugh. Beth had spent around thirty-five minutes studying our route during the Chunnel trip. She claimed her navigational skills were rusty and she was unaccustomed to the 'wrong' side of the road.

Our high spirits revived as we drove, listening to our voices from thirty-five years before. When we were living in London in 1960 and during the first trip in 1961, we had recorded tapes for our families back home, describing our experiences in detail for those who had never left New Zealand. The assurance of youth and the need to shelter our parents from worry meant our young Kiwi voices were filled with determination and conviction. The tapes had been our main form of communication on the overland journey.

Without our knowledge, our daughter Liza had taken the reel-to-reel cassettes from our apartment and had them copied onto regular tapes. Our youngest daughter, Britta, dropped them off to us in London. There was a tag attached to the package: 'Not to be opened until Day One'. The touching gift demonstrated our daughters' thoughtfulness, and my preoccupation. For thirty-five years, I had planned to transfer the tapes, but the everyday life of work and family had pushed the 1961 trip into the background.

The tapes brought the past into the present and two differences struck us immediately. This time, we knew what was in front of us (or so we thought); we weren't driving blindly into the unknown. And there was no shoestring budget. Our first night in 1961 had been spent camping in a French farmer's field. Tonight we were staying in a small hotel in the medieval city of Brugge, in the west of Belgium. Admittedly, we still had a budget and we were breaking it on our first night, too exhausted to search for a cheaper alternative. At least, this hotel was on a quiet street. There was no need to unpack the Beetle and we would receive breakfast.

After joining most of the population of Brugge for a city stroll on the cobblestone streets along winding canals, we ate *al fresco* at a pavement café. The romantic beauty of Brugge reminded us that this really was our second honeymoon, and we were free from the interruptions of our normal life. Exhausted, happy, we relaxed in our hotel room, watching the television and catching up on the results from the Atlanta Olympics.

Escaping from the Everyday

We had first discussed the idea of re-creating the trip two years before. The Beetle had been with Mum and Pop in Levin, New Zealand since we handed over the keys on the docks of Auckland in January 1962, irrevocably marking the end of our first overland trip. Tenderly cared for by Mum and expertly maintained by Terry Knowles, her local mechanic, the Beetle just went on and on.

Before Mum died, she had insisted the car be returned to us. In a way, we were both caretakers of the Beetle. While living in London, Beth and I had toured Europe in the car and then looked after it on the overland trip; Mum and Pop had taken over the driving seat for the next thirty-odd years until it came back to us. There was a lovely sense of continuity, of sharing back and forth between the generations.

With the keys in our hands once again, we had had to make a decision. Should we leave the Beetle with family in New Zealand or ship it to our home in Australia? There was a third possibility: to go back in time and retrace our steps.

We gathered our three adult daughters together for a family dinner one Sunday night, ready to announce our plans for the trip. The Beetle and its 1961 trip were a part of family folklore. Beth and I had talked about it on and off over the years, occasionally showing the slides or mentioning a suddenly remembered incident. We presumed the girls would be happy for us to go on another adventure. After all, we thought, there's nothing worse than staid, boring parents.

'Are you mad?' Shocked by our foolhardiness, Keris, Liza and Britta began shooting questions at us.

Beth's bacon-and-egg pie, their favourite dish, didn't even begin to mollify them. They simply didn't want us to go.

'It's an adventure,' Beth told them, 'and although you may think we're old, we don't feel much different from when we were twenty-five years old. You know, we still view the world through the same eyes.'

'It's dangerous,' Liza said.

'The car won't make it,' Keris said.

'What if you get sick?' Britta said.

Only later did we find out that Liza and Britta had good reason for worrying. Without telling us, they had recently been to the Turkish-Iranian border, where we were heading. It was not an experience they wanted us to share. There were guns going off around the area; men were constantly harassing them; and people had tried to break into their hotel room. With a chair jammed under the door handle, the two girls had lain awake all night, utterly terrified.

As we discussed the trip over and over with the girls, the parent–child relationship was reversed. 'Yes, we will be careful,' I found myself reassuring them. 'No, we won't drive at night. Yes, we will keep in contact. No, we won't take any risks.'

We weren't asking their permission or approval but, resignedly, they gave it.

'If this is what you really want to do, then we'll support you in it,' was the final remark.

However, there were conditions.

Keris insisted we take a mobile phone and a laptop, so we could communicate by email. We were happy with the idea. Now that the family was over the awkward, difficult stages of growing up, we all enjoyed one another's company and spoke on the phone or in person at least once a day. There was no doubt we would miss the girls and they us.

Britta insisted we do a first aid course. She was worried about me clumsily injuring myself while fixing the car, or forgetting my blood pressure pills and having a heart attack in the desert. Beth began organising a first aid course, but the timing became too difficult. In the end, our 'first aid course' consisted of my doctor's nurse throwing me to the floor of the clinic and demonstrating CPR on my chest, to the great amusement of Beth, who was laughing so hard her eyes filled with tears and she couldn't actually see.

'Don't worry,' we told Britta, 'we didn't do the course, but we're fully covered by travel insurance.' And we thought we were. Months later, however, after travelling through Turkey, Iran, Pakistan and India, we were to discover that our insurance had lapsed because the company sent the renewal to the wrong address.

Most of our friends were excited by our plans, pleased that adventuring was still a reality for our age group. A few were horrified: 'Why would you want to do it in a 1961 Beetle with no air-conditioning?' Some wanted to come along. It was a possibility for a while but, eventually, we decided against it because it would curtail our independence. We had travelled with friends over the years. This time, we were looking forward to being alone.

'Three months in a car with a husband? That's not a second honeymoon, that's torture,' one woman remarked to Beth.

We thought we'd be okay. Beth enjoyed navigating, I loved driving, and as long as we kept to our roles, there would be few disagreements. For the past few years, Beth and I had been working and travelling together. Our relationship had remained strong, and I believed it had been built on a solid basis: three months in a Beetle in 1961. At closer than arm's distance, we had gained an even greater understanding of each other, learning more and more, intensifying our three-year bond. Compromise had been an essential ingredient in survival—getting to the next town, finding the food markets, searching for petrol. With our friends and family half a world away, we had been solely dependent on one another.

I wanted to feel that sense of isolation from the 'real world' once again. The excitement, the adventure, the challenge. All of those things which made travelling a special time capsule in life. You could step outside the everyday of your own culture and get a glimpse into other lives. You could learn about people, while learning more about yourself, about your understanding of the world, your tolerances and your preconceptions.

It was an escape. Freedom.

But we still had to work around our business commitments. After resigning from a lifelong career in insurance, I had set up two businesses with Beth, aiming to give us more flexibility and the chance to travel. We could tag the beginning of our trip onto the end of a project for our incentive program company. In July, we would be running a program in San Francisco, and from there, we could fly straight to London.

Our other business, an apartment booking service, was now being managed by our eldest daughter, Keris, although I still remained 'involved'. Beth compared it to an obsession with golf. 'Some men take up golf as a hobby, but you don't, Ivan. Your hobby is the office. You wouldn't know what to do with yourself if you didn't go up there and find out what was happening every day.'

The biggest wrench for Beth was saying good-bye to Tahni, Liza's son and our delightful two-year-old grandchild. 'My little angel', as he was affectionately called by Beth, was equally upset about his grandmother's disappearance. 'Bumma,' he cried to Beth, unable to pronounce Grandma, his dark brown eyes pitiful.

Our timing also meant helping to arrange a wedding en route, for Liza was to be married in late December. We were hoping there would be no hold-ups on the long drive.

August was the month to leave London. Snow was likely to block the road in Iran from November to April. The sun would cause problems in the summer and there were monsoons in India through June and July. The route wasn't hard to plan. We still had much of the information from 1961, including the Automobile Association strip maps which helpfully described the road conditions as 'poor to fair' or 'good'. As we pulled the boxes out from the garage, we were stunned by our lack of knowledge the last time we set off.

'We just drove, didn't we?' Beth commented. 'We weren't even aware of half the historic sites. I guess the Middle East wasn't in our school curriculum in 1955.' She wanted a reason for our ignorance of world history.

'But remember what it was like,' I reminded her. 'People didn't travel much. Everyone was stunned when we said we were going to live in London for a few years. The only time your father left New Zealand was to go to war.'

1959–1961

The Extended Honeymoon

An overland journey from London to Calcutta is perfectly feasible in almost any type of car in good condition. Good springs, heavy duty shock absorbers and a high ground clearance are all, however, advisable. One month of daylight driving would be a very good time, but allows no time off for sight-seeing, accidents or hold-ups. (Report from the Oxford and Cambridge Far Eastern Expedition 1955/1956)

The first successful attempt to drive from London to Singapore was chronicled in 1956. A party from Oxford and Cambridge Universities had undertaken The Far Eastern Expedition in two Landrover station wagons equipped with powerful drum winches. Previous attempts had been thwarted by the Burma stretch, with its near impassable roads and political obstacles to entering the country.

In 1961, just five years later, we were attempting the route to Calcutta in a VW Beetle with low clearance and no four-wheel-drive option. Reading material on the overland trip was scarce. There was the university report from The Far Eastern Expedition and Tim Slessor's book *First Overland*. We sent an outline of our route to the Automobile Association in London, and they provided strip maps, mileage and brief notes, free of charge.

In 1961 the overland trip was still novel but, by the end of the decade, it was to become the well-travelled Hippie Trail to India and Nepal. Landrover had sponsored The Far Eastern Expedition, so I felt it worthwhile asking the same of Volkswagen. Sitting at the big dining room table in our rented apartment, Beth and I carefully drafted a letter asking for support. Their reply was short and polite: 'Volkswagen cannot provide sponsorship but we wish you luck on your journey'.

Although we didn't realise it at the time, we needed luck. With no handy travel guides in the bookshops, the little we did know was gleaned from other travellers and the driver of an overland bus. The advice was simple: 'Watch out in Turkey, they throw stones at the car. Don't drink the water in India.'

Our chief concern was mechanical problems. 'It is wise to be able to repair and maintain one's vehicle, especially in areas where break-down means personal risk for lack of supplies,' The Far Eastern Expedition advised. With the brashness of youth, we were certain that as long as the engine kept going and we didn't get lost, we'd make it home. We never envisaged being stranded in the desert due to lack of petrol.

According to our research, we had all the necessary provisions. The car was brimming with our new equipment: a two-man tent, stretcher beds, pillows, table, chairs, primus stove, pots, kettle and lamp. On the roof racks, we carried possessions from our fourteen months in England, wrapped tightly in an oilskin. Everyday clothes were inside the car, including a sweater for those cold desert nights; tucked behind the seats was the food: thirty-six tins of soup, twenty of meat, sixteen of baked beans, four packets of jelly, three bags of sweets and sixteen bottles of fruit juice. We also had a medical kit, a spare parts kit, a letter of credit from Westminster Bank, and a tight budget: one pound a day for the car and one pound a day for us.

I fancied myself as a radio interviewer and was recording the trip for the folks at home on my new Stuzzi transistor tape recorder. My friends had nicknamed me Richard Dimbleby, after the famous BBC commentator. On leaving London, I interviewed the VW mechanic opposite Lord's Cricket Ground ('Good luck, Mr Hodge') and talked to an ice-cream vendor near the Tower Bridge ('Two lemon ices, please, these will be our last ice-creams in London').

Driving around Trafalgar Square one final time, I recalled the young American student I had interviewed there in June. He was walking to Moscow on a 'Ban the Bomb' rally.

'We stand for equal opposition to nuclear weapons for both the Eastern and Western countries,' he had declared in an American twang. 'It remains to be seen whether we will find anyone in the Soviet Union who feels the same way we do about it.'

Some students had already marched four thousand miles

from San Francisco to Washington DC to demand unconditional disarmament. They were a scruffy, beatnik crowd claiming to be Buddhist by religion. With the haughty wisdom of a twenty-seven-year-old who had started work at fifteen, I felt these enthusiastic young students didn't fully understand the ramifications of what they were doing.

At the end of the year, we chanced on a newspaper article stating that thirty pacifists from the USA and eight other countries had arrived in Moscow, where they won permission to argue their case for unilateral disarmament. It was reported that the protesters found many Muscovites unaware of the Soviet Union's decision to resume atomic testing. Marvelling at the courage of the protesters, marching through Europe as the Berlin Wall crisis escalated, I wondered if my acquaintance had made it to the end.

I enjoyed interviewing people, but the Stuzzi machine was more accustomed to my own voice, intoning our every step. Recognising the significance of the moment, I spoke solemnly as we set sail for France, the very first step of our overland expedition from London to Calcutta.

It's farewell to England on the seventh of August 1961. We're very sorry to be leaving London. It has been a wonderful experience, and we don't know when we might be back. But what more fitting place to depart than the White Cliffs of Dover? We're feeling a little mixed at this stage and wondering if we're doing the right thing. I think when we've been travelling a day or two and starting to enjoy the wonders of Europe, we'll be one hundred per cent sure.

Our leaving was made even more difficult by our New Zealand friends, Barry and Joan. They had accompanied us from London, the four of us camping overnight in Kent.

We were all still high on the euphoria of their wedding just two weeks before. In the absence of their families, Beth and I had helped to organise the event and recorded the ceremony to send back to their parents. Our old home was to be their new one. They were moving into our flat at Clapton Common. Barry and Joan were dear friends and we would miss them terribly.

We could see them now, high on the cliffs, furiously waving the picnic rug on which we had eaten an early lunch just an hour before. It was a burst of brilliant red between the dazzling white chalk and the deep blue sky. The colours of the Union Jack.

'They're lucky it's not windy,' Beth said, laughing, 'or they'd take off and follow us right over to France.' In fact, Barry and Joan were planning to drive in our tyre tracks. They hoped to buy a Beetle and take the same route home next year. We had been dubbed 'the advance party'.

Despite her light-heartedness, Beth was hiding tears behind her large white sunglasses, the style which was later to become known as the Jackie O look. A jumble of emotions tore at us: regret at leaving London; excitement about the journey; and the antici-pation of being with our families once again.

The afternoon sun was playing in the patchwork fields by the time we found the ideal farmhouse. Down a narrow lane, a few miles from the highway, it was in a secluded position which suited us perfectly. A lady stood on the step with her young daughter, waiting, as though we were expected. Like most farming women we had seen that day, she was dressed in black; the lines on her face told of many seasons toiling under the open sky. She watched suspiciously as Beth and I clambered from the Beetle.

'Bonjour,' I called out cheerfully, using up a third of my French vocabulary. 'We are looking for a place to camp the night and we wondered if we could stay in one of your fields.'

With Beth miming the actions and me handing over four of the duty-free cigarettes we'd bought on the ferry, the woman soon led us to a spot further down the lane. With that unabashed curiosity inherent in children, the little girl stared as we set about unpacking the car and putting up the tent. By the time dinner was on the boil, the mother and daughter had disappeared, replaced by another farmer sucking on a cigarette. He wandered around the car, babbled away in French and looked closely to see what we were eating: a tin of baked beans heated up on our Primus cooker. We tried to tell him that we were from New Zealand. The chap just laughed, shook my hand and walked off down the lane.

Although we had lived in the Northern Hemisphere for over a year, the late evening light was still a novelty. For once though, the lack of darkness wouldn't affect our sleep. Exhausted from the excitement, we were craving an early night. It had been a long day—the farewell from our friends in Dover and that niggling sense of trepidation that is a travelling companion at the beginning of every journey. We had no concept of what lay ahead.

'And so ends Day One,' I mumbled to Beth, curling up to stop my feet hanging over the bottom of the new camp stretcher bed.

We had left New Zealand in September 1959 on what was to become an extended two-and-a-half-year honeymoon. Six months in Sydney, a cruise to Italy and then fourteen months of glorious London. It was not 'the done thing' for young married couples to be jaunting around the world. We were supposed to be starting a family. Beth had assumed that after the wedding we would build a house on our block of land in Rotorua, but she was soon swept away with my grand plans. Our single friends were disappearing off overseas, so I felt we should, too. Settling down seemed less and less appealing as we inspected the massive ships in the harbour waiting to take our friends across the oceans to faraway England.

Our travel plans were accepted enthusiastically by our parents, possibly due to the way we announced them. We had driven down to Levin four months before the wedding to tell our families what we wanted to do. It was a Sunday afternoon and Beth's parents had made the six-hour drive from Rotorua. All were relaxing on the rusty brown lounge suite under Goldie's painting of a Maori warrior. The mothers sipped gin and Pop had brought out a flagon of beer for the men. They assumed we had gathered to discuss wedding details.

'We've got some news for you,' I announced. Deathly silence. Beth's mum raised her spectacles. Her father straightened his dark green cardigan. Pop was staring at his lighted cigarette and Mum's eyes were fixed at a point near Beth's waist.

I stammered on, 'We're planning to go overseas after the wedding.'

Broad smiles and the chatter began.

Only on the drive back to Rotorua did Beth and I realise what had happened. They had assumed 'news' meant Beth was pregnant, a disgrace for all concerned. No wonder then they were pleased we were travelling; our plans were merely unorthodox, not a reason for social shame.

Flying into Sydney a week after the wedding, we were amazed at the never-ending suburbs and disappointed by the airport. Kingsford Smith was a collection of dusty sheds, unfit for a city of this size, we felt.

Beth spent hours in the city shops. 'Farmers Department Store is so large you could spend a whole week here and still not see everything,' I announced in awe on our first shopping outing. The solid brick houses weren't as pretty as our wooden New

Zealand ones painted and adorned with the latest fad—bright, colourful butterflies. But that didn't matter; this was a whole new lifestyle. Drive-in theatres, bars with topless women, stronger beer, the latest fashions, double-decker buses, the AWA Tower reaching up into the sky, a huge ferry to Manly complete with resident pianist and violinist. We wrote home wide-eyed, dazzled by this huge, cosmopolitan city.

But what we were really looking forward to was London . . .

1960–61—London

Royal Garden Parties and Nylon Housecoats

A month aboard an Italian cruise ship, appropriately named the *Sydney*, and three weeks catching trains through Europe finally brought us to London, the seat of the British Empire and home to the Royal Family.

We were captivated. The landmarks and streets, recognisable from films, matched our imaginations precisely. Indoctrinated through school history by the might of the Empire and the significance of the Queen, we took England into our hearts. It never occurred to us to question British rule of New Zealand or debate the role of the Royal Family.

Not long after we arrived, Beth went to watch The Trooping of the Colour with her Rotorua friend, Annie. She described its glory in one of our weekly letters home:

It was a miserable day but, luckily, right at 11am when the Queen set out, it cleared up. We got a position at the back of the footpath on Horse Guard's Parade, where the ceremony is held. We were sitting up on a rail and had a wonderful view. Firstly eight hundred soldiers complete with tall bearskin hats and red coats, accompanied by various bands, marched from the Palace up the Mall to the Horse Guard's Parade Ground. Then came about one hundred mounted soldiers, all with brass breastplates and the loveliest black horses. Sharp on 10:55am, the Queen Mother and Princess Anne passed us in an open carriage. The Queen rode in at 11am with the Duke of Edinburgh and the Duke of Gloucester. We had a smashing view of the Queen inspecting the ranks and of the formation marching. Then we ran all the way back down the Mall to see the Royal Family come out on the balcony of the Palace.

Little did we know we would soon be privileged to an insider's view of Buckingham Palace. My aunt in Hamilton, NZ, asked her local Member of Parliament if we could be invited to the Royal Garden Party. He wrote off to the NZ High Commission in London, our names were put on the list and we received a royal invitation to the party on 21 July, 1960.

It was an occasion for great excitement, one which made page four of *The Daily Post* back home:

Rotorua Couple at the Palace

Few of the Rotorua people who knew Ivan Hodge and Beth Mudge ever expected to hear of them attending a Royal garden party at Buckingham Palace. Mr and Mrs Hodge, who were married in Rotorua last September, arrived in England in May and attended the garden party recently.

In a recent letter to her parents, Mr and Mrs M.H. Mudge of James Street, Mrs Hodge described the day.

'Ivan's first visit was to Moss Brothers, specialists in hiring clothes, where he acquired a top hat and tails.'

Ann Tompkins, also a Rotorua girl, lent them her car: a

traditional English taxi which she bought for £75, and is now driving in Russia.

'When we left for the Palace, all our neighbours turned out to see us go, Ivan driving and me sitting in the back, his passenger,' wrote Mrs Hodge.

New Shirt

On the way to the Palace, the couple stopped to buy a special type of shirt to go with the tails.

'We caused quite a stir when Ivan stripped to the waist in Horse Guard's Parade to put on his new shirt,' she continued.

When they arrived, the couple were shown into an ornately designed room, where people were welcomed, and shown to period chairs.

Later, guests went out on the lawn, where the Royal Family appeared at 4pm. The crowd formed lanes through which the Royal hosts, including the Queen, Duke of Edinburgh, Queen Mother, Duchess of Kent, and her son, the Duke, and the Earl and Countess of Harewood, walked.

'We had a good look at the Duke, who is different to his photographs. He wore a huge gold ring—almost a knuckle duster—on his little finger,' wrote Mrs Hodge.

After about an hour, the Royal guests and diplomats went to one pavilion for afternoon tea and the other guests were entertained in another building.

Queen Beautiful

'The Queen looked beautiful. She has the most perfect skin I have seen, and wore little make-up,' commented Mrs Hodge.

After signing the Royal visitors' book, they left the Palace about 7pm and returned to their flat in Clapton Common.

When the newspaper clipping arrived from Mum Mudge, Beth and I giggled at the idea of the young Hodges on intimate terms with the Royal Family. If Rotorua knew how easy it was to be invited, they wouldn't have been half as impressed.

'We'll be the first to arrive and the last to leave,' we had repeated to each other, determined to make the most of our Royal outing. High tea was catered by the Lyons Corner House chain, and we delicately stuffed ourselves on cucumber sandwiches, pastries and scones. As newcomers to England, we were unsuccessful in our search for famous faces among the garden party guests; we only recognised the most obvious.

The royal invitation had stated 'no photography allowed', but an amateur enthusiast like me wasn't going to let that get in the way of this excellent picture opportunity. Beth carefully shielded me from other guests as I snapped shots of the gardens and the back of Buckingham Palace.

At 7pm, the attendants ushered the stragglers out through the gates. We were delighted with our first royal outing. Beth had fitted in perfectly, sipping tea elegantly in her rose-patterned 'going away' frock from the wedding. The pink hat, shaped much like a shower cap, and matching pink gloves were all the rage. At our flat, when I held the door open for Beth to alight from Annie's taxi, I saw the flicker of curtains: neighbours craning to watch this young couple putting on airs. Hoping to avoid neighbourly resentment, I playfully drop-kicked my top hat far into the backyard, and then had to scramble over the fence and hedges to retrieve it. Beth undressed for bed but, as I'd paid a small fortune for my hired suit, I was planning to get the most out of it. After carefully hanging up my jacket, I climbed into bed, proudly wearing my trousers and shirt all night and into the morning, until the suit had to be returned to Moss Brothers.

On moving into the flat in Clapton Common, we discovered the stereotype was true. The English really did bathe just once a week. Mrs Silverman, the Jewish landlady, who lived on the bottom floor, came to collect our first week's rent, £5/12/6, and asked when we would like to use the bath.

'Mary, the Scottish girl in number two, has a bath on Tuesdays,' she informed us. 'What day would you like?'

'Every other day,' I replied.

My answer was not received well. The landlady had to stoke up the furnace for the hot water but, as we were paying rent, she had no choice but to agree. We were flabbergasted at the thought of having to share a bathroom; at home, every flat had its own. And how could we be expected to bathe just once a week, when London was so grimy? Soot from the chimneys mixed with exhaust from the buses, building up the smog hanging over the city. After each shopping trip, Beth's petticoat was covered in dust. When the landlady went to Cornwall for a week, we crept down to the furnace and stoked it up for a bath every day.

Our one-bedroom flat soon became a meeting point for New Zealanders dropping into London. Our friends, Bev, Ngaire (otherwise known as Hoopy) and Annie, were in England before us, and once they had settled us in, they spent much of their time in our flat. Audrey and Mary, two Australian girls we had met in Italy, were a part of our ever-growing social circle. Until Barry arrived from his travels in Canada, I was often the only man amongst the highly spirited girls, who involved me in their antics.

One morning, Annie turned up at the door in her old black London taxi. We set off for Bradwell-on-Sea, seven girls and me. By the end of the trip, my hair was hidden beneath Bev's red scarf, the girls insistent that people were laughing at us because there was one man among seven girls! Adorned with paintings of a kiwi, a map of New Zealand, a tiki and Mickey Mouse, Annie's black taxi travelled all over Europe. Annie thought life a laugh, and it was only after strong objection from fellow travellers that the black taxi didn't make it to Russia. Increasing international tension meant Westerners were likely to find travel in the Soviet Union difficult and dangerous.

We had South African friends and Canadian acquaintances popping in. Weary travellers slept on our settee—or, if that were already taken, curled up on the floor—and enjoyed one of Beth's home-cooked meals.

Through our jobs, Beth and I made English friends and learnt more about the country and its habits. We never could under-stand, however, why the English wouldn't take their jackets off at the beach.

It was easy to find work with a letter of introduction from an insurance firm in Australia. I continued in my career, this time with Noble Lowndes. Mr Lowndes, himself a New Zealander, could be spotted driving through London in his black Rolls Royce Silver Cloud. With business nous, Mr Lowndes had taken offices near Harrods in Knightsbridge, on Lowndes Street. He had us believing it was named after him.

I would save up my work luncheon vouchers to treat Beth and myself to a special meal at The Stockpot every few weeks: shepherd's pie, spaghetti, and ice-cream with chocolate sauce. We would dress for the occasion, me in my stovepipe pants and Beth in her new London frock, white wool and raffia woven in stripes with a fleck of gold lurex and a gold kid belt.

Beth found various teaching jobs. In the holidays she worked at an upmarket china store. Her school children were impressed that she drove a car to work each day and nicknamed her Stirling Moss. It was in the early days of comprehensive schools when the concept of selective education was new to us. Letters home expressed her horror:

I am the Art Mistress at a Secondary Modern School. The kids have all failed their exams and can't go to Grammar School. It's awful to see tiny twelve-year-olds staggering around in heels higher than mine. They mainly wear straight, very tight skirts and blouses or jumpers. There are a large variety of hair-dos, with many wearing their hair pinned up. The boys are in jeans and leather jackets.

It was a culture shock for Beth, who thought the children were probably swearing but she'd never encountered those words before! In response to her reprimands, the boys replied that they'd 'get' their mothers onto her.

At her next school, Beth was thrilled when Mr Newell, a fellow teacher, asked if her class wanted to come to the Tower of London. We hadn't seen many landmarks and she thought it an excellent opportunity to do some sightseeing during work. On the appointed hour, the two classes arrived at the gates of the Tower and were handed into the care of the guides. Mr Newell turned to Beth and said, 'Right then, we're off to the pub until they're finished.'

Beth said she should have learnt from that experience. A few weeks later, Mr Newell's class was going in Epping Forest and, once again, he asked, did Mrs Hodge's class want to join them? *I'll see a bit of the countryside*, Beth thought, putting on her flat shoes and a light coat. As soon as they stepped off the train, Mr Newell went blundering into the forest at a cracking pace. 'You bring up the rear,' he shouted over his shoulder.

The two classes arrived at the other side three children short. Mr Newell dashed off to find the missing ones, sending Beth and the children back through the forest with no idea of the way through the massive trees and maze of paths. Cars were parked in little lanes, and Beth worried that the missing children had been taken by strangers.

Somehow they found themselves at the train station. It was a rush against time. Parents would be outside the school gates at 3pm. Speeding past one of the smaller stations, Beth recognised the two girls on the platform. They stopped the train and hauled them aboard. The third child, a boy, had conned money from the other two and caught a train by himself. Once safely back in the playground, they weathered the nervous concern of the school and the wrath of the parents. Needless to say, Beth never went on another excursion with Mr Newell.

Years later, on holiday in England with our young daughters, Beth stopped outside her old work place to show them a typical school. Peeping through the fence, she saw an older man on playground duty. 'Have you been working here for a long time?' she asked. Taking one long hard look at her, he responded with two words: 'Epping Forest'. It was Mr Newell! There was laughter all round. Neither of them had ever forgotten the horror of losing three children.

Fabulously well paid by New Zealand standards, we would spend our money on shows and entertainment. We were fascinated by the slick productions and began a ritual of seeing a show every Friday night, followed by a snack in a Lyons Corner House. It was the era of *My Fair Lady, Oliver, The Sound of Music* and *West Side Story*. We went along to the Covent Garden Opera, the Bolshoi Ballet and the Russian Circus. The glamour entranced us, but we were still sometimes shocked by the risqué costumes and dancing. *Psycho* and *Ben Hur* played on the big screens. *Lady Chatterly's Lover* was released, with bookshops selling out. Beth and I snagged a copy, battling with each other to read the book first. 'We can't quite see what the fuss is all about,' we told our parents, pretending to be worldly. The book was banned in New Zealand, so we posted a copy home, wrapped as a present.

Some of the best entertainment we created ourselves. A rowdy group of twenty-somethings making the most of their youth before conforming to society and settling down in their home country. The Londoners were charming and hospitable, welcoming us into their lives. They invited us to dinner; whirled us off to dances; accompanied us to the beach; and lent us their weekend cottages. Whatever we did, it had that Kiwi influence on it. Like the time we went to Speakers' Corner in Hyde Park.

9 August 1960, 50 Clapton Common, London E5
Dear Mum and Pop

Well, I'm afraid our letter writing has slipped a little but I can assure you we have good intentions. Our social program in London is fantastic, we hardly have a moment to ourselves. We have had people staying with us continuously at the flat—God knows what the owners think, but they have not complained.

The Saturday before last, Bev, Hoopy, Annie, Gary (a Kiwi airforce boy and friend of the girls), the taxi and us went off into the city. We drove down to Hyde Park and the soap box orators were in action—the varying subjects: flying saucers, religion, politics, etc. One group was singing Irish songs. Well, with Annie leading, we started Maori songs, and immediately people circled us for more. The poor Irish singers stopped to watch. We performed for ten minutes and had a great time. Our Irish competitors soon realised our assets and helped us on the popular tunes. There was quite an audience.

The next day we slept late but, about 2pm, headed for Henlow, the RAF camp where Gary is training. It was a lovely day and the English countryside at its best. We stopped at Bernard Shaw's home, now a National Trust place and saw the simple way he lived. Also went through his photo album—in it, shots taken when he was in Rotorua.

On the way home we stopped for a spot at a little English pub. We invaded the pub, ordered our pints of bitter and started singing Maori songs again. Well, it was not long before the whole bar was enjoying it. A chap joined us and shouted drinks. He had an interest in NZ as he had worked on Auckland Bridge, but the 'missus wouldn't live over there'. At closing time, we were made to sing 'Now is the Hour'. Outside they asked 'When can you come back again?' The chap took us to his house for a cup of tea. His wife didn't know what was happening, but she accepted us all very well.

Time is really flying by—can hardly believe we have been away from NZ for eleven months. This time last year we were full of wedding preparations. We certainly feel much 'older' now. Travel really is a wonderful thing.

Love to all, Ivan and Beth

PS Married life is okay too.

Letters to our parents didn't contain the full truth. Married life was much better than 'okay'. We were in love, happy and free, doing exactly what we liked in an anonymous city of millions. We could be who we wanted, breaking free of the constraints, the hopes and expectations of a close family and a small town.

Television, the most amazing invention, had become affordable, but it was to be a few months before we hired a set for our flat. Not long after we arrived in London, I was desperate to see the Test cricket. I went down to the local shop and asked for a 'testing'. We had a half hour discussion, and then it was arranged that a TV set would be delivered, free for a week for us to 'test'. Each night, we viewed until we fell asleep in the chair, foregoing our usual outings for the televised programs: cricket, Wimbledon and Sammy Davis Junior. 'Less blood and thunder than Australian TV,' Beth declared, particularly impressed with the BBC.

We were 'testing' the TV the same week we moved into our new flat, so we left the TV set to be picked up from Bev and Hoopy's place. The girls decided to take advantage of the situation and kept the set for the weekend. On the Friday, when the van arrived, Bev and Hoopy wouldn't answer the door. On the Saturday, the van was outside their flat when they returned from shopping, so they continued walking straight past. Finally on Monday, they let the chap take it away, after a wonderful weekend of watching.

For the next few months, we had to be invited out to see any television. The South African chap in the flat above ours would have me up to watch the rugby and the cricket. Bev and Hoopy bought a second-hand set at the markets; the picture was fine once Gary had fiddled with it. The antenna, a piece of wire hanging out the window, was secured with their iron tied to the end.

In October 1960 we hired our own set, lucky to find a shop which didn't demand the minimum four-year rental. For the first few weeks we barely moved from the screen. Eventually Beth made a rule that we eat dinner in the other room, but that meant gobbling down our food and rushing back so we wouldn't miss too much of the program. My favourite 'viewing' was sport, any kind. Beth was obsessed by cowboys and Westerns. We hardly noticed the cold winter nights as we sat inside, transfixed by the box.

At the beginning of 1961, I wrote to my family, extolling the benefits of the TV set:

Firstly all the very best for the New Year. I hope the general situation in the world improves, but with the Laos outbreak, Congo, Cuba and Belgium domestic trouble, it is doubtful if the world has entered a new year on a worse note. Television is a wonderful medium for bringing the world to your fireside. It's so easy to sit and enjoy it for the evening. The important snag is that our letter writing gets behind.

We had wished for a white Christmas, but instead it was mild, and I walked to the off-licence with neither a sweater nor a coat. In the lead-up to Christmas, we had attended parties and dances, pleasantly surprised that drinking in dance halls was legal, unlike New Zealand, where there were police patrols ready to fine those sneaking a drop within a one-mile radius of the dance. Beth had her hair 'done' at the hairdresser, back-combed until she was nearly crying. It was stuck in the beehive for days afterwards.

While it was plain murder to shop for presents, the streets of London stunned us with their Christmas lights. Huge angels blowing gold trumpets floated above Regent Street. Ladies and gents in fine fur coats stepped out of Rolls Royces and Bentleys in Bond Street. Ever fashion-conscious, Beth was most impressed by the shops and had to mention them to her mother:

The shops are beautiful. From a woman's point of view, the lingerie, the shoes and the slippers are wonderful. Thousands of sorts of slippers, furry or feathery or frilly or lacy. Another fascinating thing is they have a type of boot, it's like a gumboot, only it's on a high heel—some of them trimmed with fur. They even have it put out in white satin with white fur at the top and a matching bag.

Beth bought a pair of white lace-up boots, so tight she almost had a hernia getting them on. The sides were elasticised and came to just below her knee, impossible for her to take off when she was tired. I would unlace them and use all my strength to pull backwards while she muttered about the agonies of fashion.

On Christmas Eve, I rushed to the city to buy Beth's present, expecting last-minute mayhem, but the shops were nearly empty, the staff already setting up the windows for the after-Christmas sales. My find, a nylon-padded housecoat with slippers to match, was a big hit with Beth, nylon being the most popular fabric on the fashion scene, or so I imagined.

The Christmas preparations took weeks as Beth and I organised the logistics of lunch for nine in our little flat. We set up the tree with a few friends and a few drinks, and I recorded a Christmas tape for our families in New Zealand:

Merry Christmas to everyone at home. We're just decorating the tree which Gary got from the Henlow Army Base. At 5am he climbed the tree outside the Officers' Mess and lopped the top off, put it on Annie's taxi and brought it back to London. Left quite an eyesore apparently. We've got it in our lounge window. Beth has just informed us that it's against the law. Getting a Christmas tree in London is difficult but not for us New Zealanders. We're all buying each other a small present between 2/6 and 3 bob. Here's my darling little wife, who's suffering a little from the sherry.

Hello everyone, this is Beth and I'm not suffering at all. We've done up the Christmas tree beautifully. You wouldn't believe it—the staff at school have to put on a Christmas play for the children. We're doing Aladdin and I'm a coolie slave. You have to get up there and dance and sing and generally make a fool of yourself. We also have a party at school with champagne and sauternes and wine. But now instead of having it the day after the play, we have to have it the day before, because the school inspector is coming and it's against the law to have liquor on the premises. Anyway, here's Annie to say a few words.

Annie here and I'm going to tell you my impressions of London. Every morning we are packed onto the tube like sardines. And perhaps on the way down to the station, we'll find a bowler-hatted English gentleman saying 'Be British, buy British'. Further down on the station platform, we'll find the porters, mostly Africans and Indians, saying 'Let them off, gar, garn, move along, doors, doors, mind ya backs'. Then out on the street are the flower sellers and the newspaper men yelling 'Flowas, Getcha flowaaaass. Hellooo, Times, Daily Mirraaaa!' As I walk across Green Park towards Buckingham Palace, I find the bowler-hatted gentlemen once again who are coming from Victoria on their way to Piccadilly. 'Hmm, jolly good, Michael,' and, 'That's just not cricket, old chap.' Really, the English have to be heard to be believed!

Our cheerful Christmas was tinged with sadness. We knew our life in London was breaking up. Bev had already gone home to be married, Beth and I were leaving on our overland trip in six months and the others were talking of travelling around Europe. We'd all had such fun. It was too good to last.

Chapter 2

The Travel Bug

A Volkswagen is never outmoded. Indeed no one knows how long a Volkswagen lasts; the first VWs made have not worn out.
VW Advertising Poster, 1959

As a young couple enjoying all that London had to offer, our wages disappeared on sightseeing and entertainment. The little we did save wasn't nearly enough to buy a new car. We were resigned to doing the overland trip in a second-hand vehicle, but the mechanical aspect worried me greatly. Old cars broke down. Annie's taxi was forever coming to a halt by the side of the road although, with her looks and shapely figure, she never had any problems finding assistance. Passing motorists piled into traffic jams in their rush to help. But we were crossing the desert. We needed something more reliable than good looks.

I had a plan . . .

London, 27 July, 1960

Dear Mum and Pop,

We are thinking of buying a car as we really need one to get about and see things. However, you may be interested in a suggestion—a 'new car'! As you probably know, we can buy new cars over here without purchase tax, which makes them fairly reasonable. In twelve months, we must leave with the car or are liable for tax here. However, when the car arrives in NZ, if it is twelve months old, it comes into the country as personal property, free of tax.

I have made a few enquiries and prices here without tax are: New Anglia £436; Morris Traveller £495; Austin A40 £456; VW £439; Austin A55 £585; Consul approx £560. Freight charges from the UK to NZ would be about £90 to £100.

33

If you are interested, we would consider buying one now and in twelve months you could reimburse us, or we could pay fifty-fifty now. It is just a suggestion, but possibly a sound idea to get an almost new car home. We would, of course, use the vehicle but would pay for the use of it. By far, the best buy is the VW. It would mean getting one over from Germany but, from memory, they retail in NZ for about £930. The prices quoted are for deluxe models in all cases.

By the way, the All Blacks had a win—good show but paper coverage here is very poor, they virtually only put the score.

Love, Beth and Ivan

European cars were an anomaly on New Zealand roads, and a Volkswagen would give Mum additional status. In truth, she probably agreed simply for my sake. As the youngest child, I was the apple of her eye. She let me do whatever I liked. 'Don't go to school today if you don't feel like it,' she'd say.

My mother grew up in Raetihi, a remote farming area in the mountains, where she learnt to live by her own rules, but within limits. Beth and I were doing what she really wanted to do herself· travelling around the world. She was keen to help us experience it.

We settled on a Beetle from a dealer in St John's Wood, near Lord's Cricket Ground. Despite the appearance of smallness, it was true what they said about the headroom and legroom. My six-foot-two frame fitted comfortably with headroom to spare, possibly endorsing the advertising claims: 'you can still wear a top hat', although I never did put it to the test. My only occasion to wear a top hat, the Royal Garden Party, had already passed.

The VW Beetle was on its rise to meteoric success, with the four millionth vehicle coming off the production line that year. There were waiting lists in America where, to the amazement of industry onlookers who had predicted the 'Nazi' car would fail, the Beetle had taken over the imported car market. In England, I was told our order would be at least six weeks. It was a bother as we now had to hire a rental car for our holiday to Scotland. We were going up there with Audrey and Mary, and visiting Beth's great-auntie Allison on the way.

We went in to finalise the paperwork and choose the colour; the dealer swept open the door for us beaming, we thought, with the anticipation of the sale.

'Now if you're not too fussy about the colour, sir,' he addressed me, 'you could have your 1961 model Volkswagen by the end of next week.' Beth and I gaped at the man, a magician pulling a rabbit from an empty hat.

Over the sound of Beth's 'Gosh!', I asked, 'What colour?'

I didn't mind as long as it wasn't black, which I felt was too hard to keep clean. Really, colour wasn't an issue; the concept of actually owning a new car outweighed the choice of colour.

The dealer smiled, 'Gulf Blue, sir.'

'We can have a blue Volkswagen next week, Ivan!' Beth repeated in amazement.

'Gulf Blue, madam,' the dealer corrected her, 'Gulf Blue.'

Not only Blue, a colour we would have chosen ourselves, but 'Gulf Blue', a new shade in the Volkswagen range. Very smart, very modern. I was so excited that I didn't bother to ask how or why the car was suddenly available.

The agreement was signed for one Gulf Blue VW Deluxe Saloon Beetle 1961, Right Hand Drive, fitted with Locking Engine Hood, American Type Bumpers 94/107 and M128 (White Wall Tyres). £439 plus £7 for documentation. Our new model would be one of the first on the road in London. QJ-3951. The Q indicated it was a car to be exported.

for love and a beetle

Dear Mum and Pop,

Thursday 25/8: I picked up the sparkling new VW Gulf blue with white wall tyres. What a thrill it was, but I was sorry you could not have all been there to share it. I met Beth after work and we drove to the mall and parked the car and had tea at one of the famous Lyons eating houses.

Friday 26/8: I left work at 3pm and took a tube to Audrey and Mary's flat in Maida Vale. Beth arrived in the car. She had passed the test of London traffic in a new car and heavy rain, which I think is pretty good by any standards.

We were soon packed for the trip to Scotland and found the car held all our luggage, without much around our legs. Surprisingly, one can pack a lot in the front and the large 'well' behind the back seat. By 4:30pm we were out of the city and on the M1, which is a huge six-lane highway. The car ran like a charm. One does not have to run VWs in like other cars. You are told on delivery of the car and it is in all the books: no worries with 30 mph etc, just travel at normal speed.

I tried all the little knobs in the car. The front seats are adjustable to enable one to relax more, automatic choke (a new addition on this model!), blinkers, a peppy little horn and, my pride and joy, the heater. It's beaut, directing the heat from vents by the feet in the front, also up the window for demisting. The girls wouldn't allow me to have the heater going, much to my disgust. Why have a heater that is not in use?

We made just one modification to our new Beetle before tackling the fifteen thousand miles across mountains, deserts and plains: reclining seats. Our friends teased us about 'sleeping' in the car. The ribbing became even worse when Annie discovered Beth was sewing green and blue curtains to cover the windows.

'What will you be getting up to in that car?' the girls asked Beth, with sly expressions and raised eyebrows, causing her to

36

blush furiously. It was all innuendo. The 'swinging sixties' hadn't reached us, and sex was never openly discussed.

Camping was the plan, but we thought there might be times when sleeping in the car would be safer. The VW garage in St John's Wood extended the runners underneath so the seats could slide further forward and fold backwards. It gave us plenty of room lengthwise but, sometimes as we climbed into the car, the seats would catapult off the runners. We had to get out of the car and squat on the ground to push them back in again.

Reliability and international service points—those were the two reasons we had chosen the Beetle over any other car. Unlike some of the cheaper English cars, the Beetle was ubiquitous, sold in over 136 countries. That meant numerous VW service points along the overland route we were travelling: Europe, Turkey, Persia, Iraq, Pakistan and India. We could service the car en route and if we were unlucky enough to break down, it wouldn't be more than a few hundred miles to a VW garage.

Our first VW service on the trip was a debacle. But it wasn't the fault of the Spanish mechanics who were working on the car. The day began badly and ended worse. In our rush to be at the Barcelona garage on time, I received a traffic fine for not heeding a stop sign. Planning to leave the country before the police caught up with me, I chose to pay the fine later.

The VW garage was neat and the mechanics appeared efficient, so we left the Beetle with them for the day, trusting that nothing could go wrong. To pass the time until 4pm, we wandered along the wide, leafy promenades of the town, glancing at the shops and admiring the stately, old buildings. When the shops closed from 1 to 3pm, Beth and I made our way down to the harbour, pleased to have a cool breeze on our faces.

After eight hours of walking, we returned to the garage to

discover that the mechanics hadn't even started the work. Through the language barrier, I soon realised why. The key to the Beetle had been in my pocket all day! Feeling terribly stupid, I handed it over and was told to come back in another four hours. We spent the time at a bullfight, gaining free entry because some English people left at half time and gave us their tickets. While the fight was interesting, one could hardly call it enjoyable. The poor bloody bull had no chance.

In the intense heat of Spain and Portugal (we had detoured south to see the Rock of Gibraltar), we were pleased with the Beetle's air-cooled engine. Unlike us, desperately thirsty for one of the many bottles of fruit juice we were carrying, the Beetle didn't need water. Ignoring our dry mouths, we saved the fruit juice for when we would be in the desert, never guessing it would be cooler there, and never imagining that we would end the journey with ten full bottles of the stuff!

1962–1996
The Beetle Becomes a Kiwi

From when we left London, Mum had been following the Beetle's route on the wall map near the back door, vicariously living out her dreams of travel, fuelled by the stories and pictures in her National Geographic magazines. When we arrived home at the beginning of 1962, Beth and I had to uphold our side of the bargain. Devastated by our loss, we handed over the car.

It transpired that the Beetle was passed from one set of adoring owners to another. To a woman who had never left New Zealand, the strange-looking German Beetle was foreign and exotic. Mum loved the little car, cherishing it and sparing no money on its upkeep, despite Pop's modest income.

She puttered around the small town of Levin in third gear with the air of a celebrity, the locals waving on instant recognition. A country girl, driving since the age of fourteen, Mum was confident handling the car and only had one accident in the Beetle. Thankfully there was not a scratch to be seen. Jumping from the car, she blamed the other driver, tossing her dark wavy hair, shouting in anger that her precious Beetle had been touched.

She never considered selling it, upgrading to a new model or another car. Beth joked that she would trade in Pop before she was forced to trade in her Beetle. It was an unusual loyalty in an era when the Australian and Japanese car industries were emerging, offering vehicles that were faster, bigger, better. As the Beetle shape remained the same, her 'old' car was indistinguishable from the newer versions. Indulging in a little Beetlemania, she kept a few miniature VW cars in a kitchen drawer, bought from the local toy store.

In her pink high-necked blouses, calf-length skirts and sensible shoes, Mum would set off on picnics or fishing trips with Pop, the black and white dolly on the rear vision mirror swinging along with the rhythm of the road. Horse racing was a favourite. They preferred the smaller country races and would drive into Levin or Otaki or Foxton. Mum, always a rebel, used the police phone in our house to place bets with her 'unacceptable' friend, Jack the bookie, while Pop tried to have Jack's illegal business closed down!

Pop was a good old country policeman, serving Levin and the surrounding region of Horowhenua. He had his own vehicle, a Ford Prefect in 1962, but he dreamed of driving the Beetle. Possessive of her car, Mum made him ask her permission every time.

It didn't stop him. He borrowed it frequently, to drive around 'in luxury' on police business. Even with the windows down, not one strand of his slicked-back hair was ever out of place.

The unique Beetle worked to Pop's advantage. Fights would end before the car door opened. The troublemakers didn't need to see the navy police uniform with its bright silver buttons to know who they were dealing with. It was the days before police cars were issued, and the Beetle became the region's de facto official police vehicle.

Ferrying criminals back and forth around the countryside, Pop would turn to his passengers in the back seat and ask how they were enjoying the drive in a Volkswagen. He sometimes dropped in at our Wellington house for a little sustenance for the felons he was transporting to Mount Crawford. Barely stopping to put out his cigarette, Pop would rush inside, saying, 'This man has had a drive in the Beetle, but I think he needs a good Scotch before going off to prison.'

Years later, glancing through Beetle memorabilia, I saw that Pop's 'police car' was just one of many Volkswagens in the service around the world. In America, they even made an advertisement about one:

Don't laugh. A Volkswagen police car may seem like a funny idea to you, but it makes a lot of sense to the city of Scottsboro, Alabama. They wanted a car that could take Police Officer HL Wilkerson on parking meter patrol; all day, 6 days a week, in stop-and-go traffic. Without breaking down. And without breaking the taxpayers. So, in 1964, they bought Car S-5: a VW with a dome light, siren and 2-way radio.

That was the year of Scottsboro's only 12" snowfall. The other police cars were in trouble up to their hubcaps. But Car S-5 was a

credit to the Force. It went uphill. And downhill. And Officer Wilk-
erson didn't even bother to put the chains on.

Officer Wilkerson isn't supposed to go after speeders. But one day
in 1965 he chased one. And caught him. It's hard to say who was
more surprised. Car S-5 still averages 29 miles per gallon. It still
doesn't use any oil between changes. And it's never had a breakdown.
After a year and a half of continuous use, it had its clutch replaced,
and its valves readjusted. That is all.

Our Beetle never broke down but, of course, Mum and Pop
didn't drive it hard. Occasionally they took short trips, up to
Auckland and once over to the South Island. When we were
living in NZ, they would pack our three little daughters into the
Beetle and set off on excursions across the hills, the girls bouncing
up and down on the back seat, pushing each other aside to look
out of the small rear window.

If it hadn't been for Mum, the Beetle would have disappeared
years ago. Returning to NZ with so little money after our overland trip, we would have sold it. If, by some chance, the car had
stayed with us, it would have been upgraded to a larger one when
our children were born. Beth had always said, much to our daughters' annoyance, that if they had learnt to drive in it, the car would
be in a scrap heap by now. She wasn't criticising the way our
daughters drive, Beth just knew the effect of teenagers on a car.

Only weeks before going into a nursing home at the age of
eighty-two, Mum was still driving. Although sometimes forgetful
and confused, she found her way to the shops and back home
again. Pop, with his ingrained police background, argued with her
to give up her licence as he had done years before. She refused.

When she died a few months later, the Beetle stayed in the
carport, a symbol of her determination and spirit. Alone at home,

Pop would go and sit in the car, remembering. Sometimes he started the Beetle and reversed carefully down the drive. Later he told us that in spite of his police background, he did drive the Beetle out onto the road once or twice. My brother, Leo, or I would come up for visits, to take him on an outing. Mum's picnic basket and blanket would still be in the back of the car. Before we arrived, we'd ring Mum's mechanic, Terry Knowles, to make a house visit and check that the Beetle was running.

A friendly, trustworthy man, Terry came to know the inside of that Beetle better than any of us, chronicling its long history in his head. Mum first met him when he was an apprentice working in a garage in Levin. Later, he had his own service station, specialising in VWs, and Mum's business went with him. At one stage, the Beetle even became a part of Terry's family, living with him for six months. We were worried about the car being stolen from Pop's house, so we had Terry do some work on the Beetle and look after it at the same time.

One day I asked Terry if the Beetle would make the 15,000 kilometres from London to Bombay. 'Of course,' he answered without hesitation. We discussed him coming with us in a support vehicle.

'Wire and a pair of pliers—that's all I need to fix anything,' he said, reinforcing my mechanical inabilities and reminding Beth of her ceaseless amazement that she had married a man with no practical skills whatsoever. Her father could hold a car together with a piece of chewing gum. It eventuated that Terry had other plans and couldn't accompany us. He was retiring from old cars to take up restoring old furniture.

There was work to be done on the dear old Beetle to prepare her for the journey. The electrical system was changed from a six-volt battery system to twelve volts. Terry went through the engine, piece by piece, cleaning and replacing valves. We had a petrol gauge added. It had become standard on the 1962 VW model. Up to that point, each car came with a dipstick to check the level and a reserve tank for another thirty miles. The sharp memory of being stranded in the desert with no petrol was enough to convince us that the cost of a petrol gauge was worth our peace of mind. (We took the dipstick with us anyway, just in case.)

A fracture in the doorjamb on the right-hand side was probably from when we had run off the road after hitting the donkey in Turkey—unless, of course, Mum had had other accidents that she neglected to mention. A semi-circle was worn into the paint below the glovebox, the spot where Beth had hung her olive green handbag during the entire three-month overland trip. Swaying with the motion of the car, it had left an indelible mark.

Beth sat inside the car to check the seats and found herself staring at the top of the windscreen. Over the years, as Mum and Pop clambered in and out of the car, they had pushed their weight heavily against the seats, causing them to angle back. With their height, they probably hadn't noticed the gradual movement. Likewise, I had no problem seeing out, but Beth felt as if she were lying back in the dentist's chair. We decided to leave the seats as they were and use pillows and woollen seat covers to make them more comfortable.

The lining on the ceiling needed replacing. Once grey, it was now stained yellow with the curling smoke from Pop's roll-your-own cigarettes. We kept the original netting, designed for maps and papers; it was easier to reach upwards rather than fumbling around in the back seat. New tyres, new paintwork and some new panels to replace the stone marks from the first trip completed the renovation. The Beetle looked in better shape than when she had come off the production line, thirty-six years and 250,000 kilometres before.

With the silver, aerodynamic jetbag on the roofracks, the car perfectly fitted its 1960s label of a cockroach or a tortoise. And I was confident that under its hard shell, we'd make the trip safely again. We were older and slower, but there was no hurry to get to Bombay. The joy was in the journey, not in the destination.

'You're not as fast as you used to be and neither is the Beetle,' Britta reminded us. There were no illusions of drag-racing semi-trailers across the open plains or overtaking a new Mercedes on the Autobahn.

1996

A Feel-Good Story Makes the Newspapers

I felt young again, different from those in our age group who were taking 'safe' weekends away at their holiday houses on the coast. Excited and enthusiastic, I told anyone and everyone of our plans. Some feigned polite interest, but generally people were keen to hear more.

'It's not just a travel story,' I would begin, 'it's a love story, too. Beth and I have been together for almost forty years, that's a pretty good innings these days. And we still have the Beetle. The three of us are older now, but it's a chance to go back in time and do it all over again.'

A chance remark to an acquaintance in public relations, and our story appeared in the local newspaper, *The Mosman Daily*. From there, it was picked up by other papers, radio stations and a television channel in New Zealand. I wasn't surprised by the interest—it was a happy, feel-good story in the midst of the constant bad news favoured by the media.

Apart from the ego aspect of seeing our names in print, I felt that the media coverage could protect us. We would be travelling through a war zone in Turkey and facing anti-Western sentiments in Iran. As 'celebrities', we might be given assistance if there were difficulties. Beth took the opposite view.

'If we're well-known, then surely we're more likely to be taken hostage.' She preferred the anonymous approach. Months later, she would be proven right.

In the meantime, I enjoyed talking to reporters and showing photos from our first trip. We were described as 'an intrepid couple on an epic journey in a love Bug'. It was a 'trip of a lifetime'. I revelled in the media, while Beth reluctantly agreed to be involved. Not expecting many journalists to take an interest, she thought there would be just one interview.

When we were interviewed by Elizabeth Heath on ABC radio's midday show, we were stunned at the response: an enormous number of phone calls from friends and colleagues.

'It beats me how many people heard us on the radio,' Beth commented. 'They're supposed to be at work in the middle of the day. When I was talking to that tiny microphone, I didn't imagine anyone actually listening.'

With my past experience as a marketing manager and an insurance industry spokesman, I was accustomed to dealing with journalists. Chatting about our trip was a pleasant change from speaking on the insurance industry.

The Holmes Show, a current affairs program on NZ television, decided to track us on our journey. They would do a series of three segments—a show before we left, one en route from Pakistan and another when we returned. Their continuing interest in following our story was slightly surprising as it was a relationship which had started badly.

'Where the hell are you?' the producer had yelled down the line at me. Lost, I was calling from a phone box. 'I have a whole camera crew waiting for you.'

I was in NZ organising shipping arrangements for the Beetle when the producer of *The Holmes Show* suggested it was a good opportunity to do some filming of the car. He particularly wanted a shot of the Beetle driving over the long Auckland Bridge. The plan was to meet at 9:30am in a road near the Takapuna end of the bridge.

Beth was at home in Sydney and I was lost, literally lost, without my expert navigator in the passenger seat. I drove around and around, searching for the rendezvous, knowing I was close. Finally, I decided to find a phone box and call *The Holmes Show*.

An hour late, the Beetle and I met up with the crew. We had always been within a few streets of one another, but coming and going at different times. Once we had our directions, the Beetle and I performed beautifully, and there were no more complications that day.

My Pop and Beth's mother were chuffed to see their children on the television. It gave them status in their respective nursing homes, with everyone talking about 'Beth and Ivan's trip'. When the stories went to air, the other occupants of Pop's lounge were told they had no choice but to watch *The Holmes Show* that night. Pleased to see us looking happy and well, he felt the segments went too quickly. 'It was too short,' he told everyone, confused about where in the world we were.

Beth's mum was very proud. It gave her something to boast to her sisters about. Even the nursing staff took an interest, asking us how we were, before passing the phone to our parents. While we were concerned about our parents becoming sick or dying while we were away, we had to do the trip. I felt that we could never know how much time we had left when we would still be fit enough to do the things we wanted.

As a result of the media coverage for our 1996 trip, letters flooded in to us. We had bought our car at the beginning of the sixties, before the 'Vee-Dub Beetle' was to become a cultural icon of the decade as a symbol of freedom, of rebelling against the establishment. In those years, thousands set out on their own Beetle journeys. For some, it was a challenge to see how much the car could endure before it self-destructed. The original game of 'how many people can fit in a Beetle' was replaced by 'how many miles can it go'.

The love affair with the Beetle held a special place in many memories. 'We drove around Europe in our Beetle in the sixties, too,' the letter-writers proclaimed. Past and present owners told us of the terrain, the mileage and how their Beetle just kept on going in any conditions. In a way, the famed reliability was proven by the Volkswagen company itself when it sent a Beetle on a 1963 Australian National Antarctic Research Expedition. According to Volkswagen, it was 'the first car at the bottom of the world' and 'started without a tremble' at -50° Celsius.

Beth and I found that one of the most adventurous journeys mailed in to us was by Hansjuergen Enz, a friendly fellow who invited us to visit him in Tasmania. He had been travelling by Beetle just after us in 1962, undertaking an overland trip from Berlin to Hobart, clocking up nearly fifty thousand kilometres. Judging by the pictures he sent us, Hansjeurgen had chosen the most dramatic seasons to travel: the photos showed his white Beetle fjording through monsoonal floods in Thailand, juddering over baked-dry mud in Iran, ploughing through snow in Yugoslavia and disappearing under a cloud of red dust in the Nullarbor Plain in southern Australia.

The photo of his Beetle half crushed by a taxi in Istanbul reminded us of the unavoidable risk of driving through chaotic traffic. To his cheerful caption, 'lucky—no mechanical damage, only bodywork', he added that it had taken three weeks to mend and then he was on the road again. Like us, Hansjuergen still had a taste for travel. As we were setting out to re-create our Beetle journey, he was returning from a trip around the Arctic Ocean on a Russian ice-breaker.

Despite the famed reliability of the Beetle, there was a good chance that our thirty-six-year-old car might decide to break down. Hoping for more success than in 1961, I once again contacted Volkswagen to ask for technical support. It was a long drawn-out process. Volkswagen was a busy organisation, involved in its new range of cars; I was an old Beetle owner asking for assistance, with only publicity to offer in return. We sent requests to New Zealand, Australia, England and finally, the head office in Germany.

Paul Buckett, the manager of public relations at Volkswagen UK, arranged for us to visit the VW factory in Wolfsburg on the fourth day of our trip. We had rather ambitiously hoped he could also provide help with obtaining third party insurance for the car in Europe. But that was not to be.

Insurance was to become an obstacle which almost ended the trip before it began.

The St John's Wood dealership in London was still in operation. There were more glass windows and more cars out on the footpath than I remembered in 1960. The popular Beetle had been replaced by Golfs, Audis, Passats and VW Transporters. Bemused staff watched as we rolled up in the Beetle, trailed by cameras from TV NZ.

Brandishing the original receipt, I demanded a refund on the car. There was laughter all round and comments on the impressive condition of the Beetle. Without hesitation, the mechanic presented us with a MOT slip, the roadworthy check we needed to apply for third party insurance. Last time, the staff had chatted into my Stuzzi tape recorder; this time, it was captured on film to be beamed back to New Zealand.

Then came the frustration.

We wanted to do the long drive on our NZ number plates, but the UK had no agreement with NZ on the registration of vehicles on temporary entry. Obviously, there were few Kiwi cars coming in and out of England. Before we left Australia, I had inquired about the insurance process and was told there would be difficulties. One insurance agency went so far as to suggest: 'It would be easier and more convenient to buy your car in England.' I had to laugh. It would also be cheaper than shipping it across the world, but as the Beetle was the protagonist of the trip, the car could hardly be left at home. I managed to convince myself that the insurance process would be a minor obstacle.

'You'll have to register the car with UK plates and then you can get insurance,' we were told by the Driving and Vehicle Licensing Centre. This, the only apparent option, would add weeks of processing and thousands of pounds on to the cost. Import tax. Registration fees. Car inspections. We would only be driving in the UK for three days but the insurance would cover the car across Europe until we reached Iran.

I was stressed. My aim to leave on the first of August appeared impossible; this insurance problem was looking to take three weeks.

TV NZ filmed us as we spoke with yet another insurance agency. Added to our frustration was the potential embarrassment of our well-publicised journey being aborted at its first step! One insurance company suggested we 'do a runner' and get it worked out in Belgium. The risk-taker within me briefly considered the idea, but then a lifetime career in insurance held me back. We couldn't afford being uninsured in an accident.

As I became more depressed about the situation, an unexpected solution arose. Down Under Insurance Services convinced Norwich Union to insure us on our NZ plates through them. Our green card was issued; the departure date postponed by just two days.

But before we could set off, we had to finish our publicity commitments. Paul Buckett wanted photos of us 'doing London'. With the sunshine reflecting off our polished Beetle, we posed in front of London Bridge, Trafalgar Square, Big Ben and St Pauls. On Albert Bridge, I stopped a 'London Grand Tour' double-decker sightseeing bus. The photographer snapped away as I nosed the Beetle up to the front of the bus. On the upper deck, the Japanese tourists laughed at the incongruity of the red bus towering over our minuscule blue car.

1937–1948—Germany
The Strength-through-Joy Car

When we had bought our Beetle in 1960, little was known of the history of Volkswagen and the Wolfsburg factory. Due to World War II, there was a general bias by many people against German products, but we were the new generation.

'The war's over,' we declared, unaware of the effectiveness of the propaganda on our young minds. Had we known that the Volkswagen factory was used to build the Buzz Bomb which had killed thousands of English civilians, our choice might have been different. It was unlikely that we could have been impartial; that we would have realised any country at war would turn its factories over to armaments production. We had been weaned on cartoons of the German baddies and the Japanese fools. In Auckland Harbour, a young Beth greeted her father disembarking from his ship, the HMS *Leander*, which had been ripped apart by a torpedo. Her father survived but, like most, the war altered him. Beth's mum was conscripted to work in a factory while the grandmother brought up the children. Anti-German songs echoed in the playground.

Fifteen years later, we bought a German car, not fully aware of the political aspects. Some historians have noted that the Beetle succeeded where Hitler failed: the little car overran the world.

The Beetle story began in the early 1930s, when automobile designer, Ferdinand Porsche was working towards an affordable small car; one which was *designed* to be small, rather than a scaled version of a larger vehicle. The concept seemed destined to fail as the Depression took hold and car companies everywhere battled for survival.

Hitler gave Porsche the opportunity to continue his work. An admirer of the records set by Porsche with his Mercedes S and SS, Hitler had his own dream of a small car. He thought a *People's Car* would give hope to the struggling population and, more importantly, it provided an excuse for building autobahns. Porsche was told to create a small car which cost a third less than the cheapest vehicle then on the market.

But Hitler was demanding the impossible. No German automobile manufacturer could make the Volkswagen for the required price—less than 1,000 Reichsmark.

The Fuehrer found the solution within his German labour front. It would build a factory, produce the cars and sell them to the people. There would be no distributor costs, no sales commission and no manufacturer's profit. Factory door sales only. It was a futuristic concept.

The factory site was chosen for its transport network. Mittelland Canal ran through it; the Berlin Autobahn was being constructed a few miles away; and the east-west railway line to Berlin was 120 miles to the east. The government bought farmland from Count Werner von der Schulenberg, despite his arguments. (After the war, the town took the name of Wolfsburg from Schulenberg's castle, by then crowded with refugees fleeing the Russian-occupied zone of Germany.)

Around the factory, architects designed a city for ninety thousand people. At the cornerstone-laying ceremony in May 1938, Hitler declared the Volkswagen would become known as the Strength-through-Joy car, bearing the name of the labour movement which made it all possible. As a result, the town was to be KdF-stadt, Kraft-durch-Freude stadt, the Strength-through-Joy town.

Only 630 Volkswagens were produced during Hitler's reign, yet the Nazi propaganda machine had the world thinking the dream was a near reality. In July 1938 the *New York Times* used the 'beetle' imagery, probably for the first time in print:

> *In a short time Der Fuehrer is going to plaster his great sweeps of smooth highways with thousands and thousands of shiny little beetles ... the new automobile is already nicknamed the 'Baby Hitler', but its proper name will be the KdF: Kraft-durch-Freude or Strength-through-Joy ... judging by the pace at which things get done in the Third Reich today, citizens will not be long in getting theirs.*

It would be ten years before the car was actually sold to the German people. As Hitler went to war, priorities changed. Most of the factory was turned over to armaments work, producing aeroplane wings, bomb casings, land mines, rockets and sheet-metal stoves. Porsche, in fear of losing the small car concept forever, re-designed it as an open-bodied utility vehicle, the Kubelwagen, to be used by the army. An amphibious version was created, and these two vehicles rolled off assembly lines, replacing the KdF car.

Against the odds, the Volkswagen factory survived the damage of Allied bombings during the war and English occupation afterwards. Categorised as a war plant, the factory was to be dis-assembled within four months but an English major convinced his superiors of its potential worth. He completed the half-finished Volkswagen cars which were languishing on the factory floor and set about building new ones for English use in governing the region.

Despite the usefulness of the factory for the English occupying forces, Volkswagen had to make a profit, otherwise it would be dismantled. The English put Heinz Nordhoff in charge of the near-impossible task.

Unexpected success came with the introduction of the Deutschemark which set the stage for the birth of the Volkswagen phenomenon. In 1948, the Reichsmark was converted to the Deutschemark, and every German was given forty DM. Amidst the post-war poverty, the cheap Volkswagen suddenly became affordable. The re-opening of a free market meant the German people no longer required a British permit to buy a vehicle and Volkswagen orders came flooding in.

Although tainted by its association with Hitler, the little Beetle became a success story across Europe and eventually America. It crept into the hearts of the young, who somehow identified with the small, cheap, ugly duckling.

Porsche, destitute after being imprisoned by the French, requested financial backing from the VW company for his next venture, the Porsche sportscar. As he was never paid for the rights to his Beetle design, Porsche was allotted 200,000 DM and a one DM royalty for every car produced. In February 1972 the Beetle hit fifteen million. It was the first car to break the record set by the Model-T Ford in 1927.

6 August 1996
Wolfsburg, Germany

We spent our two days in the town of Wolfsburg under the wing of the staff from the International Press Office. They expressed great interest in the 1960 Gulf Blue Beetle.

'What a lovely car! And in what beautiful shape, too,' Sabina Ellert exclaimed. Recently appointed to the press office, she was extremely enthusiastic about us, her first project. Sabina was enchanted by the romance of our story. Smart, and smartly dressed in a white trouser suit, she brightly led us from appointment to appointment. We liked Sabina, her cheerful manner and eagerness to help winning us over immediately.

Sabina's manager, Gunther Scherelis, took our Beetle for a spin and confidently announced, 'You'll have no problem driving that car to Bombay'.

Gunther was charming and fast-moving, working on numerous projects at once with the nervous energy of the highly successful. Gunther and Sabina escorted us to lunch with eight journalists, translating for us when necessary. The newspaper stories which appeared the following day attested to the German love of the Beetle. We were front-page news, a well-balanced, well-groomed mature couple driving an old Beetle for a three-month second honeymoon. We didn't realise the legacy of this publicity would follow us to a tiny village in Turkey.

With the Beetle, we posed for photos under the massive Wolfsburg plant. The backdrop—four factory chimneys from the old power plant—apparently was a recognisable symbol throughout Germany.

Although Wolfsburg was an industrial town, trees graced the planned streets. It was a regimented environment, neat and tidy; signs on every corner pointed to the Volkswagen factory. There were only two reasons to be in Wolfsburg—Beetle business or Beetlemania.

The Wolfsburg plant no longer manufactured the world's most popular car. The cost of complying to noise and safety standards set on larger cars had led VW to design a new family of small cars—the Golf.

Watching cars on a production line was not high on Beth's list of holiday experiences and she approached our tour of the factory with an air of resignation. But soon she was listening and watching in rapt attention. The size of the place was the first shock. I read the figures but they didn't translate to images in my head. Eight square miles, nearly a quarter of it undercover; 45,000 employees—the largest plant under one roof in the world. It was far bigger than my home town of Levin.

Part of it looked like a gigantic red brick high school with students rushing between classes. I was impressed by the obvious pride the employees had in their work. It made the evidence revealed in the new book, *Volkswagen and its Workers during the Third Reich*, all the more shocking. Commissioned by the company itself in a spirit of openness about its Nazi past, the book renewed discussion of slave labour used during the war. It proved that some workers were beaten to death and others died from starvation at their posts.

The factory tour took us along a caged-in walkway high above the machines. No noise, no smell, no dust, no dirt. It was hard to believe we were looking at a car production line.

Mesmerised by the massive machines churning out pieces of car, we were told that ninety per cent of the work was now done by robots. It all appeared so simple. Car pieces were carried by robots through the air, moving mechanically between halls.

Beth liked the way the process of car production was humanised; it seemed 'right' from a factory that had assembled the Beetles with their lovable personalities. The 'Place of Birth' was the body shop. When the chassis number was stamped on the engine, that was the 'Baptism' and the area where the engine was turned over for the first time was called the 'Birthing Room'.

On a wall, there was a poster for the New Concept Beetle. Beth asked to photograph it and was given permission. The plant was under stricter security than usual due to the development of the new Beetle. We heard murmurs that hidden 'spy' cameras had been found. Still, the staff were thrilled to talk about the New Concept Beetle. The design had been unveiled at the 1994 Detroit Motor Show to an enthusiastic response. A few diehard fanatics labelled it a travesty, saying the Beetle could not be re-created and especially not in a new shape. Intrigued by the New Concept Beetle, we were hoping to see it. We weren't to have our wish on this trip.

Volkswagen agreed to check our Beetle, and I assumed we'd explain what the problems were. But, without discussion, the car was matter-of-factly taken away from us by a white-coated worker. His white beard, round glasses, cheery face and clean fingernails gave the appearance of a local pharmacist. We learnt that he had been working at the factory back in 1960 when our Beetle had rolled off the line!

Returning from the factory tour, we were greeted by the white-coated fellow, now smiling and praising the condition of the car. 'It's fine,' he said, seemingly unwilling to explain. With questioning, we discovered that he had fixed the heater which, once again, had shown its endearing and enduring trait of not turning off. I often wondered if I had cursed it by worshipping it so on our first drive. The heater had been a problem in the very first prototypes tested in 1936—although back then it wouldn't switch *on*, rather than refusing to switch *off*.

There was an oil leak which, the fellow said, could be expected in a car this age, and a petrol smell, which he had also investigated. Beth asked him about carrying luggage on top of the car, and he replied that it was advantageous to the performance of the Beetle. 'The more weight, the better.' He waved at the silver jetbag on the roof, with little notion that he'd just given Beth the green light to shopping heaven.

'Keep putting oil in it and if it's not broken, don't fix it!' were his parting words, as he assured us the Beetle would make it to India. I was relieved; Beth would now be more confident about the trip.

'You can't doubt a man in a white coat,' she said as we drove away.

On Dieselstrasse, we dropped by a place of pilgrimage: the Volkswagen AutoMuseum. Not being fanatics, just in love with our own little car, we were pleasantly rewarded with a fascinating exhibition and a friendly archivist, Herr von Witzleben. I was intrigued by the Beetles that had done journeys like ours. One had driven from Alaska to the bottom of South America.

The museum showed the development of the Beetle and the

history of other Volkswagen cars. There was a prototype from 1934 and the very plain 1942 model, one of the first off the production line. The war years were represented with the army version of the original design. Incongruous against the range of basic Beetles were the snazzy white VW racing cars. I still admired the sleek Karmann Ghia, the one I had dreamed of owning when I was twenty-seven.

Beth's attention was caught by the specialty cars: a white wrought iron Beetle through which we could see the engine; a green and white Polizei vehicle; the 'Buggy Australien', sand-bashing at home in the red dust of the outback. Beetle miniatures were replicated in incredible detail.

Herr von Witzleben presented me with a book, *The Beetle—A Most Unlikely Story*, and graciously told us he would be happy to display our well-travelled Beetle if we ever decided to donate it to the AutoMuseum. I explained to him that I hoped the Beetle would entertain a few more generations before ending up in the museum.

That evening, we were invited to the Käfer-Club, the local VW Beetle Club, which met in a café set amongst beautifully tended gardens. The communal gardens had been designed during the war for workers to grow their own produce. We were warmly welcomed to the club night by the informal chairman, Michael. In response, across the language barrier, Beth and I demonstrated the four-fingered wave favoured by Beetle drivers in New Zealand and Australia. We assumed it was a universal gesture. The club members assumed it was a rude one.

In the summer evening half-light, the twenty members ventured outside to examine our Beetle. They climbed in, testing the seats (thankfully empty, as we'd left all our belongings at the hotel) and sticking their heads under the boot to look at the engine.

'You shipped it all the way from New Zealand?' they confirmed, approving of the fanaticism.

The oldest Beetle amongst the group was a 1954 model. The tall, thin owner was keeping it for his three-year-old. I reiterated my wish of passing the Beetle on to our grandson, Tahni. Not quite joking, I added, 'Maybe he could do the overland trip in another twenty years, and Beth and I could fly to meet him at the big cities.'

It would be a wonderful gift if Tahni were to derive even half the pleasure we'd experienced from the car—yet another link through the generations. Before we had shipped it out from NZ, the Levin newpaper had taken photos of the whole family around the Beetle with Pop in the background and Tahni at the wheel, his tousled blond hair almost covering his eyes. I imagined him following our tyre marks, planning the third Beetle trip, reading our maps and diaries, stunned at the changes in the world.

Chapter 3

Beetling through Europe's Turbulent History

Humans were redefining their world in 1961. The Berlin Wall went up; the Algerian independence movement was put down. Syria broke away from Egypt, while America moved into Cuba. The USSR set off the largest nuclear explosion in history. African colonies set up their own republics.

Without English papers to read, we were unaware of the turbulence: the re-escalation of the Cold War and the one issue which would directly affect us: hostilities between Syria and Egypt. Blithely we continued, driving the Beetle on through Europe.

Berne, the city of bears. Ours was a brief visit. Switzerland was not a country in which budget travellers like us luxuriated. Under the gaze of gawking tourists, caged bears paced restlessly in the Bärengraben, the 500-year-old pits. The symbol of the animal adorned the sandstone buildings. It was said that the city's founder, Berchtold of Zähringen, went out on a hunt and named the town after his first trophy. With its neat streets and rows of beige blocks below red roofs, the city of Berne had little in common with its wild namesake.

Hoopy was the reason we were there. At the Berne Youth Hostel she had fallen head over heels for the manageress' son. Her vivacious personality had charmed Mama, the manageress, who had given her a job in the hostel—general duties. We were never sure if Mama knew of Hoopy's ulterior motive.

In her white smock, brown curls flying, Hoopy ran out to greet us. She was enjoying herself, learning a little German, meeting other travellers, and still happy despite the son's disappearance from the scene.

'You have to play table tennis with Mama,' she whispered discreetly as an enormous woman thundered towards us. Mama hugged us to her huge bosom and said that as Hoopy's friends, we could stay, regardless of the twenty-six-year-old cut-off point for Swiss youth hostels. Even with the proof of our marriage certificate, there was no possibility of sleeping together, however. We were sent off in separate directions to the male and female dormitories.

'So we play table tennis,' Mama said. It was more of a demand than a suggestion. For the next two days, we slogged it out across the table. I was taken by surprise. She was good. Her bulk disguised quick movements. It would have been political to let her win, but it wasn't in my competitive nature. As it turned out, we were a good match, the wins and losses spread evenly.

In the late hours of the night, we stayed up talking. The following week, Hoopy would be returning to London to find a new job. She was sorry to be leaving Switzerland, although relieved to be done with peeling potatoes and washing dishes. For the first week back in London, the tables would be turned. Grabbing at the opportunity to improve her English, Mama was accompanying Hoopy to England, so it would now be a case of Hoopy instructing Mama. This lively woman could barely contain her excitement, counting down the days until their departure.

As we left Berne, even the pleasant countryside couldn't quite lift our spirits. It would be a long time before we would see our friend Hoopy again. We hoped she might return to NZ the following year, but we well understood the fascination that kept her abroad, wandering around Europe.

Travelling through the Swiss landscape, we were overwhelmed by picture book images. Wooden chalets with tiny balconies nestled on the lower slopes of rugged mountains. Villages hid in the winding valleys. Flowers dotted the gardens. The chalets had window boxes coloured with red geraniums and white petunias. Streets were spotless and shopkeepers immaculate in their white smocks. Business was conducted in a friendly, easy manner.

Everyone spoke some English. I was impressed with their language skills; most knew three languages, French, German, English or Italian. With my knowledge of just one language, this country of five million people seemed particularly intelligent to me.

The principality of Liechtenstein was a place we'd never heard of. We only discovered its existence when we found ourselves driving through this tiny region. It was a link between Switzerland and Austria, a land of yet more mountains. Our first few hours in Austria were spent debating which was the more rugged—the Swiss or the Austrian Alps. My money was on Austria, but Beth defended Switzerland. That night, we camped outside Innsbruck and managed a little sightseeing in the morning, before setting off for Vöcklabruck.

Our destination for the day meant forgoing the historical town of Salzburg. We passed through the pretty villages of the Salzkammergut, amidst a paradise of steep mountains hugging deep lakes. Motoring on to Vöcklabruck, a working town of 10,000 people, we drew it all in with hungry eyes, learning more and more, aware of the contrasts with New Zealand.

We had come to Vöcklabruck to see Uda and Frederick, a couple we had met camping, on a beach near Lisbon, in the first week of our trip. We had spent two days together there, sharing dinners, pouring their wine during the meal and our brandy after dessert. Frederick, an English-language teacher at a grammar school, leapt at the chance to speak with us, testing his ear against our Kiwi accents and expressions. His German wife, Uda, could understand only a little English, and communicated mostly by shy smiles and nods. At first, we were unable to pronounce Uda's name. By associating it with the English word 'udder', we finally remembered it, although we had to twist the accent slightly and stop ourselves from laughing at the image of a cow's teat.

Frederick had invited us to visit their home in Vöcklabruck, insisting in his serious manner that we must come. Upper Austria was not exactly on our route, for we were heading south to Yugoslavia, but there was no set itinerary, no place we absolutely had to be. We turned the Beetle north. To venture inside an Austrian home and enjoy a real bed instead of a tent was too tempting.

And what a bed it was! The likes of it we'd never seen before. The only similarity with ours back home was the mattress. There were huge pillows scattered across the bed, wider but thinner than ours. The eiderdown was what fascinated Beth and me the most. Stuffed with feathers, it didn't have the sewn-in sections of our eiderdowns and, as a result, it was two feet thick, the same height as the mattress itself. We found it wonderfully warm to crawl underneath this massive eiderdown, with pillows plumped around us. I imagined it to be perfect for an Austrian winter. Beth laughed at my delight in the continental bed. 'You look like the cat who got the cream,' she said, punting a pillow in my direction. 'It's going to be impossible to get you out of this bed tomorrow!'

The morning brought with it a new curiosity. Breakfast. In addition to the usual coffee, bread roll and jam, Uda served up three types of cheese and various cold meats—ham and some kind of spiced garlic sausage meat. We weren't sure whether we could stomach such meats so early in the morning, nor how we were supposed to eat this interesting breakfast. Closely watching Uda and Frederick, we copied their every move.

During breakfast, Uda's parents arrived from Germany. They professed to speak no English, but we found that they were actually excellent in the language and had no accent whatsoever.

Uda was running the family business: a hat shop below their flat. I was amazed by the concept of a shop just for hats! No such 'extravagance' existed in Levin. There must have been some in London, but Beth had never dragged me into any. I guessed hats were more important in the Northern Hemisphere, essential in winter instead of a mere fashion item.

The shop sold traditional Tyrolean felt hats. Uda showed us around, and we watched her at work: encouraging customers with a warm, friendly smile to try another hat; massaging the felt to sit at the right height, the right point; shaking her blonde head—no, this feather would be better. She gave me a feather to keep. Long and elegant, it survived the journey back home, where Pop stuck it in his grey hat and wore it for years on shooting expeditions for pheasant and duck.

While Uda worked and chatted with her parents, Frederick took us to the clear lakes near the town. We lunched by the shore at an outdoor restaurant under a chestnut tree. Frederick ordered our first-ever wiener schnitzel, and we savoured the combination of the golden fried breadcrumbs and veal. A typical Austrian dessert followed: a delicious, frozen combination of meringue, cream and ice-cream.

On the last night, we shared our part of the world with Uda and Frederick, showing them slides of Australia and our families in NZ. Afterwards, the girls went off to bed, while Frederick and I discussed World War II. I found it exciting to meet someone from 'the enemy side', but Beth warned me about asking too many sensitive questions.

Frederick said that when the Nazis had invaded Austria, Hitler promised to improve living conditions. He put the unemployed to work on the autobahns that were built across the country. According to Frederick, the standard of living improved, but the Austrians never saw eye to eye with the Nazis. In the later stages of the war, Frederick was conscripted into the German army. Seventeen years old, he went to fight against the Russians and the Americans. When the war finished, he found himself in the Russian zone of Austria. He threw down his arms and decided to walk home. But, said Frederick, the winning forces which occupied Austria were also problematic. The Americans treated people badly and looted what they could.

I hadn't realised that Austria was once a major power. Frederick explained how the Austrian empire had covered parts of Hungary, Czechoslovakia, Yugoslavia, Romania and Bulgaria, totalling around forty million people. It had been a mighty force in Europe, and Frederick was displeased that this great empire was now a small country with seven and a half million people.

The following morning, Frederick, Uda and her parents fare-welled us with tears and promises to keep in touch. We felt restored after the stay with our new friends, pleased to be seeing local ways and eating traditional food, which was certainly a change from the 'meat and veg' cooked on our little primus. We never guessed that in fifteen years we would be on a return visit, and introduce our three daughters to Uda and Frederick's son.

It was in Vienna that we received snippets from the outside world. At the tourist centre, the visitors' book fell open to a page from the previous year, and we saw that it was the very page Hoopy had written upon when she was in Vienna! It was such a miraculous coincidence, we thought, especially as the book went all the way back to 1957. I suddenly felt that our friends were with us on this journey, either leading the way or following behind. There seemed such a strong link between us. I knew that even if Hoopy and Annie stayed on the continent for years, our friendships would never dissolve.

The *Voice of America* on the radio was another interruption from the 'real world'. One morning, I managed to pick it up. The news was good: a Western response to the escalating communist aggression.

This is the Voice of America. *Opinion Round-up is a cross-section of editorial opinion on the reports and views of press, radio and television commentators, whose programs and syndicated columns serve to keep their readers and listeners well-informed on the important issues of our time.*

Congressmen, newspapers and millions of Americans are showing quiet but strong approval of President Kennedy's order to start atomic testing underground again. The Summit Democratic Leader, Senator Mansfield, said, 'The Soviet Union has forced us to do it.' And the Republican Leader, Senator Dickson said, the President must go ahead with testing. 'The nation expects him to go ahead.' Others, Republican Senator Cooper and Democratic Senator Gore, added that if the Soviet Union continues making its tests in the air, then, although we hate it, America might be forced to test above ground also.

President Tito today gave separate messages from the Conference of Neutral Nations to the Ambassadors of the United States and the Soviet Union. Reports say the messages urge an immediate meeting between President Kennedy and Prime Minister Khrushchev to stop the atomic race towards war.

Listening to this news in the city of Vienna was pertinent. Only three months previously, Kennedy and Khrushchev had met here in Vienna. It had not been a successful discussion. Now, we were heading south into communist Yugoslavia, where the Conference of Neutral Nations was underway. In the last few days, the United States had increased the number of American troops in Berlin. The reality hit us hard. Atomic war over the issue of Berlin could happen. It made me see exactly how isolated our islands of New Zealand really were—a good isolation, oceans away from the turbulence of Europe.

September 1961—Yugoslavia
Reds under the Bed

It was nearly dark when we reached the Austrian border post: two huts on a bleak pinnacle of the mountain. The weather conditions were equally bleak: wet and cold, indeed very, very cold. The Austrian customs officials glanced at our papers, dashed out for a quick glimpse of the car and waved us on, unwilling to expose themselves to the elements.

Crossing the Alps on both sides of the border, we hoped to see the beauty of the mountains, but the terrific rain meant concentrating solely on driving. The unsealed dirt road snaked through the rugged terrain, just wide enough for two cars. Fortunately, there was no oncoming traffic. We were the only ones foolish enough to attempt the road at this late hour.

'Let's get into Yugoslavia tonight,' I'd said to Beth before we began the ascent in Austria. 'We can just keep driving until we find somewhere to camp.'

The heater was on, we were wrapped in jumpers and still we

were cold. But in the diminishing light, as we came over the highest point of the mountains, a magical view of Yugoslavia stretched out below. The craggy peaks dipped down into a gentle valley laced with mist. Since the light was too dim for photos, it was a scene only Beth and I could share.

Although it seemed impossible, the descent was even steeper than the upward climb. As we rounded one of the many hairpin bends, a striped pole barred our way. Yugoslavian customs. Surrounding the Beetle, protected by their greatcoats, these officials were more thorough than their Austrian counterparts. We had to declare anything and everything.

Further down in the valley, darkness descended and, with it, forms leaping by the road. Rocks. Overhanging trees. The rain confused our vision, our windscreen wipers inadequate for the downpour.

The little we could see surprised us: clean, proud villages and, in the larger town of Ljubljana, beautiful shops. Yugoslavia was communist. We expected it to be shabby, a police state with spies on every corner. When would we encounter the guards, dressed in their grey uniforms and red stars? We'd been told to stay in approved camping grounds, but how did we find out where they were? This was an alien culture, a political system we knew nothing about and yet, here we were, driving right into it, in the dark.

Exhausted from battling the weather on the difficult gravel roads, we wanted to stop for the night, but it had to be away from the towns. Finally, we found a spot just off the road. No traffic and no buildings meant a little privacy while we slept. Using the gas burner we'd bought in Gibraltar, we cooked soup inside the Beetle, ate it quickly and prepared for bed. A bucket was put out for rainwater; Beth pulled the green and blue curtains across

the car windows; I squashed our belongings onto the floor, man-
oeuvered the seats into the sleeping position, and we fell into a
welcome sleep.

The chattering woke us up at 5:30am. Gingerly, Beth lifted the
curtain and peeked out. The response was peals of laughter.

'We're parked in a bus stop,' Beth giggled, 'and there are about
forty people waiting for the next bus.'

'God knows where they all came from,' I said with a wry smile.
'I couldn't see any buildings last night.'

The crowd watched in silent fascination as I emerged to take
in our rainwater. 'Good morning,' I shouted, smiling in every
direction. They nodded back, containing their amusement
for a moment. We decided to find a quieter spot for breakfast and
a wash, a site without an audience of bus passengers!

Heading westwards to the coast, we stopped at the caves at
Postojna. Our AA strip map, the only 'guidebook' we had, briefly
listed places of interest:

Postojna: *The grottoes of Postojna, remarkable and most extensive.
About two hours should be allowed for a visit, which can be carried
out to a great extent in wagons running on rails. The grottoes are lit
by electricity and the outstanding chambers are the Ballroom, the
Calvary, the Sepulchre and the Grotta Nuova.*

Tickets for foreigners were six hundred dina, twice what the locals
paid. We realised that the Yugoslavian government was doing a
shifty deal: attracting tourists by offering a special exchange rate
and then charging them double for sightseeing and accommodation. I felt it gave the bad impression of a country sneaking its
money back.

An open train took us down into the caves. We had to duck
our heads as the track wound a path through the rock formations.

It brought us to a magnificent cavern, the walls reflecting a warm glow from the enormous chandeliers. Orchestras would play in the cavern, the rock provided amazing acoustics for the privileged listeners.

The caves were reputed to be the best of their kind in the world. Staring in wonder at the elegantly lit stalactites and stalagmites, Beth and I appreciated the claim. Our guide, a local student who had learnt English at school, explained that the caves near ground level had scrawlings which dated from 1217; however, the lower sections of the caves were only discovered in 1818. During the war, the Nazis had used one of the top caverns to store petrol. Unbeknownst to the Germans, there was another entrance to the cave. One night, a handful of locals had crept in and blown up the stores. Unfortunately, the explosion had blackened the cave and destroyed some stalagmites.

In the darkest depths of the caves, our guide showed us yet another marvel: an amphibious fish, unique to Postojna. It was an ugly thing, about six inches long, similar to a lizard, with four legs and five toes on each. A few of these blind, transparent fish were kept in a tank for visitors but the creatures on display had to be swapped every so often, otherwise they died. In the blackness of the underground river, the fish lived for forty to fifty years but, when exposed to light, they survived only a few months.

Our guide intrigued me. Here was a fellow in a communist country who could speak English, so I took the chance, in the half-light, to ask a barrage of questions. He was twenty-one years old, and this was his holiday job during the university break.

'Are you a communist?' I asked.

'No, I'm not,' he said, confusing me. I assumed most people in this country would be.

'Well, do you think communism is good for your country?'

'Of course it is,' he replied earnestly. 'Our country is poor, but life is growing better and better. It is difficult fourteen years after the war, it is not a long time. Tito good man. Everyone likes him and he has good relationship with Khrushchev.'

The lights went out to demonstrate the pure blackness of the cave. A few shouts of surprise and concern echoed through the chamber.

I ventured one last question, trying to understand this commitment to communism. 'Are you jealous of people in other countries, like Britain, who have more than you?'

'Yes,' he said, adding that people were only allowed to take thirty dollars with them when they travelled outside Yugoslavia. Twenty people from his village had gone to Australia, but he had faith in the government to build up industry and create prosperity.

A few days later, I spoke with a chap on a motorbike who shared the same view. He had even been living in a Western country for some time, but still was sold on the idea of communism. According to him, the older people were less enthusiastic about the regime. I feared for the young. The government was destroying their minds with this communism.

Driving through the countryside, we could see the struggle ahead for the government. Most people relied on a peasant way of life. Women sat by the roadside spinning wool. Shepherds herded their goats across the road. Where the barren land was cultivated, the fields were ploughed by donkeys. In the village squares, the men stood around after dinner. I wondered what they were waiting for until I suddenly realised that this was their social interaction, their evening entertainment. Everyone was friendly to us. Foreign tourists were a novelty.

Our first glimpse of the Yugoslavian coastline was at Rijeka, a popular tourist centre. From here, ships cruised through the islands down to Dubrovnik. Near the beach, we found a marvellous camping spot, which we shared with three other tents, all belonging to Germans. I commented to Beth, and on the tape recorder to my parents, that Germans were everywhere. Although they had lost the war, they seemed to have come out on top, very wealthy. They all had cars. The German travellers we met tended to be pleasant people with a good command of English.

After a long soak in the sea, we decided it was time to wash our clothes. While Beth scrubbed and pummelled, I traipsed back and forth from our tent to the well behind the church. It was an old-fashioned well. I would drop the bucket down, fill it with water and haul it back up with the old rope. By the afternoon, we had three lines of washing strung between the Beetle and two trees. The Germans were lazing about, amused by our industriousness. With the hard work over, I swept Beth into my arms, carried her to the beach and threw her into the sea. Between spurting out mouthfuls of water, she warned me that I would be sorry. The retaliation didn't take long. As I was relaxing on my camp chair, Beth grabbed a bucket of water and poured it over my head. By now, the Germans were laughing outright at our antics. The best was yet to come.

Beth began washing her hair, using shampoo and a bucket. I asked if she would do mine and she agreed, sitting me down as though I were in a barber shop. One German chap was guffawing so loudly at the scene that I felt he should join in. The bucket of soapy water which we'd just used for our hair was by my feet. In one swift movement, I covered him in bubbles and water. Stunned and silenced, he looked at me and then erupted in another round of ear-blasting guffaws.

The road from Split to Dubrovnik down the Dalmatian Coast was rough but magnificent, taking us high up on the cliffs with a view over the islands, and then back down to sea level for a close-up of the rocky beaches. Clear water beckoned us. We could see the tiny fish shimmering under the surface.

Near the towns, the coast was marred by construction sites of big tourist hotels and restaurants. All this development was a promise of prosperity from the communist government.

At Dubrovnik, we camped above the city in an olive grove, paying the farmer the price of three cigarettes. Vehicles were banned in the centre, and so the beautiful old walled city radiated an atmosphere of peace and serenity. We strolled through the alleys, buying grapes, tomatoes, potatoes and beans for next to nothing. Speaking into my tape recorder, Beth commented on the shops for our parents:

> *The shops do have everything that we're used to in life, but of very inferior quality. The shoes are shocking.*
> I added: *'As in Red countries, the selection of goods for sale is very poor, and luxury items so high-priced that locals can hardly afford them. When there's anything to do with tourists and tourism, the cost is very high. They give you a good rate of exchange, but they certainly get it back. They charge tourists double for everything.*

When we were planning the trip in London, we hadn't been sure which route we would take through Yugoslavia. We had requested four AA strip maps, but all of them went via Belgrade. Now, we were on the other side of the country with no map whatsoever. We chose roads on the basis of direction and size. All road surfaces were terrible, but the main ones slightly less terrible. As we crossed over the mountains towards Pec, we discovered the answer to our dreams: a modern, sealed highway. We should have known it was too good to be true.

Driving along the highway brought relief. We didn't have to avoid potholes or breathe in dust. Our bodies, accustomed to constant jolting, thanked us for the smooth surface. The Beetle hummed in happiness.

People working in the fields waved and pointed as we went by. But we were used to that. Inland, away from the 'tourist' coast, people were always staring at our Beetle, because there were fewer cars. And that accounted for the lack of traffic, we thought. The Beetle was the only car on the road.

'This is fantastic!' we kept telling each other, beaming with our good fortune.

Forty miles later, we came to the end of the road. Literally.

It wasn't finished yet! The dark tanned men, stripped to their waists, turned from blasting rock to see a Gulf blue Beetle come to a sudden halt. Others put down their picks to look and laugh. They grinned, toothlessly, pointing to the solid rock ahead, the road behind us and the Beetle. It was a great joke. Maybe we were the first ever to have driven along that road. While the men investigated the car, Beth and I walked around the site. Happy to be filmed, the men proudly posed with their equipment, still laughing and pointing at the car. And then it was time to back-track down forty miles of excellent highway, with the knowledge that we had to return to the rutted road.

That evening, we stayed in a field just outside Pec. Like most of the camp grounds we had seen, the one in Pec was too expensive for us, and a vast contrast to the reality for the locals, who could barely afford clothes. After a dinner of tinned meat with fresh beans and potatoes, I recounted the highway experience into the microphone and brought the family up to date:

We eventually arrived in Pec about 5:30pm and found the only petrol station in town. There was only one pump, a hand one. So few vehicles, and this is a town the size of Palmerston North! It's probably the dirtiest town we've seen. Once off the tourist coast, we found a poor Yugoslavia, so poor in fact that people are dressed in rags. They are so thin, the children gaunt-looking, and living in mud huts. There's lots of water and mud and slush around. Frankly it's been quite a shock to us, the first time we've seen such poverty in Yugoslavia, and probably the only time we've seen poverty of this kind since we started travelling.

We continually pass cartload after cartload of gypsies, literally hundreds. The children are very inquisitive. They all come and stand by the car and have a good look at you to see what you're doing. The people in southern Yugoslavia are dressed in national costume all the time. Here comes a man on a little donkey. All the men wear little felt skull caps, but everybody is so dirty and in such rags. Beth, what is today, darling, is it Thursday? I think it's the 14th of September.

In Skopje we came across some travellers who weren't German. A middle-aged Australian couple had bought a car in England and were travelling the continent. We thought them very adventurous, considering their advanced years. Just south of the town, we noticed two motorbikes flying the Dutch flag, the first other overland travellers we had met. Well-equipped, they were heading for Singapore, and then Darwin. They hoped to go to Burma, but did not know whether it was possible to obtain a visa and whether the roads would be passable. Travelling as cheaply as possible, the two chaps were living on rice and potatoes and had covered Europe in just ten days. It made us feel we were driving in luxury, detouring to Spain and Portugal, eating fruit and vegetables and spending five weeks to make it this far.

We had driven around the border of Albania. The country could have been a shortcut to Athens, but it was a closed communist state, eschewing Western influence. Communism in Yugoslavia wasn't so bad, we decided, amazed by the openness there. Our preconceptions of a police state were proven wrong; we saw few police and guards. None of our friends had been to Yugoslavia, and so our imaginings had been based on travel stories from the USSR.

Some travellers to communist states said they tired quickly of the difficulties in buying food and doing simple daily tasks. Others said the drabness depressed them. From an Australian couple, we heard the story of an English chap who had been approached by the KGB. It confirmed our suspicions of the tyrannical rule of communism.

The chap, a communist himself, lived in Britain with his wife. He went to the Soviet Union frequently, on the pretence of work but, really, to visit his girlfriend in Moscow. When our Australian friends met him, he was frightened. A few days before, he had been approached by two men, presumably the KGB. They had asked if he'd do a couple of jobs in Britain, such as investigating the backgrounds of English tourists before they came to Russia. They only wanted tourists who were sympathetic to communism and would not spread negative stories back in England. The chap replied that he didn't want to act against Great Britain. So then they offered him a permanent job in Russia, but he said, no thanks.

The next evening, he was walking his girlfriend home when a fellow jumped out in front of him, took a flash photograph of the two and disappeared. The English chap was very concerned and didn't know what to do. He told the Australian couple that he didn't want to tell anyone at home, not the authorities and particularly not his wife, but he did think the Russians would twist his arm when he returned to England. He felt he was definitely heading for trouble.

Although we were wary of communists, we hadn't actually met any. Stories of the Russian threat filled the papers. Yuri Gagarin had beaten us in space, while on earth it seemed that the Soviets would go to war over Berlin. Everyone was looking to John F Kennedy for hope and the righteous victory of democracy.

In New Zealand those who spoke against the Government were labelled 'commos'. It was a word to be used with caution. Commos were evil and a threat to political and social order. They infiltrated unions and created labour problems. When a friend joked that Beth's red frock was a 'commie' dress, it was an insult which caused great distress. Beth never wore the frock again.

The two main political parties in New Zealand were National and Labour. Inheriting our parents' preferences, Beth and I voted National. In my teens, I joined the Young National Party, not due to any burning ambition for politics, but because I had heard the Young Nationals held great social events with good-looking girls.

With forty years of hindsight, I could see that we had been indoctrinated during school, and those views were reinforced through the media and society. Critical thinking and questioning the status quo were not encouraged in our education system. We remained accepting and ill-informed.

The disarmament protesters were forward-thinkers, who had broken the boundaries of their upbringing. Perhaps it was university that had taught them to question. They were dreaming of saving the world; I was dreaming of earning enough money to drive around it. After being labelled 'not the intellectual type', I had left school at fifteen, before the end-of-year exams. I was slightly envious of university students and determined to prove I could be just as successful. At the time, I believed I was a man of my own making, with my own views, not recognising the social conditioning which had formed me.

Back then, we knew communism was bad. Every newspaper and television report told us of the Red threat. Years later, Beth and I travelled through the Soviet Union and China, holding in check our learned anti-communist attitudes, hoping to understand the countries through our own personal experiences. Regardless of the leaders and their political aspirations, we realised it was a hard life for the average person. Outside a Moscow shop, we joined a queue, hoping to buy some food to take on the Trans-Siberian railway. We ended up with a pot plant, the only item on sale that day.

The propaganda of the sixties presented one unified communist bloc that was preparing to paint the globe red. It was only later that we could see the reality: each government, each country and its people were different, with different political goals. I developed a healthy cynicism, a thriving distrust of the views presented by the government and media. I often wondered what realities society would discover in another thirty years when it looked back on its current propaganda.

1996

The State of Southern Europe

Yugoslavia exploded into civil war in 1991. We watched the televised scenes in horror, seeing little connection with the country we'd visited three decades before. Ethnic cleansing. Death camps. Tanks. Snipers. Mercenaries.

As we made our travel plans in 1996, one country had become five: Slovenia, Croatia, Bosnia, Macedonia and Yugoslavia. I wanted to re-visit the Balkans, not to see the effects of war, but the change in the region from 1961. Had the government lived up to the expectations of the trusting youth in its post-World War II optimism? Was rural peasant life now modernised? Did massive hotels and apartment blocks obliterate the beauty of the coast? But the instability worried us. We decided against going.

Our disappointment at not seeing the Yugoslav region was tempered by the excitement of our first visit to the Czech Republic, another former communist state. Unlike Yugoslavia under Tito's policy of non-alliance, Czechoslovakia had been dominated by the Soviet Union. It was interesting to note that both of these former countries were created after World War I, from the Austro-Hungarian Empire, that mighty power which my Austrian friend, Frederick, had once explained to me. And since then, these countries had broken up into even smaller nations.

With the Beetle's clean bill of health from the Volkswagen factory in Wolfsburg, we headed south-east through Germany towards Prague, past the tall chimneys of industrialised regions and then into lush meadows, fields of sunflowers and wild pink roses. At the border near Teplice, we faced a short queue to buy our Czech visas and go through customs. Three agitated English fellows were hoping to speed up the process. They'd arrived at another border post only to discover that visas weren't available there. In a hurry, caught short, they had thus lost a day by going to the wrong crossing. We heard a number of tourists had experienced the same problem, stuck at a border post unable to enter the Czech Republic because they had assumed visas could be bought everywhere.

During our picnic lunch by the road, we realised the Beetle would be at home in the Czech Republic, a country full of old cars. However, there was still the possibility of it being stolen. In the city of Prague, we needed somewhere safe, in the suburbs, where we could leave the Beetle while we went sightseeing.

A friend had recommended the Penzion Ivana, on the outskirts of Prague. Beth joked, 'Ivan just wants to stay at the Ivana'.

Armed with images of Prague's majestic spires and arched bridges, we were slightly taken aback on our arrival at the Penzion Ivana. It was in Jinonice, an outlying suburb consisting of grey, Soviet-style apartment blocks and very few patches of grass and garden. As with most cities, the stunning tourist office photographs obscured the reality of a city surrounded by people living in ugly flats and ordinary houses.

The Beetle rested at the Penzion as we set off to explore Prague by train and foot. With its thirty baroque statue groups, we found the Charles Bridge to be the most splendid of the bridges which spanned the River Vltava. We weren't the only ones enjoying its charm on this glorious sunny day. Tourists in bright shorts and T-shirts posed for photos against the statues. The air filled with the sounds of buskers and stallholders touting their wares. In an attempt to sell her ceramic flutes, a long-haired girl was playing a haunting tune from the musical, *Cats*. Artists sketched mediocre images of their customers. Gypsies, dripping in gold jewellery, begged for money. Ducks and rowing boats glided beneath us while, on both sides of the river, spires glinted in the sun.

The tourists streamed towards Prague Castle to see all the architectural styles of Prague in the one place. The Cathedral, with its massive stained-glass windows, had taken six hundred years to build and was only completed in the 1930s. We wandered through the brightly painted workmen's cottages, the tiny rooms now full of arts and crafts.

While Beth feasted on the artworks in the National Gallery of the Palace, I unpacked my new video camera and filmed the square. A palace guard, immaculate in his blue-and-white uniform, the gold crest reflecting the sun, stood motionless in his guard box. His rifle wavered slightly, and sweat trickled on his forehead, but apart from that, there was no movement from him. The cool, short-sleeved tourists posed with him and still he did not flinch. I filmed him for a full five minutes, waiting to catch the moment when he would wipe his brow or adjust his gun. He remained rigid. Eventually, I pressed the stop button. He had outdone me! I couldn't hold up the video camera for that long, let alone stand still in the one position. My silly game had given me great respect for his skill and discipline.

We walked back down the steep hill to *Staromestske namesti*, the wide city square dominated by the old Town Hall. A well-dressed wedding party and a band of trumpets and drums competed for the tourists' attention. But, on the hour, it was the Town Hall clock which drew the largest crowd. Twelve apostles and a bell-ringing skeleton danced out under a golden bird and stone angel. The clock face itself boasted gold numerals, a world map in its centre and carved stone animals around its edge. The intricacy and beauty of the clock caused sighs of appreciation, followed by grunts of disgust on learning that the architect's eyes were plucked out so he could never create a rival piece of work.

Not far from the Town Hall, we discovered the surviving buildings of *Josefov*, the traditional Jewish quarter. During World War II, *Josefov* had been emptied by the Nazis and the buildings used for storage. Almost ninety per cent of the Jewish population in Prague had been killed. Hitler's aim was blatant in Czechoslovakia. It was said he ordered Jewish artifacts to be collected as the basis for a future exhibition of 'an extinct race'. The artifacts were now on display at the State Jewish Museum, which included five synagogues and a cemetery.

Czech crystal, jewellery and salami beckoned from the shop windows on *Na prikope*, the main shopping street near Wenceslaus

Square, the site of mass demonstrations during the communist rule. I filmed the meat shop, amazed at the hundreds of salamis hanging from every possible point. Beth bought a garnet ring for herself and a crystal bell to be rung for silence before the speeches at Liza and Rob's wedding. Liza had efficiently organised most of the wedding before we'd left Australia, so we expected only a few international phone calls and emails discussing the dress and the guest list. I assumed that I would be told what suit to wear.

Green gnomes with lanterns; red gnomes fishing; blue gnomes giving the finger; gnomes flashing their chests; sunglassed gnomes relaxing in chairs—the village gardens were bursting with them. The uniform red caps and white beards smiled at us from almost every village, as we drove south from Prague towards Ceske Budejovice.

Five hundred carp lakes dotted the countryside under the gaze of fairytale gothic castles, which appeared to float on the hills above. The heavy rain reminded us of driving into Yugoslavia, and we put the tape from 1961 into the cassette player. We had a sudden inclination to try out our brand new tent, perhaps due to the mention of camping on the tape. But as the rain bucketed down, the basic hotel near the camp ground became more and more appealing. There was to be no sleeping in the Beetle this time—too uncomfortable for our older bones! That night, the new tent stayed neatly folded in the jetbag up on the roof. And it was to remain in this position for the entire trip.

Founded in 1265 as a royal town, Ceske Budejovice's real claim to fame was as the original home of Buduar (Budweiser) beer. Appropriately, we escaped from the rain by dining at a beer hall and enjoying the beverage.

Because it was a brief visit, we only managed a quick walk around the massive town square bordered by Renaissance and

Baroque houses. Beth and I decided this was an excellent base for exploring the castles in the nearby towns of southern Bohemia. We had time for just two: the medieval town and palace of Cesky Krumlov and the rococo facades of the village square in Telc. Both were stunning examples of architecture, but I was pleased it was Monday and the palace was closed. It meant I didn't have to follow Beth around the interior. While she loved to see the furniture and artworks and tapestries, I preferred to wander around outside, chatting with people.

August 1996

Hot Baths and Hungarian Hospitality

As we drove across the border into Austria, we vowed to return to the Czech Republic. We knew we hadn't done the country justice, but this trip was about moving onwards. Unlike the 1961 journey, we had an itinerary and a time limit, and we had to keep on moving. It was a different sensation from a normal holiday because there was a purpose, a destination which had to be reached.

Vienna offered the chance to do chores: washing clothes and sending faxes. We had been to this gracious, sophisticated city before and delighted in the sightseeing rounds of magnificent palaces and cathedrals. We stayed with Liza's friend, Doris, enjoying her hospitality and catching up on each other's news.

At Demel, the most famous bakery in Austria, I indulged in my favourite sweet, vanilla slice. With boyish impatience, I couldn't wait to eat, so I had a vanilla slice on the way and then another when we arrived at Demel. While Beth commented on the fashionably dressed Viennese, I announced that I felt extremely sick and would never have vanilla slice again. As was to be expected, Beth refused to take me and my illness seriously.

A three-hour drive from Vienna and we were in Budapest. As we had lived most of our lives in New Zealand and Australia, the cluster of different countries and cultures in the small space of Europe never ceased to amaze us. It was the reverse experience had by many English visitors to Australia who, in flying the five hours from Sydney to Perth, couldn't believe they were still in the same country with the same language and accent.

The proximity of Vienna and Budapest meant we compared the two cities, Budapest coming off as the poor cousin in desperate need of money to restore its run-down treasures. Its turn-of-the-century charm, however, was still evident: the wide boulevards and myriad architectural styles. We walked over the not-so-blue Danube, across the Chain Bridge, its entrances guarded by fierce stone lions, and up the steep hill to the impressive Royal Palace. Our legs complained that we should have caught the funicular. The thirteenth-century domed Royal Palace had been constantly re-built and reconstructed following sieges by the Tartars, Turks, Nazis and the Red Army. Virtually in ruins after World War II and suffering further damage in the 1956 uprising against the communists, the city's recent reconstruction work had unearthed centuries of artifacts, even some from the earliest palace.

I had read that 'taking the waters' was a must in Budapest, a historical reminder of the Romans and Turks, and an excellent way to relax. There were all sorts of baths catering for every personality and pocket. Beth went off to the Government Folk Art Store, and I found some baths in the middle of a park.

It was the most unpleasant experience.

Maybe I chose the wrong bathhouse. Maybe it was my Western

perception of being pampered in a hot spa. I was expecting so much more.

Masses of bodies bumped against one another in the hot, dirty water of the old pool. Too risky to swim, I thought, picturing the germs multiplying in the heat. And the people were so old and ugly. Beth always teased me that young bikinied women featured heavily whenever I was videoing on a beach. She was right, but they were far more attractive than this collection of sagging bodies, which must have been, well, at least a few years older than mine.

I realised my disappointment stemmed from my own misinterpretation of the baths concept. People came here for medicinal reasons, arthritis and the like, not as a pampering luxury. Deciding to make the most of the situation, I endured a pedicure from a woman in a white smock and then left, without ever 'taking the waters'.

Budapest's public transport system was efficient. We'd caught a tram and buses that day, and now we took the metro for dinner at the New York Café, a favourite meeting place of artists and writers since the early 1900s. It was a living memorial of what Budapest once was: a buzzing atmosphere with the formality of chandeliers, violins, crisp white tablecloths and well-dressed waiters. The guidebook said no-one came here for the food, but we relished our tasty veal goulash, salad and beer.

To avoid having your car ripped off, take the usual precautions. Most Hungarian thieves are not after fancy Western models, as they're too difficult to get rid of. But Volkswagens, Audis and the like are very popular, and they're easy to dismantle and ship abroad. Don't leave anything of value inside the car, even if it is hidden.

Lonely Planet Guidebook, Hungary

Harshegyi, a camp ground in the Buda Hills, promised the highest level of safety for the Beetle. We chose one of the 'first class' cabins, rearranging the single beds to be next to one another and dealing with the hand-held showerhead and lack of curtain by taking it in turns to stand and direct the spray onto each other.

In the camping ground, we noticed an overland truck with a pair of bare female legs sticking out from underneath the engine. Ruth, a slim attractive Australian girl, was the driver, mechanic, manager and guide for the trip. With her truckload of mainly New Zealand backpackers, Ruth was on her way to Nepal via Egypt, Syria and Iraq. Trouble was blowing up in Iraq but Ruth seemed confident, despite this being her first tour. Romania and Bulgaria, on a route known for hold-ups and problems, were also on their itinerary. Beth worried that they had so little information and gave them her *Lonely Planet Guidebook* of Eastern Europe.

We chatted to Ruth's passengers, who were enthusiastic and happy. One Kiwi fellow said he'd paid $7,000 for the truck trip. It seemed an expensive overland camping trip to us, recalling our budget of two pounds a day in 1961. When they left the next morning, we felt a degree of trepidation. Would they make it? So young, keen, ill-informed and going through all the hotspots— much like us thirty-five years before. We hoped to catch up with them in Pakistan, mainly to reassure ourselves that they were okay.

Memories tugged at us of the three overland buses we had come across in Turkey in 1961. The bus drivers/owners had run short of finance for the trip and disappeared one night in Turkey, leaving the buses with the passengers. Booked on a ship from Colombo, the Kiwi and Aussie passengers had a month to get through Turkey and Pakistan, with little cash on them. They had all paid the £55 fee for the bus trip and hadn't expected to need much more.

In Lahore, we had met them again, begging for help from the British Consulate. Two mechanically-minded Australians had driven one bus on to the Pakistan border, hoping to have it impounded so the owners couldn't get it back. The two other buses had fallen to bits, with the passengers resorting to third-class train travel, £2 for 1,000 miles. They said the train officials had been fairly decent and given them a section to themselves. It would cost them another £5 to travel from Lahore to Colombo but they expected to make the ship in time. Despite it being a public holiday in Pakistan, the staff at the British Consulate had stayed open to sort out the problems of those bus passengers minus their bus. By that stage, the travellers had resigned themselves to their unplanned adventure, but were still concerned about running out of money.

Hungary, now so accessible to tourists, was aggressively chasing the foreign dollar, and Szentendre was the perfect example. Situated on the Danube bend, with a varied cultural history, the town had become an attractive artists' colony, pulling in hordes of tourists. Around the cobbled square, the bustling shop assistants, in traditional dress, sold embroidered dolls, blue-and-white linen and bright red chillies.

As usual, Beth and I compromised our sightseeing preferences. Beth went to see three of the art museums, including the works of the popular Margit Kovacs, a well-known artist who combined traditional Hungarian styles with modern themes in her ceramic works. Beth described Kovacs' work as different from any other pottery she'd seen and beautiful in an unusual way. Generally, I didn't mind art galleries too much, but my lack of art knowledge always made me feel I wasn't quite 'getting it', and so I tended to lose patience. Instead, I wandered around the town square, people-watching and videoing the colourful buildings, as well as a brass band in full uniform with a plain-clothes conductor.

The countryside by the road up the Danube to Esztergom was lush. Purple, white and yellow flowers were hidden in the long green grass. Oak trees towered above us. We stopped to buy peaches for eighty cents a kilo from a roadside stall. Through the language barrier, we chatted unintelligibly to the stallholders, a middle-aged couple who insisted on showing us their garden. I grabbed the video camera and filmed the large man, clad only in black trunks, his huge stomach hanging over the top. Talking in Hungarian to the camera, he proudly showed off his beans, tomatoes and fruit trees. We assumed the house, overlooking the Danube, was a weekender. As we left, saying a cheery goodbye, the wife piped up and, with many giggles and much difficulty, said, 'Thank-you-very-much'. We were touched by her effort.

By mistake, we almost entered Slovakia, the other part of the former Czechoslovakia. We lined up for the car ferry at Esztergom, paid for our tickets and looked forward to driving back down the other side of the Danube. Beth stared at the foreign signs and said, 'That's odd. I think that sign means we're going into another country.' Dashing back to the ticket office, she asked if we were heading for Slovakia. The man nodded and then burst into bellows of laughter as Beth tried to explain we didn't want to go there, and could we have our money back please? Eventually we managed to manoeuvre the Beetle out from the ferry queue and drove back the way we came, to catch the ferry at Visegrad.

'There's a billboard for a Volkswagen,' I shouted, slamming my foot on the brake. The car pictured was almost identical to ours and we copied the pose for a photo: bonnet up, boot up and me pointing off into the distance. I couldn't understand why there was a Beetle advertisement when the car was no longer made.

Leaving London first time round. August 1961.

About to set off on the second honeymoon! Copeland House, Kensington, London. August 1996.

My two loves — Beth and the Beetle — ready for a long drive down memory lane. London. August 1996.

Ivan and Beth posing for German newspapers at VW headquarters in Wolfsburg. August 1996.

*E-mailing from the Austrian
campground, near Graz.
20 August 1996.*

*The hospitality of a stranger: relaxing at Agnes' cottage in the Hungarian countryside,
near Kohdorfa. August 1996.*

Meeting Italian Volkswagen staff in Verona for a Beetle check-up. 23 August 1996.

Our modern cabin in Fiesole, outside Florence. Drinking Italian wine while watching the sunset. 28 August 1996.

By asking directions, we finally found the small village of Paciano, Italy, twin town to Mosman, Sydney. 30 August 1996.

A welcome break on the road in Eastern Turkey. 1961.

Fording a river near the Black Sea coast, Turkey. October 1961.

Coming to the end of the road literally! Yugoslavia. September 1961.

On the ferry to Kos when bad weather threatened to push the Beetle overboard. 1996.

Rhodes harbourside, waiting for the ferry. 1996.

About to cross the continents, driving into Turkey. 1961.

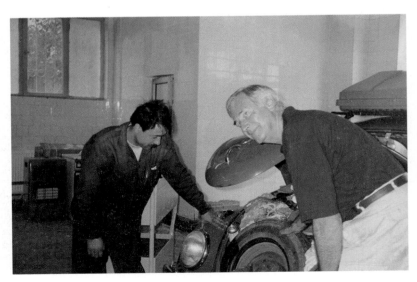

The Beetle gets a check-up in Ankara. 1996.

Then we spotted the mobile phone in the corner of the poster. Presumably the Hungarian caption said something about breaking down. Hopefully it wouldn't happen to us. We had a mobile phone, but could only use it to access voice mail messages at the moment, or so we thought. Beth decided to try ringing Australia as we were crossing the Danube, and to our surprise, succeeded in speaking with Keris and Liza.

'What does NZ mean?' A young woman with a large silver medallion hanging around her neck was pointing to the sticker on the back of the Beetle. We were in a small village in the hills, ten kilometres from Budapest, stopping to check our directions. When I explained it was New Zealand, her reply was 'Jesus!'

'Come and join us for lunch,' she suggested, in a flamboyant manner. 'We're going to a good restaurant.'

We'd only been talking for a few minutes and had already witnessed Agnes' generosity. She was open and welcoming, a woman curious about people and travel. It was a delightful lunch with her and Josef her friend. They had met up a few days ago, after not having seen each other for fifteen years since working together in Budapest. Josef was now in Stockholm and Agnes, a jewellery designer in Munich. She felt it was important her son know his Hungarian heritage and returned frequently to see her mother in Budapest or to stay in her weekend cottage near Szent-gotthard, close to the Austrian border.

It was a meal of conversation. We fed on talk of Hungary, Munich and travel. Agnes and Josef shared local stories and asked about our own journey and why we were doing it once again. By dessert, Agnes had invited us to stay in her cottage, saying she would ring the neighbours and organise for them to give us the key. We were overwhelmed by her kindness. She trusted us, total strangers.

On the way to the cottage, we expected a beautiful drive along Lake Balaton, 'Hungary's inland sea', but we were sorely disappointed. Barely an inch of the seventy-seven kilometre lake had an open shore. Wall-to-wall caravan parks meant we could hardly see the water, let alone sit by it. And this was on the northern shore, supposedly the less touristy side. Not stopping, we continued on to Agnes' cottage, discovering verdant, sleepy farmland, a world away from the chaotic tourism of Lake Balaton.

The neighbour happily provided the key, and the farmer down the hill sold us eggs for breakfast. They had all been 'warned' of our coming by Agnes and accepted us into their community for a few days.

The tranquillity captivated us immediately: birdcalls, a barking dog and women scything the hay were the only sounds. The white cottage, with its red-tiled roof and homely furniture, contained everything we needed to be comfortable. The sun was warm as I sat in our picnic chair on the verandah, reading and gazing over the low, green hills.

In her spontaneous gesture, Agnes could not have realised what she was giving us. A chance to unwind completely; to relax, away from the demands of driving, navigating and sightseeing. Almost an escape from our holiday, with its daily effort to orient ourselves, find a hotel, search for markets or a cafe dinner. While we did enjoy the challenge of arriving in new places, Agnes' cottage was a breathing space. We could get back into an organised state, wash our belongings, clean the car and re-pack it. It also gave Beth some time to catch up on her writing.

19 August 1996

Beth's Diary

By the time I awoke, Ivan had breakfast ready and was surveying 'our estate'. Fresh peaches and yoghurt, with toast made on the gas burner using a fork. I wish I hadn't left our camping toaster in Australia. I thought I'd put in a toasting fork but can't seem to find that either.

Great joy again—we have just accessed our email and sent mail back. We tried using the mobile, but no service, so connected to Agnes' phone and will leave some cash. Several emails from Keris, who is going ahead in leaps and bounds at the office. I washed my hair and could use a hairdryer, a small thrill, and then washed some clothes. Tidied up inside the car and the box on top. Now I've caught up on my diary, and Ivan is still playing with his computer.

We drove about ten kilometres to the next village and found a nice little 'pub' for lunch: soup, beer, salad, schnitzel, for $21. As we went through several other villages, I noticed that the gardens are very colourful, in contrast to Budapest. In one of the villages, on top of a lamp post, there was a huge stork's nest, complete with stork. On the hillsides, the cottages are Hansel-and-Gretel style, and the land seems to be divided into long lean parcels.

Back in Kondorfa, a National Day celebration had started in the local park. A band and vocalist were doing their best, and two large cauldrons of goulash were on the boil. The men were drinking seriously and the women chatting. Elderly ladies wore kerchiefs of various colours.

Behind 'our cottage', a local family was turning their patch of hay, and then the father appeared with a wooden cart yoked to two cows. Ivan went down to film and delighted them by showing the replay on the camera. I took a toy koala to the child. Tonight we were serenaded by the sounds of the local celebrations as we ate our toasted baked bean sandwiches.

for love and a beetle

Because of the problem with Ivan's credit card, we're carrying a lot of cash, so have spread that between us and inside the coffee bean tin. I'm writing this clad in my T-shirt and face plastered with masque—must keep up the routine! Reading and enjoying Midnight in the Garden of Good and Evil.

It hadn't occurred to us that the celebrations meant a two-day public holiday, and the country was virtually shutting down. The usual St Stephen's Day national events were particularly important this year, as Hungary celebrated its 1,100th anniversary. The following day, as we searched for the necessities of bread and petrol, we could hear celebratory gunfire in the distance. We left Hungary and its festivities behind, heading for Italy, via Austria.

'We've clocked up nearly 2,000 miles,' I informed Beth, as the odometer ticked over another ten miles. Quite an achievement, I thought, until I realised we hadn't covered even one fifth of our 11,000 mile trip.

Chapter 4

Feasts, Wine Festivals and the Mod Cons

Emails From An Austrian Camp Ground

Sent: Tuesday, 20 August 1996
  To: Keris
  Subject: Now in Austria
  Dearest Daughters Keris, Liza and Britta . . . and not forgetting Tahni and Rob

We had only a short distance to drive into Austria; sad to leave our country cottage, but any more silence would have caused nervous tension! Beth selected a most scenic route not on the main roads. It was still a holiday in Hungary, and when we crossed into Austria, they were also closed, but it was just their lunch break and they re-opened for business again at 2:30pm. The border post was not busy; the Austrians were interested in the number plates, the original English one, which we attached below the NZ plate.

It was not long before the comparisons of an affluent nation against a developing country were obvious. It started in the supermarket, with prices double that of Hungary. Streets were cleaner, signage better and far more orderly. Cars were faster. In Hungary, the Beetle could hold its own with the many old models.

Well, we're now in a camping ground outside of Graz. A cabin with a small bed, costing about A$45. It's small but the people are nice, and we are parked right at the door. Our self-catering dinner will be fruit (apricots, peaches, apples), bread rolls with ham and vine-ripened toma-toes. We had lunch in Hungary to get rid of our 500 florins (about A$5), *and still there was one dollar left over, so we bought ice-creams!*

Temperature today: 32 degrees Celsius. We rolled down the car windows a little further. The land is so green and lush. It has been a wonderful drive today, in both countries.

Love to you all, Daddyo and Mum

The cabin, with its corrugated roof and proximity to the camp ground toilets, didn't make an ideal home office, but I pushed aside the teapot and basket of tomatoes and set up my laptop computer on the red-and-white plastic tablecloth.

Unsure of the reliability of universal attachments for electrical sockets, we'd bought a plug for the different systems of each country. Beth up-ended the bag and we searched for one to fit Austria. In the absence of a power point in the cabin, I resorted to the light socket, putting the plug in above me, the cord hanging down next to my head. With my slow, two-fingered typing, I tapped out a short message to our daughters. They were the reason we were carrying so much technology.

Then came the task of connecting. As to be expected, there was no phone cable in the cabin. I attached the laptop to the modem and to Beth's mobile phone and dialled in. We shuddered to think of the cost of connecting over the mobile. Keris received the bills, generously paid them and refused to reveal the damage. From the home front, she was handling everything for us—credit card problems, bookings and reservations, Volkswagen and media contact, the posting of films and other necessities, and the informing of family and friends as to our whereabouts. Only afterwards did we realise the enormous strain we had placed upon her; it was our only misgiving of the entire journey.

In our cabin in the camp ground, the connection worked! Each time I successfully downloaded emails, feelings of relief surged through me. Still new to this game, I was learning as I went along. Today I had emails from family, friends and strangers. The one from Keris included a fax from the Australian Embassy warning about the situation in Turkey. I wanted to print it out. It was impossible in this cabin without another power point.

Outside their campervan, a German couple around our age, in the holiday uniform of shorts and T-shirts, were enjoying a glass of wine as the hot day gave way to the cooler dusk. I had an idea that their campervan must have at least two power points.

Once I'd explained my predicament, the couple were only too pleased to have me connect up. Laptop, printer and mobile phone all plugged in, we showed them our emails and the Internet. As far as I could understand, they'd never seen any of this before. They craned over my shoulder, watching in fascination, only turning away to summon friends from a nearby van.

'Das ist Wünderbar!' they exclaimed, clapping me on the shoulder and smiling broadly at Beth. Wine was passed around, and I proudly beamed at my camp ground display, not letting anyone else touch a single key.

We printed out the fax forwarded to us by Keris. The news wasn't good:

AUSTRALIAN EMBASSY TURKEY—FACSIMILE
MESSAGE
Dear Hodges
We have received a letter regarding your travel. Following please find the travel advice for Turkey for your information.

The Department of Foreign Affairs and Trade recommends that because of the continuing dangerous security situation in Eastern and Southern Turkey, Australian citizens should defer all non-essential travel to those regions.

There have also been isolated security incidents directed at tourists else-where in Turkey, including in Istanbul and on the Mediterranean coast. Australian travellers are advised to observe local instructions and exercise caution at all times.

Australians who visit Turkey are encouraged to contact the Australian Embassy in Ankara or the Australian Consulate-General in Istanbul for advice on current developments.

NB. While every care has been taken in preparing these Travel Advices, neither the Australian Government nor its agents or employees, including any member of Australia's consular staff abroad, can accept liability for injury, loss or damage arising in respect of any statement contained herein.

'They're overreacting,' I announced haughtily to Beth. 'It's their job to be excessively cautious.'

She agreed that was probably the case, but thought we should look at other options for our route. I didn't want to even think about it. There was no way I was turning back, especially not from Austria. We hadn't even left Europe yet. What sort of over-land trip would that be? Excited, determined and stubborn, I had no intention of cancelling this journey.

'We'll reassess the situation when we get to Turkey,' I told Beth. 'At least then we can speak to the Embassy and read the papers and see what's really happening.' I muttered that we could always do the trip again next year, but the thought of having to give up made me angry. Knowing that there was little chance of my turning the Beetle around, Beth hoped the political situation wasn't as dangerous as it appeared.

While I was pleased with the technology we were carrying, at this point I wished we were ignorant of the Turkish situation. Then we could just keep driving until the point of no return. Instead we were continuing, against Embassy advice, with our daughters worried for our safety, and Beth and I aware that we were acting irresponsibly. It was exciting for young backpackers to charge headlong into areas of political unrest and live to tell the tale, but the more mature travellers like us were expected to exercise intelligent caution. 'Bugger that,' I thought and tried to dismiss everybody's concerns.

Our 'mobile home office' amazed me. I was thrilled to be sharing the trip with others through the Internet and extremely proud of my new technological status. Few other travellers were hooked up like us, and I knew no others of my age who had their own personal home page. Fascinated by the power of the Internet, I imagined the possibilities in business, the ability to break down international boundaries, to make contacts and sell products across the world, all from a home computer.

Through the media and our home page, we were receiving emails from well-wishing strangers the world over. Stunned by the number of interested people, I made the effort to reply to every one. In Australia, our home page became popular when the address appeared on the front page of *The Sydney Morning Herald* in Column 8, a section providing amusing snippets. Anthony, a friend's son, was updating this home page of ours. It was he who told us of the paragraph in the *Herald* as we were setting off from London.

Sent: Monday, 8 July 1996
  To: hodge@fl.net.au
  Hello, I trust you had a safe and comfortable journey. Well at about 1am last night (yes I am always on the job!) I received an email message checking the address of the web page before a small article gets printed in Column 8. The article was published today and reads:
  In 1961, as newlyweds, Ivan and Beth Hodge, of Balmoral, drove a VW Beetle from London to Calcutta. Yesterday, Ivan and Beth left for

London, where they will pick up the same VW (it has served the family here for 35 years) when it arrives by ship. Then, on August 1, although being of sound mind, they'll set out on the same journey, including the passage of the Khyber Pass. Friends will keep track of their progress on the Web—http;www.hodge.fl.net.au

I am a bit grumpy—the above semicolon should be a colon, but I think most people will work it out. Some time between 1am this morning and 11:59am (when I got up) your web page had about 50 visitors. I'll update the log and map now with your current position, London.

Kind regards, Anthony

Emails from New Zealand began rolling in after the segment on *The Holmes Show* had gone to air. The television program mentioned we had an email address, and the station was inundated with calls. Beth and I puffed up as we read comments admiring our adventurous spirit and courage; it was more flattering than our daughters labelling us 'foolish'. Many people found parallels between our lives and theirs:

Sent: Thurday, 12 September 1996
  To: Ivan and Beth Hodge
Greetings, We saw the item on The Holmes Show *the other night. We are extremely jealous, having been part of the way down the road you are now travelling. We lived in Cardiff from 1968 till 71 and bought a 1967 VW 1500 (the first of the 1500s in a 1200 body shell) and planned to do the overland trip. However, events got in the way and we never made it.*

Holmes, in his closing remarks, said something along the lines of who would keep a receipt from the 1960s? Jan, my wife, immediately said that she would and—in fact—had. We still, or rather Jan has the ignition key for a car we used in Cardiff. Not in a drawer as a memento, but still on the key ring she uses every day. So don't feel guilty about hoarding things!

Our Beetle was the most reliable car we ever had, and we ran it for twelve years after arriving here with it. The two children were heartbroken when we finally sold it, and I have said that should we ever win Lotto, we will buy it back.

We would love to be on the trip with you and wish you both all the very best. TVNZ said that they had many requests for your email address, so there is a lot of interest out there in cyberspace in your journey. We are hoping to get back to the UK in 18 months and stay for a year or so, but I doubt if we will have the courage to do what you are doing.

Wishing you both all the very best and God speed, Nevile and Jan

During the journey, we wrote to Nevile and Jan a number of times, learning more about their Beetle and they about ours. Friendships evolved over the Internet, emails whizzing back and forth between strangers with a common love for travel or a Beetle. Often we couldn't figure out which country they were from. And it wasn't just folk our age, yearning for past adventures. Much younger people wrote in, expressing their dreams of making a similar journey. Some even commented on our marriage:

Dear Ivan & Beth, I am a Kiwi who has been watching your progress on TV with a lot of interest. I admire how you have kept your original car all these years, I only managed to keep my first car for nine years (ie, it was over twenty years old then). My Mum thinks it is lovely to see how you two are so close after thirty years of a wonderful marriage. I guess there must be nothing more challenging in a marriage than to go to the ends of the earth together! Wishing you all the best, Warwick.

This chap, Warwick, echoed my thoughts exactly. I felt that our marriage had worked so well because of its grounding in the first trip. Travelling in a car and sleeping in a two-man tent provided no chance for escaping from one another. Quite simply, we had to get along. Now, on the 'second honeymoon', we were enjoying that closeness once again, delighting in the uninterrupted hours we had to talk, discussing the world around us or life back home. We had time to reflect.

People we'd lost contact with over the years heard of our trip and suddenly sent email messages wishing us luck. A German couple wrote, wondering if we were the New Zealanders who had camped with them in 1961 near Alicante, Spain. We weren't, but the message reinforced what we already knew: so many people fondly recalled their travel experiences as young people in a world before responsibilities.

Hello Ivan and Beth, I saw the beginning of your trip from London tonight on Holmes. *What a wonderfully adventurous couple you are! Thank you for sharing your experiences with us. It reminds me of my big Overseas Experience in 1967 in a little Minivan. Have a great time, and hopefully no VW naughtiness! I look forward to the next episode! Bon voyage, and safe travelling, Robyn*

An Australian couple, Jim and Colleen, dropped a line after reading our story in the *Daily Telegraph*. Their Beetle was a year younger than ours but, unfortunately, not faring as well. It was in the car wreckers in Mt Isa—after the engine had blown up on the way back from the Northern Territory! Despite the incident, Jim and Colleen still held their belief in Beetles and were hoping to convince their son to buy one.

We discovered that Sue, a woman in America, had exactly the same model as our Beetle, in exactly the same colour and it, too, was still in good working condition. The Beetle owners who wrote demonstrated their passion for the cars, even for old Beetles they had since sold. An email from a car club summed up how the peculiar-shaped Beetle had made such an impact on so many people, from Germany to NZ:

Subject: Honeymoon in 'Herbie'!

We have all been following your story (and updates) with interest and a great measure of nostalgia! The distinctive VW has featured in many of our lives, and I personally learned to drive in one, and was captivated for life by its charismatic charm and distinctive personality! No other car, before or after, has left such an impression on me! Your story on The Holmes Show *tonight was really heartwarming! The roses were a timely and romantic touch!! Happy holiday, both of you. From Susan Brennan-Hodgson on behalf of The Micro Car Club of New Zealand*

With the NZ well-wishers, it often eventuated that we had mutual friends or that I knew people in their towns. Occasionally, I emailed back, asking them for a favour. Janet, who lived in Otaki, kindly agreed to call Terry Knowles, the Beetle's mechanic, and let him know the car was running perfectly. Nevile phoned my old friend, Les, whom I had worked with for many years, to give him an update on our journey. Les was a Beetle man himself—he had bought a new one almost every year, in exactly the same colour, so his clients wouldn't think he was doing too well!

With her teaching background, Beth was particularly interested in one email we had from Dunedin, NZ. We were going to be used as a geography lesson! Having seen us on *The Holmes Show*, a teacher of a tourism course asked if we could send him a regular progress report of our travels. He felt it would be a great use of the Internet to teach world geography to his students.

It was wonderful to receive emails from the countries we were travelling through. A German family had read about us in the VW company magazine and suggested we drop in for dinner if we were near Cologne. Another offer was from an English girl who said she could keep us informed on 'significant' events in that country:

Greetings, I hear you are intrepid explorers, travelling overland to New Zealand. Well, good luck with your endeavour. I will follow your progress as you travel. I am based in Cambridge, UK, so if you want updates on Coronation Street *or* Charles and Princess Di, *let me know. Good Luck. Syl*

Email made it so much easier to connect with people, and it opened up doors that wouldn't have otherwise existed. One evening, we received a message from John, a typesetter on a newspaper in South Africa. John had just finished setting an article on us for the *Cape Times* in Cape Town. He assured us we would complete the trip because we were driving 'the best car in the world'. I assumed the paper had heard of us through a press release from Volkswagen. From then on, we communicated regularly with Les, the motoring editor of the paper, sending in a few paragraphs about where we were. It was odd to be writing to a person we had never met, for a paper we had never seen, in a country we weren't travelling through. Once again, the international interest in the Beetle trip astounded me.

It was Keris who had insisted we take a laptop and mobile phone to stay in touch. With her computer knowledge, she had researched what we should buy and which email service provider to use. She had spoken with computer salesmen and technical experts, deciding on the right equipment so we could connect anywhere, from an Austrian camp ground to a beach in Turkey.

I took her advice because it was all over my head. I'd used computers before, but never email or the Internet. I had a steep learning cliff to climb into the technology of the nineties. *Dialling-up*, *modem* and *downloading* soon became words I understood. That wasn't to say it was easy. Keris spent tortured hours teaching me; without her, it would never have been possible.

The technology side of our trip had been finalised only a few days before we left Sydney. Events had conspired against us: the first modem didn't work and then a shipment didn't arrive in time. Because we wanted to use the modem on a mobile phone, there were set-up problems, as dialling sytems had to be altered. If we were a huge company with money to spend, it would have been far simpler—a satellite phone was the best option, but that was out of our league. Eventually it was sorted out. We connected through Microsoft and had a list of numbers to dial for email access in each country.

Beth was amused by my enthusiasm for my new toys. Between cleaning the apartment and packing for the trip, she had watched me playing but rapidly disappeared when I began swearing because I couldn't make it work. Beth also learnt how to use the system, but she barely had a chance to send one email because I closely guarded my new possessions, watching over her shoulder, terrified she would do something wrong. Those few days were the beginning of endless hours of frustration as we tried to connect during the trip. In the end, it was worth it. The opportunity to share our journey with so many people, especially our family, was priceless.

We had agreed to the communication network mainly to assure our daughters we weren't at risk. Realistically, the risk factor was my reason for going: a buzz, a thrill to set off into the unknown. As it was in the old days—the Beetle, Beth and I dependent on

each other. But even back then, I had a hankering for technological gadgets. And it was the same idea of wanting our family
to share our experiences in places so far from home.

September 1961

Gregarious Greeks

I was really chuffed with my brand new Stuzzi tape recorder in
1961. None of the other travellers had anything like it, let alone
a movie camera as well. It was all insured, just in case. I wasn't
taking that risk again. On the ship to England, the tape recorder
we'd bought in Singapore had been stolen, probably by the crew.
We'd only used it once. Now, on this trip, I was making the most
of my Stuzzi, interviewing as many locals as I could. They were
impressed with the equipment, too.

One Greek chap we met in a café in Athens had been living in
Australia for thirteen years and this was his first visit back home.
He described his life to us in quite good English:

*When I first went to Australia, I didn't like it because I couldn't
speak the language, but the more I stayed, the more I like it. The
people were very friendly. I worked for my brother in a milk bar and
then I save enough in four years to start my own business. I have a
shoe shop in Muswellbrook. My first visit back to Greece and I rather
live in Australia because I am stranger here but I got lots of relatives
here. Everybody wants to go to Australia!*

Our camp ground was excellent. It had one thing we'd been
craving: hot showers. Originally we had planned to stay with an
acquaintance of our friend, Bev. But the camp wasn't at that
address any longer, so the man who was there graciously took us

to a cheap hotel nearby. Either he had never been inside, or he was having fun at our expense, because when Beth and I climbed the stairs to check the room, it was disgusting. Our eyes fell on a tiny leaking sink and dirt all over the floor. Men loitered in the corridor, eyeing up Beth. Then we noticed the room next to us. It didn't have a door, just a sort of curtain, and a girl was lounging there with barely any clothes on, obviously soliciting. We were horrified! I told the fellow we didn't want the room and when he asked why not, it was too embarrassing to try to explain in English, so I said we'd rather camp, and we were very glad we did.

A wine festival was in full swing next to the camp ground. Three bands were playing and there were hundreds of wines to taste. We didn't even have to go in there because we could hear the music and George, the night manager, would come and look at our dinner, go to the festival and bring back a decanter of wine he thought appropriate for our meal.

George was a character. His family lived in Istanbul, but he had been thrown out of Turkey about five years earlier for writing on a wall: 'Cyprus belongs to Greece'. He had moved to Belgium, then to Australia for three years, and now he was living here in Athens with his Greek wife. Very proudly, he told us that his wife had been pregnant when they married, but none of her family realised until the baby arrived three months early. When the family became upset, he had said that it was 'one of those things'. We were a little surprised at his pride in mentioning the incident.

According to George, when a man was wed in Greece, the bride gave him a house and all the money she possessed. George's wife actually did provide a house, and he thought it was a pretty good idea. I joked to Beth that I agreed. George said that a girl had to be a virgin when she was married and, if by chance she wasn't,

then she must explain why not. If the husband found out afterwards, he could have the marriage annulled immediately. It was
simply a matter of a doctor certifying that she wasn't a virgin.

One morning I interviewed Dionys, the boss of the camping
ground. George had to act as a translator, speaking English for
Dionys. 'I am happy because everyone say they find the best
camping ground in the world here in Greece.' (It was no lie—
endless hot water was the saviour of any weary traveller!) 'I was
in the war with Australians and New Zealands in the same place
where we are camping here in Daphne. I am pleased to see Australians and New Zealands here now. The wine festival is on now
for seven years. Everyone get happy. The people dancing and
singing and be joying every night.'

There were others who also remembered the ANZACs fondly.
An old chap explained he was from Crete. 'When the war starting
in 1918, the New Zealands and Australians comes to Crete. I meet
him and help him and hide him from enemies. I give him food
and help him because he is good person.'

By Athens, the Beetle had 22,000 miles on the clock and was
due for a service. The clutch needed adjusting and I became
slightly worried as the mechanics took the whole engine out of
the car. But they were very efficient. Three men worked on the
car, and little Nicola, the apprentice boy, ran here and there,
getting his backside kicked by the chief mechanic for bringing the
wrong tools. When it was time to check the engine, a violent
argument broke out. Eventually I understood that the leads to the
spark plugs had been put on wrongly, and the chief mechanic was
looking for someone to blame.

Generally, we'd found the VW service points to be very good,
and there was always someone who could speak a bit of English.
The garage in Athens was excellent; it even had a coffee lounge.

We took advantage of the spotlessly clean toilets, the likes of which we hadn't encountered for some time.

By day, we saw the sights of Athens, awed by the history of the city. New Zealand was so young by comparison. By night, we relaxed at the camp ground, spending time with George or our new Australian friends, Anne-Marie and Michael. This couple had spent some time in Russia and other Red countries. In Moscow, they had watched a celebration in Red Square with Khrushchev at the microphone on a high platform. Michael said the crowd had been bored, fidgeting, uninterested in Khrushchev and the parade. It was as if they had no choice but to attend.

One evening, we planned to pop into the wine festival, but after a camp fire dinner with Anne-Marie and Michael, we couldn't tear ourselves away from their fascinating stories. After talking about Russia for hours, they moved on to Turkey. There, they had met a chap who couldn't afford a ticket home, but was unable to get a working visa to earn enough money for it. He kept complaining to the officials, yet no help was forthcoming. Finally, he became so fed up that he threw a brick into the window of a camera shop. He picked up a camera and then stood there in broad daylight, waiting to be arrested. The police took him away and, a few days later, he was put on a plane home. When he unpacked at the other end, he discovered that the police had carefully placed the stolen camera into his bag!

We were enjoying Athens so much we didn't want to leave. The wine, the food, the friends, the hectic city and the ancient sights could have kept us there for weeks. But it was time to drive on towards Turkey. We farewelled Anne-Marie and Michael at the camp ground and then dropped by George's apartment. His wife served us vanilla sweets and thick coffee in a tiny cup, while George spoke into my tape recorder, dictating a message for his mother in Istanbul. Chatting to George and his wife, playing with the baby, we lost track of the hour. As we waved from the Beetle, Beth and I voiced the same thought: 'It's late. We're having such fun, it would be a shame to go right now'. With the luxury of spontaneity, we changed our itinerary on the spot and headed back to our favourite camp ground.

Hello to everyone at home. We're still in Athens, so we'll explain it a bit more to you. I spoke cheerily into my Stuzzi. *It's one of the most modern cities we've been to. It has a population of two million, but you can drive from one side to the other in 15 minutes because they utilise one-way streets. One street is six lanes and you can travel quite quickly. As with other continental cities, driving is a little hazardous and, when the heavy vehicle drivers see you have a foreign plate, they tend to bluff you, but we give way anyway. Here's Beth to tell you about the shops.*

Hello, Mum and Pop Hodge and Mum and Dad. I hope this finds you all well. Athens is rather unusual—there doesn't seem to be many ladies' shops. The shops close from 1pm to 5pm and then re-open until 8pm. We discovered they make rather nice ice-creams, so we've been sampling those. On Sunday we went to the Acropolis. I think it would be even more wonderful if we understood the very long history of Greece. We saw the changing of the guard at the Royal Palace. The men didn't look at all effeminate although their national costume is a tiny skirt (to the length we'd wear our shorts) and long, tight stockings. Ivan has been having many 'conversations'. He has a great belief that people can understand him and carries on a lengthy conversation and then tells me the results. I'm buying Ivan some shoes for our wedding anniversary and he's giving me a handbag. Love to all.

From Athens, we drove back up north to Thessalonika and Alexandroupolis. On the way, we met a carload of New Zealanders, who informed us of road conditions and the whereabouts of others we had passed on our travels. It was amazing how the network of news was passed among the overlanders!

Driving through the countryside, we were intrigued by the rural life. Sheep and goats grazed in the fertile valleys. We were constantly passing carts pulled by donkeys, horses, cows or oxen. One cart had a special load. Behind it, attached by ropes, two huge grizzly bears were waddling along. Sometimes, we would see tortoises in the grass, and twice we had to swerve to miss the reptiles as they rested upon the road.

In Alexandroupolis, Beth and I lived it up for two days. A policeman noticed us parked in the middle of town, pondering how to find accommodation, and he suggested a little hotel. It was a good one, clean and comfortable, although the water didn't work particularly well. Each morning, we were woken at 5am as the market below us came awake. Carts clattered back and forth, bringing produce and wares to sell.

When we finally set off towards the border of Turkey, I wondered if we had been delaying our departure from Greece subconsciously. This was our last European country. From here it was into the unknown: Turkey, once a great empire and the gateway to Asia was also the only country to span two continents.

August 1996

Opera in a Thunderstorm, Italy

As we listened to our tape recordings, thirty-five years later, we marvelled at the memories returning to us; memories which had been forgotten in the intervening years.

This time, however, we weren't to enjoy Greek wines and talkative locals. Our trip took us down through Italy.

The romance of Romeo and Juliet's town of Verona was not immediately apparent, as our first stop was Autogerma, the Volkswagen representative, in an industrialised part of the city. Sabina, our VW public relations friend in Wolfsburg, had contacted Frederica Bennato, another very attractive PR employee, to meet with us. Frederica, it turned out, knew of our friends in Florence. She treated us to lunch in the cafeteria, organised photos for the company magazine and a press release for the media.

Meanwhile, the Beetle was undergoing a check-up. It had started backfiring recently and the mechanic discovered a small hole in the manifold which was causing the problem. He covered the hole with aluminium, added some oil, adjusted the carburettor and declared, 'I think she will make it to India!' The service was provided 'under warranty', with VW generously refusing payment. Cornello, the Chief Engineer, gave us his business card and said to show it at any VW garage in Italy and we would easily get anything fixed that we needed.

In addition to the helpful service, Volkswagen booked us in for a two-night stay at a hotel nearby. We appreciated the accommodation, but the location drove us insane. We got lost getting there. We got lost leaving there. We got lost coming home that night. We got lost going out the next morning. Beth denied fault on the part of the navigator, insisting that the freeway exit system was just too damned confusing!

In July and August, Verona would present a summer festival of opera and ballet in its 22,000-seat Roman Arena. *Aïda* was on the program the previous night, but some very disappointed Japanese tourists informed us that it had been rained out. We were hoping to see *The Barber of Seville*, a less popular opera, which meant we were able to buy tickets that morning. Declining the $250 plush front-row seats with champagne and hors d'oeuvres, we took the option of the $35 concrete steps on one side of the vast stone amphitheatre.

The excitement of attending the opera in this remarkable arena was magnified by the fact that our companions were our old friend, Annie, her husband Luciano and daughter Isobella. Despite the intervening decades, Annie was the same character from our London days—vivacious, flamboyant and frequently outrageous. Possibly more so. Now an Italian, she had a national right to be larger than life, gesturing wildly in the emotive Latin tradition.

It had been eight years since we'd seen Annie when we'd stepped off the Orient Express in Venice, a very special birthday trip for Beth. Annie had taken us out on that occasion for an incredible meal of polenta and black squid. She still called me 'Slim', my youthful nickname now a mockery of my middle-aged spread. It was mutual, we'd all grown older and wider. Even so, our smaller Australian appetites couldn't keep up with the Italian love of eating and their never-ending meals of four or five courses.

Beth still cringed at the memory of a dinner with Annie and our three daughters twenty years before. It was on a campervan trip of Europe aimed at giving our adolescent girls an appreciation of culture, history and travel. We'd been looking forward to seeing Annie and her new baby, Isobella, and for a few days beforehand, we had entertained the girls with stories of Annie's travels in her black London cab.

After a happy reunion, Annie and Luciano took us into the countryside to their favourite restaurant. In a flurry of singsong Italian and dramatic gestures, Annie ordered nearly every dish on the menu. The food kept coming. Piles of it. Plates balanced on one another across the table. Pasta, meats, fish, herbs, sauces, vegetables—the aromas steamed into the room, combining in an orgy of incredible flavours. Accustomed to plain camp dinners, we were overwhelmed and unsure whether we could do justice to this feast.

We began the first course, an unrecognisable texture fried with garlic. Guessing what it was, I glanced fearfully at the girls, hoping they would eat it without question. They didn't ask the dish's origins, but Liza noticed the menu board on the wall and saw a picture of a frog. That did it. In unison, the three girls put down their forks and crossed their arms.

'Eat it!' Beth whispered fiercely.

'Frogs' legs, yuk! We won't,' came the defiant reply.

'Have something else on the table then,' I suggested, wishing the hare dish were further away from their accusing gaze. We didn't even eat rabbit at home.

'No.' The teenage arms remained folded, the cutlery on the plate.

Beth and I surveyed the feast with dismay. There was no way our children were going to waste this amount of food.

'Eat it or you can go to bed right now,' Beth told them, mortified by their behaviour in front of Annie. Isobella was only a few months old; Annie and Luciano had years before the experience of teenage sensitivity and stubbornness.

The three girls walked out to the campervan, with Beth following to make sure they actually got into bed. Embarrassed, I made excuses and apologised to our dining companions, who responded graciously.

Even with Beth back at the table, we couldn't finish the huge meal. Annie insisted we take some with us and ordered the waiter to pack it up into containers, 'for the girls to eat tomorrow'. She didn't understand their mentality. There was no way our girls would eat this food—not tomorrow, not next week, not ever, not when frogs and hares were involved.

After numerous attempts, I gave up trying to pay the bill, as Annie and Luciano generously persisted in saying it was their treat. We stacked the pots of food inside the campervan, knowing it would all be thrown out in the morning.

This time our epicurean delight was at a vineyard restaurant in the hills outside Verona. Sitting in the garden, a glorious starry sky above us, we indulged in a sumptuous dinner and sipped the local wine. Beth and I only had to ask about a dish and Annie would call the waiter to order it. 'Wait, Annie, I just want to know what it's like,' we'd stall. 'It's nice, we'll have it,' she'd say.

Annie, Beth and I were all brought up in the 'waste not, want not' era of 1950s New Zealand, but Annie had managed to transcend this ingrained behaviour through her Italian way of life. For us, food left on the table was a waste; for the Italians, a groaning table was a chance to sample a multitude of dishes and tastes.

We joked that Annie was more Italian than the Italians themselves. She'd never been back to live in New Zealand since leaving for London in 1959. Annie had gone to Mantova to study singing under a maestro and had fallen in love. The fair-haired Luciano was a lift serviceman and, with Annie, he set up a successful lift construction company. When Isobella was born, she was much adored by both parents. Later, the family moved into the beautiful home they had built near the factory.

Along with the more serious discussions of business and family, Annie regaled us with a story of attending the school reunion in her small hometown in New Zealand. At school, Annie had always felt her schoolmates thought she would never amount to anything, and so she was determined to show how well she had done. Carefully choosing a good Italian outfit, she adorned herself with every piece of expensive jewellery she owned and paraded into the reunion, dazzling in diamonds and gems. She never knew if her schoolmates were impressed but, when she arrived back in Mantova, she was thankful. Her need for an ostentatious jewellery display had been fortuitous. The house had been robbed.

As evening approached, *The Barber of Seville* looked unlikely to go ahead. Rain clouds had been gathering ominously and, at 6pm, the deluge began. It was a 9pm performance, and the 'rain procedure' was that the opera could be delayed for half an hour. If the performance were cancelled, we still had to turn up and have our tickets stamped to receive a refund the next day.

In trepidation, we watched the clouds. Luciano directed us to the Arena. We arrived at 9:30pm, expecting a cancellation and that we'd all go for pizza instead. But by 10pm, *The Barber of Seville* was underway. Entranced, we sat on the wet concrete, the damp soaking through our hired cushions into our clothes and right to the skin. After the first act, Luciano went scouting for better seats, and we moved around to the front, pleased that the threat of rain had kept others away. Along with the singing, the costumes and the orchestra, the rain commanded centre stage. Occasionally, lights would flicker and flash as the wet residue caused shortages in the fuses. At one point, a few droplets anointed our heads. We watched in amusement as the entire orchestra ran maniacally for cover, dragging their instruments with them. When five minutes had passed and no sign of rain, the orchestra decorously walked back to their seats and the performance resumed.

The majesty of the Roman Arena and the emotion bursting from the stage couldn't quite banish the cold creeping through our seated bodies. By midnight, the 'oldies' were ready to leave, but Isobella was thrilled by the *Barber* and desperate to see the end. The sky cleared and we stayed, enjoying the rest of the opera, but ready for a hot pizza in one of the restaurants hidden in the little lanes surrounding the Arena. Beth and I finally got to bed around 3am, absolutely exhausted, our body clocks struggling with the demands of the Italian lifestyle.

1960—Florence

We remembered that Annie always had energy. In 1960 she had camped overnight outside Buckingham Palace to be in the front row for a view of Princess Margaret's wedding. Her peering face was in the crowd on the television news, astounding the folks back home who had gathered around the precious television to see glamorous Margaret, not their own Annie.

At the time of that 1960 wedding, we were in Florence, having disembarked from the ship in Naples, and were making our way to London. Rome had fascinated us with its ancient ruins, but in Florence, the main attraction was a TV. The folks at home heard all about it through a letter from Beth:

Friday 6th May, 1960. We left the hostel early (you have to be out by 9am) and went into town hunting for a bar with a TV lounge. We found one right at 11am and settled back for two-and-a-half hours to watch Princess Margaret's wedding. The TV program gave an excellent coverage. We saw most of the important guests arrive, the whole drive to the Abbey, the ceremony, choir and all, the drive back to the Palace and the appearance on the balcony. It was really lovely. It made us realise how near we are to Britain. In the afternoon, we wandered around the Florence markets, where lovely handbags are between £3 and £4.

Saturday 7th May. *We spent the morning walking through the back streets and through an old palace. In the afternoon, we went to the markets once again, and Ivan bought me a pair of shoes for £3 10s, which was a really good price to pay in Florence. They are black kid, plain pointed fronts, but the sides of the shoes are cut out, which is one of the latest fashions. We cooked our evening meal in the hostel kitchen, met some interesting folk and spent hours talking.*

Sunday 8th May. All art galleries and museums are free on Sundays, so we left early and went to the Uffizi Galleries, which hold one of the most important art collections in the world, including work by Rubens, Van Dyke, Michelangelo and Rembrandt. Some of the work was really wonderful. About midday, we went back to the hostel and sat on the lawn in the sun, catching up on our diaries. The evenings in the hostel we usually sit and talk. We've made two particular friends, Audrey and Mary, two Australian girls who have travelled the same way as us. Usually in bed early (separate rooms).

Monday 9th May. We left Florence early but certainly hope to return. Travelled by tain to Bologna and then hitchhiked to Venice.

Little did Beth realise that Florence would etch itself into her heart. She loved the sense of style, the fashions and the shops, the history and the Renaissance art, the coffee and the food and, of course, the swarthy Italian men.

It was through our daughter, Liza, that Beth's fondness for Florence blossomed. Liza taught English there for three years. With Liza in Florence, we leapt at the chance for another trip and discovered our daughter Italianised, introducing us to her many Florentine friends and showing us the secret nooks and crannies of the beautiful town.

1996—Florence

Now we were returning to Florence, with the Beetle, unexpectedly becoming confused in six-lane single-way traffic, as we tried to find a parking station near the railway. It was a scene from the Chevy Chase movie, *European Vacation*, as we drove round and round the roundabout, unable to cross the traffic and turn off. Our impeded vision in a right-hand-drive car was compounded by the fact that no-one actually used the lane markings as a guide.

Beth was pleased it was her same old Florence—the mad traffic, crazy scooters, scaffolding on many of the palaces, locals standing up to drink coffee at streetside cafés, summer tourists rushing from the Duomo over to the Uffizi, crowds pushing in to see the gold jewellery on the Ponte Vecchio, bustling markets and peaceful, exclusive shops.

Bearing in mind the comments from VW Wolfsburg, about weight on top being good for the Beetle, Beth was determined to shop the streets of Florence and fill the jetbag. Partial to Alessi kitchenware, she came back to our cabin one afternoon with a pair of kitchen scales in green. She was hoping for blue to match the Beetle, but the shop had run out. I guessed they would come in handy for weighing food in the markets in Turkey and India but, then again, probably we'd carry them home without ever using them, like much of the other stuff on the roof. There was a special shopping excursion for a black scarf for Beth to wear as a headscarf when in Iran. Another shopping trip took Beth to the tiny jewellery shops on the Ponte Vecchio. Keris had asked for some gold earrings, and Beth decided on a stunning pair in a combination of yellow, white and rose gold. A pair of shoes for young Tahni took two more shopping trips, as the size of his growing feet was disputed.

Beth shopped until she dropped, while I mostly stayed back in our delightful camp ground, reading, emailing, relaxing and catching up on the BBC world news. There was a terrible paedophile

case in Belgium, a hijacked plane from Sweden landing in Stan-
stead, and Israel was building nine hundred homes on the West
Bank. The rest of the world seemed a long way from our idyllic
existence. We were there for five nights, eating light summer
meals on the little balcony of our wooden cabin, drinking local
red wine, as we watched the sun set over the Florence skyline.

The camp ground was in Fiesole, a village on the edge of Florence. It was a friendly place, full of holidaying European families
and friends. Various languages drifted from tents and campervans.
We wandered through the terraced camp ground, looking at the
number plates from different countries, chatting to fellow travellers and their young children. I talked slowly to a German couple,
with Beth laughing afterwards, saying that I still believed everyone
could understand me if I just talked slowly and loudly. Here in
Europe, with so many people fluent in two or more languages,
we both felt slightly embarrassed by our lack of multilingual skills.
At least Beth had tried to learn French, but she had failed the
course. I just knew that I didn't have the ear or the mind to grasp
another language.

There were a few other Beetle owners on Beetle journeys. One
guy had bought his Beetle new in Brazil about five years ago.
Having a look over it, I felt it probably wouldn't make thirty-five
years, but could provide good spare parts for us once it died.
Obviously, I didn't tell him that. Another couple with a Beetle
were from Leibzig and had only been allowed to travel outside
Eastern Bloc countries for the past four years. Now, they were
making up for lost time, travelling into Europe as much as possible, using up their four-weeks' annual holiday.

On the Friday we awoke at 6am for a radio interview with 2BL
back in Sydney. The time difference meant our responses were
slightly slow; it was too early in the morning for a couple on

holiday! We enjoyed the short chat, though, describing the camp ground at Fiesole and the Beetle's recent adventures in Italy. I also repeated a conversation with a German fellow we'd met in Florence.

'I know you,' he had said, leaning out from his shiny, black BMW. 'I saw your little car and I read in a German newspaper about you. I recognised it was you! Congratulations on thirty-five years of car and marriage. About twenty-five years ago, when I got my driver's licence, my first car was a Beetle.'

Finding Paciano—by Luck

In our local library I had first read about the tiny village of Paciano, nestled in the Umbrian region of Italy. Apparently, it was the twin town to our suburb of Mosman. I had suggested to Beth that, as it was near our route, we might as well drop in and meet the Lucks, the couple who had arranged the link with Mosman.

Unfortunately, it wasn't that simple.

After staying an extra night in Fiesole because we liked it so much, we set off for Paciano. An easy two-hundred-kilometre drive, we thought. Beth navigated the Beetle along the picturesque back roads, far from the rushing autostradas. The undulating Tuscan vineyards gave way to the tobacco and sunflower crops of Umbria. Paciano was too small to be marked on our European map, but Beth and I both assumed it was on the outskirts of Perugia. Wrong, wrong, wrong.

Beth accosted a taxi driver for directions and learned we had to go back along the road we'd come, down the other side of Lake Trasimenos. After thirty kilometres, we stopped and asked directions again. This time, the woman rang the post office in Paciano for specific directions and sent us on our way once more.

Finally, we saw the sign: *Paciano—Gemellata con Mosman, Sydney, Australia* (Paciano—twin of Mosman, Sydney, Australia). It was strange to see the name of our Sydney suburb and the Olympic symbol of Sydney 2000 on a sign in the sleepy Umbrian countryside. From our research in Mosman library, we knew to go to the chemist, where Ivana, the pharmacist, also doubled as the public relations officer in this village of nine hundred people. Once we mentioned 'Mosman', Ivana was extremely helpful, booking us into the *pensione* on the hill and leaving a message on the answering machine for Geoffrey and Audrey Luck.

We didn't hear back from the Lucks and, assuming they were out, settled down to dinner in our rustic hotel. The only complaint was about the woman on the table next to us. Six cigarettes were consumed along with dinner, inflicting smoke on our own meal. 'It's Italy,' we consoled each other, spoilt by Australia, with its non-smoking sections in restaurants.

Stepping through the gates into the medieval walled village of Paciano, we entered a time capsule of 14th-century towers and 16th-century churches and houses. One of the cultural and historical centres of Umbria, Paciano nestled on the slopes of Mount Petravella, overlooking Lake Trasimeno and the Chiana Valley.

In 1992 it had been chosen as a finalist in a competition to find the 'Ideal Village' in Italy and had won an award for Best Village in Umbria. Only a few *stranieri* (foreigners) lived among the locals in the village, including the Lucks from Mosman and Canadian David McTaggart, the founder of Greenpeace International and hero of the first Mooraroa protests against French nuclear testing in 1971. In *Airone*, an Italian nature magazine, David had said, 'Here I have the things that I have always believed in: silence, nature and peace. I have bought a house and land, an olive grove that I cultivate solely with my own bare hands.'

The Lucks had bought their farmhouse just outside Paciano in the mid-eighties, when the trend was Tuscany. The good houses had been snapped up and the rest were over-priced, a fact which had led Geoffrey and Audrey to this serene region. Retiring early, the Lucks had moved to Paciano in 1990, renovating their farmhouse and forging a twin town link with their old suburb of Mosman.

The following morning, we actually put faces to this couple we had read so much about. Over coffee, the Lucks told us of the huge renovation their farmhouse had undergone. Before re-flooring the terracotta tiles, they had had to lay a special concrete so the floor could hold the weight of modern furniture. It had taken them ten years to obtain approval to move a road from outside their door to forty feet away. The village community was environmentally aware and protective of its historical buildings.

We learnt the reason for the deserted appearance of many houses: the shutters had to be closed during the hot weather because the walls were so thick that once the house heated up, it was impossible to cool it down again. From the Lucks' cool farmhouse, we could see their olive grove. The fifty trees had produced about thirty litres of oil that year.

The tranquillity of the countryside was shattered by a downpour of torrential standards. Geoffrey and Audrey directed us towards Ancona, the port of departure for our Mediterranean cruise. We were referring to the cruise as a 'third honeymoon' for us and a nice rest for the Beetle. The fierce storm did not bode well for a smooth passage.

Chapter 5

The Charms of Sea Travel

When we first began planning the second trip, we had hoped to stay faithful to the 1961 route. It just wasn't possible. With the upheaval in the Balkans, we had to look at other links from Europe to Turkey. The route through Romania and Bulgaria was a possibility, but that region was also unstable. We heard there were delays, bad roads and problems with thieves and dangerous gypsies. Had we been in a four-wheel-drive vehicle with a group of people, like the overland truck commandeered by Ruth, we might have risked it.

Our final choice of route was designed as a holiday within the trip: a three-day Mediterranean cruise on the *SS Charm* from Ancona in northern Italy to Kusadasi on the western coast of Turkey. We had images of sampling seafood buffets and sipping cool white wine, as we lounged in deck chairs, admiring the lush, green islands jutting defiantly from the sparkling Aegean Sea.

It would be a pleasant break from driving, a chance to stretch our legs and relax in the open air, away from the Beetle's confined interior. Sea voyages were one of our favourite ways of travel, and we were looking forward to three days in a luxury cabin.

Flexibility was an essential trait for enjoying long journeys. Luckily, Beth and I were both able to make the most of any situation. When anticipating places and conditions on the trip, we tried to be realistic. I felt that great expectation was a dangerous item in a traveller's suitcase. It should be left at the airport with the left-behind relatives. Otherwise, it was bound to lead to intense disappointment.

31 August 1996

Beth's Diary

The Lucks kindly directed us out of Paciano and pointed us on the right road to Perugia, around the southern shore of the lake. Our ship was due to sail from Ancona at 6pm, and we planned to get there by 3pm. The road to the coast went through an amazing series of long tunnels, which gave Ivan a rest from peering through the rainy windscreen. The Beetle's wipers were not quite up to the task.

Still in the rain, we had no trouble finding the docks, where it was utter chaos. Huge articulated trucks, cars, campervans, caravans all heading in four directions on the one piece of dock. Five or more big ships were trying to load.

I left Ivan in the Beetle in the middle of the mess and asked a policeman where to go. He threw up his arms and I think he said, 'Five ships, 2000 vehicles and you ask me for Charm?!' He was almost in tears, and it crossed my mind to join him. Running around trucks and through rain and puddles, I eventually found the right office about half a kilometre along, and discovered we had to check in first. I ran back for the documents, worried I wouldn't be able to find Ivan. He was stuck behind some trucks and it was obvious he would never be able to move along the dock, so he somehow turned the Beetle, pushed his way back onto the road and drove up to where I had told him I would be.

A number of splendid ferries were loading. They looked just like the brochures: magnificent, sleek and shining white even in the rain. I searched for the words SS Charm and couldn't find them. Finally, when I asked at the office, the fellow pointed behind him. My heart sank. The poor little Charm was badly named: old, dilapidated and grubby.

The 6pm departure became 8:30pm. Ivan made sure the Beetle was *chocked properly. Only two other cars were aboard. Mostly there were huge refrigeration trucks. The* Charm *was obviously more a cargo ferry than a passenger cruise ship. Due to the poor weather, it had arrived late and hadn't been cleaned. Our "luxury" cabin—top price—was three flights down under the car deck and with no portholes! Two bunks, one chair, one table and a questionable bathroom/toilet. A good spray with my Dettol soon made things look better. We took our own towels from the car, pinched a chair and a rubbish bin, and we were installed in our windowless home. After a self-service meal in the buffet, we negotiated the shower, which just hung down, so it was a two-person job.*

During the night, the storm calmed down, and we woke to a gentle lulling motion. Without a window onto the world, we had no idea of time or weather. Breakfast was served between 8am and 9:30am and, although it didn't promise much, judging by last night's dinner, we were hungry. We arrived at 9am to find a sign: CLOSED. *That's odd*, we thought, deciding that the crew were a little lazy about timing, with only eighty passengers on board, instead of a possible seven hundred. Cold boiled eggs and a thermos of hot water for tea in our cabin sufficed.

We almost missed lunch as well—not that 'missed' was quite the right word—as the menu was the same for lunch and dinner. Then we made a startling discovery: this was a Greek ship, so we were running on Greek time, an hour ahead of Italy. Once that had been cleared up, meal times were easy, although the fare was very ordinary: lamb kebabs, pilaf, spaghetti and fetta.

Many of our fellow passengers were truck drivers, chatting about distances, road conditions and the constant strikes in France. An English chap regularly drove loads to Turkey, away for four weeks at a time and back home for just one. He said the success of a truck journey depended on backloading, but he didn't expect to take much out of Turkey back to Britain. At midnight, numerous trucks unloaded in Greece. It was a spectacle to watch under the bright lights: the huge articulated trucks manoeuvring around one another and out of the *SS Charm* onto dry land. I gained a new respect for the European truckies who, up to that point, had just seemed hell-bent on intimidating us in our little Beetle.

When we set off again, the ramp at the back of the ship stayed down. The truckies didn't seem concerned—perhaps it was standard practice—but my head filled with visions of the *Zeebrugge* disaster, when the ferry had sunk after water flooded in through the ramp. I tried not to think about it as I checked our little Beetle, an ant against the remaining trucks on the car deck.

Out on the deck, we met other travellers, about ten years younger than us. Retired army officer, Graham and his wife, Dindy, were escaping from the English rat-race to spend a year in Crete, studying the Greek language. Dindy, an artist, was eager to paint on the island and run in the Athens marathon.

A Swiss couple planned to drive around Turkey for five weeks and had all the mod cons aboard their campervan. Michael was a banker and a whiz on currency exchange, which put my long calculations to shame. We accepted an invitation to visit their 'luxury' cabin with which they were most pleased. Our mouths gaped and our complexions turned a shade of green. Their cabin was delightful. It even had windows. *Just the spot for a third honeymoon*, I thought. When booking, we had been told there were two luxury cabins aboard and one was ours. We vaguely wondered if there really was another cabin and who had won it.

The romance of a Mediterranean cruise depended upon attitude and, despite our airless cabin, we were happy. Sea travel smoothed life into slow motion. We calmed to its pace, relaxing, chatting with passengers. The greeny-blue water drifted by as the sun set over distant islands. On the deck, Beth and I toasted the *SS Charm*, our new stemmed glasses from Florence filled with a fruity red wine we'd bought in Verona.

There was no service on the mobile phone, so even the frustrating joys of connecting and emailing were taken away. I typed a long 'VW Beetle Travel Report' to send home to friends and family. It was fun to write, reminiscing about our first sea journey and, for once, I wasn't concerned about the tricks of memory sentimentalising the past. I knew we had had a splendid, carefree cruise, marvelling at our first glimpse of the world outside New Zealand and Australia.

3 September 1996

Beetle Report from the *SS Charm*

Beth and I experienced our first sea voyage in 1960, from Sydney to Naples, on the Flotta Lauro liner, Sydney. *The voyage took four weeks and included visits to Colombo, Bombay and Port Said. It was a brief introduction to the East. We were astounded by Bombay, in particular. Back home, we had some Indians at school, and Mr Aktar was our neighbour, but somehow Bombay was very different and unexpected.*

The Sydney *was not a luxury cruise ship, but it did have a range of shops, a florist, hairdresser, captain's table, deck games, balls and parties. Impressions were formed on that journey. We tasted the Italian way of life: spaghetti, zuppa, gelati, bread rolls for breakfast and lots of strong coffee in small cups.*

We met Liza and Mama, Germans returning home from the Snowy Mountain area. Liza, single and very attractive, was like honey to the crew, and she borrowed our cabin on several occasions to meet with

126

'friends'. We liked Liza, the girl and the name, and subsequently recalled her when naming our second daughter in 1964.

Nora and Dudley from Rotorua were travelling first class, and they invited us to share their facilities in the more elite areas of the ship. There, the Italian officers shared their favours, dancing skills and romance with the several young mothers who were accompanied only by their small children. Although older than us, Nora and Dudley became great friends, and we caught up with them once we reached London. When our youngest daughter, Britta, was born in 1966, Nora and Dudley became her godparents.

We were travelling economy and had a twin berth cabin with a hand basin, but no other facilities. We were introduced to squat toilets, something quite new for a young married couple from New Zealand.

We approached Naples and our security blanket was taken from under us when we disembarked. We had to find our way to London carrying two suitcases.

The car deck was almost empty when we packed up the Beetle and closed the door on our windowless cabin, ready to arrive in Kusadasi, Turkey, at midday. When noon passed with no sign of a busy port, Beth checked with the crew. 'Maybe five o'clock,' they said. And 5pm it was when we drove the little blue Beetle off the ship, back onto dry land.

Shell-shocked, we wondered if we'd alighted in the wrong country. Kusadasi bore little resemblance to our memories of Turkey in 1961. It seemed to be a town of shops, all along the waterfront and down every street. Among the shops, restaurants and bars competed for business. Above it all rose tall holiday apartments and hotel blocks. Cruise ships and daily ferries haggled for space in the harbour and business on the docks, as they carried the day-trippers for excursions to ancient cities.

In just this one city, we could see the incredible effects of the 'discovery' of Turkey as a cheap holiday destination during the 1980s. We knew that Mediterranean Turkey was quite different from the rest of the country and hoped that, by driving inland, we'd find the 'real' Turkey again, with its traditional customs and rural culture.

After our windowless cabin, we deserved a treat, so we booked ourselves into a three-star hotel. The deck on the roof of the hotel, looking out over the sea, made me feel we were still aboard the *Charm*. We slept in snatches, the sounds of the restaurants and bars drifting up to our room, and the early morning call to prayer reminding us that we were now in Turkey, 'the cradle of civilisation'.

In 1961 we had no guidebooks telling us of the wealth of history passing us by as we motored through Turkey. Now in 1996 we were well aware of the vast empires and kingdoms which had battled through time, wrestling for control of this strategic region. While my understanding of the numerous historical periods was slightly lacking, I was fascinated by the multitude of ruins dotting the countryside. There were stone tablets protruding from fields of sunflowers and crumbling statues by the road.

With such a huge number of ancient relics across the land, the Turkish people seemed to take them somewhat for granted, and obviously had neither the resources nor the inclination to undertake the massive restoration task of the less-touristed sites.

Ephesus was our introduction to the ruins of the ancient empires. Under the pounding sun, jostling through the hordes of tourists, we wandered along the marbled Arcadian Way, flanked by colonnades and statues.

After the Roman legion had invaded and wrested power from the Anatolian kings, Rome declared Ephesus the capital of its new province of Asia in 129 BC. Forcing their own gods onto the Ionians, the Romans transformed the temple of Artemis, the virgin goddess of the hunt and the moon, into a temple for Diana the Huntress. The temple became one of the Seven Wonders of the World.

While the Temple of Diana no longer stood, Ephesus was the best preserved classical city on the Mediterranean. Beth and I sat in the Great Theatre, which could hold nearly 25,000 spectators. Cooled by the hard stone seats, we marvelled at the architectural prowess of the Romans and imagined ancient performances.

'What a glorious city it must have been!' Beth exclaimed as she studied the intricate carved detail in the stone facades of the buildings. I was more interested in the ancient toilets; they were stone and very functional, although one couldn't suffer from modesty, as each sitting bowl was a mere metre from the next.

We chatted with two Swiss backpackers, brothers, both with very long hair, also heading for Iran and India. Discussing travel plans, I told them of our journey thirty-five years ago. One asked, 'What did you do that for?' I wasn't sure if it was a simple question or a response implying it was a crazy thing to do. Among the many other nationalities of tourists, we spoke to a fellow New Zealander who didn't want to talk about his holiday and was offended by my filming him. Beth hid from the sun, and my embarrassing behaviour, under an umbrella.

That night we picnicked on the roof of our hotel at Kusadasi. Half a roast chicken from a restaurant, with olives, cheese, tomato, cucumber and Turkish bread. Watching the cruise ships sailing out at sunset, we could almost forget our worries about crossing the Kurdish–Turkish war-zone in eastern Turkey. The relaxed scene was suddenly interrupted by a power failure in the hotel. In our hot, stuffy room, we tried to sleep without air-conditioning and with the noise of a huge generator pounding outside our door, its diesel fumes irritating our breathing.

The two-hundred-and-twenty-kilometre drive from Kusadasi to Pamukkale took us through a fertile valley with rows of figs and roadside stalls selling tomatoes and apples. As we neared Pamukkale, the sound of a rifle shot cracked through the car. I pulled over quickly. After a stunned moment, we realised a stone had smashed the small window on Beth's side.

Pamukkale was famous for its snow-white travertines, cascading cliffs with pools of warm, mineral water. We hadn't realised the waters actually ran through the ruined city of Hierapolis, a spa town which was founded around 190 BC and then deserted in 1334 after a bad earthquake.

Our hotel room opened out onto a balcony by the hotel pool, and then onto the travertines and the valley below. The view was astonishing. The only problem was that we had to walk through the hotel pool to get to the travertines! We bathed in the warm, calcium-rich pools, photographing the bizarre blue and white landscape, which looked like a great slab of icing dripping down an uneven wedding cake.

It reminded us of the thermal areas in New Zealand. We imagined that the pink and white terraces of the Rotorua spas had once appeared like this before they were buried under volcanic lava. The long tradition of thermal waters in New Zealand was carried on in my backyard in Rotorua. A small, man-made pool had mineral waters pumping up into it. It was wonderful for rejuvenating a tired body. Beth, Annie and I often relaxed there after our basketball games.

Night fell in Pamukkale and we watched, transfixed, as the travertines were illuminated by massive floodlights. It was an impressive sight: the calcium-encrusted pools, cold, white and eerie, and suddenly it seemed an alien landscape without the bathing tourists.

In the hotel restaurant, a bus group was enjoying the talents of a local belly dancer. The waiter insisted on moving Beth and me closer to the show, although the whole affair was commercial and badly done. We were disgusted by the behaviour of the male tourists, pawing and grabbing at the belly dancer.

Once again, the issue of tourists in Turkey bothered me. I wondered if it were possible, in the early stages of tourism, to find a balance between attracting the traveller and protecting the country's culture.

And there was a dilemma for the traveller to face as well. Beth and I were luxuriating in this hotel, walking across the travertines, bathing in the pools. We read that the government had announced it would close the pools to swimming and remove the hotels on the top of the ridge in order to decrease erosion and possibly uncover further ruins of the ancient city. Four years later, the closure hadn't come about, but should we have been taking that responsibility on ourselves, avoiding actions that caused further deterioration to natural and historical sites? Travellers tended to rationalise their sightseeing choices with issues of distance and cost: 'We've travelled halfway across the world, we have to climb it, see it, swim it'. The reality was tourist sights would soon disappear as a result of the tourist impact.

The next day was devoted to practicalities rather than sight-seeing. The broken window on the Beetle had to be mended urgently. While the additional breeze was welcome, the hole was a matter of security. Everything we needed was in the Beetle and we couldn't risk losing it, especially not my computer equipment. Beth was amused by my concern for the car in its injured state.

'The Beetle has finally become your fourth daughter,' she laughed.

Denizli was a large, industrial city and we found an auto glass repair shop after thirty minutes. When asking directions or advice, the locals led us on a trail to their friends. Another half an hour and the window was fixed, for just A$9. One fellow did all the work, five others came to watch and talk to the foreigners.

We realised that window repair was big business. The dangerous road surfaces, combined with fast cars and determined buses, fed a lucrative industry in the glass repair trade. Turkish drivers were often quite mad, overtaking on blind corners, apparently trusting their fate to Allah. Our worst enemy, though, was the bus or *dolmus* (minibus). Masters of the road, the buses pushed all other vehicles aside, using the white centre line as their own personal space. Travelling on the right in our left-hand drive Beetle meant Beth had to be on a constant lookout for buses and cars overtaking and heading straight for us.

Beth commented that she hadn't seen any women driving. In the villages, we passed women wearing loose blouses, their hair hidden under scarves. The colourful printed skirts were often pulled up into impromptu trousers, tucked into the waistband to form a pocket for carrying. The women walked barefoot or sat on the back of carts pulled by donkeys.

After driving through inland villages, fertile valleys and pine forests, we came back to the coast, down to Bodrum, aiming to catch a ferry to the Greek isle of Rhodes. We had decided to relax in Rhodes for five days and then begin our drive towards eastern Turkey. It would be a break before making our decision.

I was reading the newspapers and speaking with officials about the Kurdish situation, and the news was not good. Although I didn't want to concern our family, I felt we should keep them up to date.

From: Ivan Hodge
Sent: Sunday 8 September, 1996
To: Keris and family

Tell all who called we are safe and pissed off! I spoke with the Australian Embassy yesterday. It is uncertain at present that we will be able to get across to Iran from Turkey. Next week we will call the Australian Embassy in Tehran to get their view. The guy in Ankara was most pessimistic.

We will be on the coast for at least two weeks and I am hopeful that things will look brighter after that. It leaves us with few options to get through to Iran. We had a similar problem thirty-five years ago and made the decision to travel via the Black Sea instead of Syria, Jordan and Iraq.

Tonight, we're staying in Gumbet just outside Bodrum. Beth's guidebook said it was a nice spot, but it's like living on a building site. Obviously a few years ago, nothing was here, but now every part of the hill is being built upon. I wouldn't like to see it in another few years. What a price to pay for the tourist dollar! There's a pretty awful beach covered in sun lounges. It's like sunbathing on the highway, on hard gravel instead of sand.

It seems that cheaper hotels are not such good value, as that's the backpacker market and demand is higher. As we move into the off-season, it will be interesting to see how the prices change.

Beth's credit card is playing up now. The magnetic stripes are a real problem. I'm not sure what the banks and shops do, but somehow they keep damaging them. We'll keep you posted if we need another card issued.

I will send this now as you are probably at the office; it's 3:30pm your time, 8:30pm here. We will be very, very disappointed if we do not get a green light to pass through eastern Turkey but, at worst, we will repeat the journey next year.

Love to all. Thank Britta for her message . . . Daddyo

Five kilometres from the construction site of Gumbet, we found Bodrum, a far more pleasant town, with its fifteenth-century

Castle of St Peter guarding the port. The word 'mausoleum' originated in Bodrum, or rather Halicarnassus, as it was known in 360 BC. King Mausolus had planned an enormous tomb as a monument to himself. His wife organised its construction after his death, and the marble slab topped by a pyramid came to be known as another of the Seven Wonders of the World—until it was knocked down for building materials in 1522.

After arranging a ticket for the following day on the vehicular ferry to Kos, Beth and I walked the streets, discovering that the veneer of sophistication on the waterfront fell away rapidly as we entered the old back streets. A photographic shop offered film developing in twenty-three minutes. Although we were a little suspicious of the precise time limit, we put in our film and were pleased when the photos were ready exactly twenty-three minutes later and were of good quality.

In the evening, as we returned from our restaurant with its splendid view over the floodlit castle, we were amazed by the liveliness of the town. Each bar and nightclub was trying to blast its music louder than any of its neighbours. We expected the cacophony to go on late into the night and were relieved to have chosen a hotel in a little backwater away from the main drag.

September 1996

Rough Seas and Wedding Anniversaries

With each swell, sea water washed over the deck and Beth's plastic chair skidded slightly towards the side of the boat. The Beetle, the only car aboard the tiny ferry heading for Kos, was chocked underneath the wheels, but no ropes secured it. Each time we hit a wave, the Beetle rose alarmingly on its suspension. I had visions of it jumping the chocks and flying off backwards into the sea.

There was no gate or chain across the back of the ferry, so I rushed to sit on the front bumper of the car, hoping my weight would steady it. Nearby, the German tourists began vomiting over the railings and inside, under the small covered cabin, children were screaming.

'We're turning back,' shouted the captain, but he actually kept on going, occasionally slowing the boat to find a calmer passage. The other crew member took off his heavy windproof jacket, and Beth and I wondered if he expected the ferry to capsize.

The captain had decided it was too late to go back, and so we ploughed on, the wind tearing at us from every angle. I was wet from head to toe, and the Beetle was drenched in salty sea-spray. More tourists came out from the cabin, desperate for fresh air to stop them from being seasick.

The one-hour trip became an hour and a half, but finally we arrived at the Greek port on Kos. I pitied the day-trippers who would be returning on the ferry that same afternoon. Passengers rushed off the boat, eager to be on solid land. I was the only one to thank the captain for getting us (and the Beetle) across safely.

Before we could relax on the island, there was one more hurdle to overcome: customs, for we had now entered Greece. The customs woman was furious. She had intended to go to the bank, but instead had been forced to wait an extra half an hour for our delayed ferry. The trauma of the crossing meant nothing to her— she was determined to punish the passengers with her bad temper.

Because of the Beetle we were the last to be processed and, by that time, her patience had drained into the nearby harbour. She stamped our passports and then looked at the carnet for the Beetle. 'What's this?' she demanded. We wondered if she was just being contrary, for other cars must surely have arrived on the island.

We had to walk over to the Customs House so they could look at the files and determine the purpose of a carnet and what they were supposed to do with it. Fed up with the issue, the woman finally ordered us to leave, her plans for the bank ruined.

We had one night on Kos, as a stepping stone to Rhodes. Scattered with ancient historical sites, Kos was also known as the birthplace of Hippocrates, the father of medicine, who was born on the island in 460 BC. Finding accommodation was our first priority. We booked into a modern hotel, ten kilometres from Kos town, overlooking the beach and islands in the distance. Next, we needed the car washed. Otherwise, encrusted with salt, the Beetle would soon start rusting. With directions from the hotel staff, we found a group of lads set up with buckets and soapy water. They gave the car a thorough scrub, and the Beetle was back in good shape after the rough crossing.

Most tourists whizzed around on little mopeds, so we felt quite sedate in a VW. Our leisurely drive took us through the centre of the island, amongst tiny villages and Hellenic and Roman ruins. Narrow lanes wound between whitewashed houses. Villagers were selling carpets at roadside stalls.

We were driving up one hill in the countryside when Beth shouted as a rooster darted under the car. It was too late. I didn't have time to avoid the bird, and we heard a thud as it hit the wheel. There were no houses close by, so we nervously left the rooster dead by the roadside, uncertain how to make amends. Two hours later, we had to come back the same way. We watched out for a furious farmer on a vendetta, but there was still no-one around.

It was comforting to see a large ferry when we arrived at the dock the next morning for the four-hour trip to Rhodes. As we were loading the car, a German fellow ran up to us.

'That's the car!' he shouted, his round face nearly hidden under a hat. 'I saw that car with its luggage on top. I know it must be the car I read about in the newspaper in Germany. I find it very nice that you have a second honeymoon trip.' Like the German man we had met in Florence, this guy was also a fan of the Volkswagen Beetle and had owned one when he was younger.

Rhodes beckoned from the flat sea: two columns crowned by bronze deer watching over the entrance to the harbour of Mandraki. The columns marked the supposed site of the Colossus of Rhodes, a 32-metre-high bronze statue and another of the Seven Wonders of the Ancient World.

The grand buildings in Mandraki were a reminder of Mussolini's control of Rhodes, when Italian was designated the official language of the island. The Italian rule of Rhodes was just one of the most recent tussles for power over this strategic island. Rhodes has been invaded by Romans, Goths, Persians, Saracens, Turks, Genoese and Ottomans—to name but a few.

We were welcomed to Rhodes by the cats, strays living by the harbour and searching for scraps. Friendly and alert for the possibility of food, they walked near us, keeping a close eye on our movements. These gangly creatures were to become our constant companions, particularly when lunch or dinner was being consumed.

It was refreshing to stay in one place for a few days. There was no unpacking and re-packing the Beetle each night. We blended in with the British tourists, taking life easy on the beaches, occasionally arising from the sun lounges for a touch of sightseeing.

Following in the footsteps of the package tours, we visited Petaloudes, a cool, wooded gorge, dappled in sunlight. Here, the strong scent of the sytrax trees attracted a particular species of butterfly (*Callimorpha quadripunctarea*) for a few months each year.

Leaf-shaped, the butterflies camouflaged themselves against rocks and trees, visible only by the cream veins radiating from their spines. The surprise came when they set off in flight: underneath, the wings were a magnificent scarlet.

Once we were past the tourist traps of Rhodes city, we delighted in the winding lane and bustling squares of the old town. While there were still dozens of tourists, the summer season was winding down, and apparently it was quieter than normal but that didn't stop the restaurants and bars. Their blaring music competed with one another for custom, destroying the relaxed holiday feel of the beaches.

Faliraki, the nearest beach to our hotel, was crowded with beach umbrellas and sun lounges which could be hired for A$7.50 a day. If we moved to another beach, we could transfer our ticket and use it once again.

It was on our wedding anniversary that we came across Haraki, a tiny fishing village with a small strip of accommodation and tavernas facing directly onto the pebbled beach. Above the town, there was a rocky outcrop which may well have been ancient ruins but it was too hot to climb up and see. The clear blue water was peaceful. Only a few people were swimming and two or three boats bobbed at anchor.

A quick dip and we cooled down completely. Unlike at most of the other beaches, I didn't see any nudist swimming. Beth and I were following the fashion, and would swim naked where others did. Without staring offensively at anyone, I had noticed that some men had clean-shaven pubic regions, and there were women with ribbons tied in their neatly trimmed pubic hair. I had pointed this out to Beth as a matter of interest. She wasn't impressed by the direction of my gaze.

The day of our thirty-seventh wedding anniversary continued

wonderfully. Lindos, with its bright white, red-roofed buildings, shone in the afternoon sun. The seventeenth-century houses were nestled below an ancient acropolis built high on the rock peninsula, the sea on three sides. Most tourists hired a donkey for the steep trail to the top. We contented ourselves with the alleyways of the village and the stunning, secluded coves.

At 1pm, standing on the cliffs above the sea near Lindos, we rang home on the mobile phone, as promised. The three girls had gathered at our apartment for the phone call and to discuss Liza's wedding plans. Away from home, my priorities had changed and, while I was pleased the plans were going smoothly, I had little interest in chatting about them. Beth spoke to Liza about dresses and menus, and thought it lovely that the girls were discussing the wedding on our anniversary. We didn't know it then, but two years later, our youngest daughter, Britta, would choose to be married on the very day of our wedding anniversary.

That evening, we celebrated by returning to Haraki and dining at an idyllic restaurant perched on the rocks. Gentle waves lapped beneath us. As on the Turkish coast, fish was still ridiculously expensive. We didn't understand why, but assumed it had something to do with over-fishing in the area. We had a meal of chicken instead, with vegetables, salad and bread, accompanied by a good bottle of Rhodes white wine. Beth's tan was accentuated by her low-cut blouse, and I knew we both looked and felt fit and relaxed after our days on the beach and our walks through villages.

1958

The Rotorua Water Ski Club
Dine and Dance

In 1957 Bev had come home one night and announced to Beth, 'I've found a man for you and I'm bringing him home on Sunday!' Beth laughed, but Bev insisted on inviting me to their house. On first sight of me, Beth ruled out any chance of a relationship—the difference in height was ridiculous.

We all began playing indoor basketball together, along with our friend, Annie, and eventually I asked Beth out. After a year, it was time to pop the question. Beth's mother was keen for her daughter to be married and kept asking young men to the house to meet her lovely Beth. Thus far, I'd managed to stave off her interrogations about my intentions.

Down by the lake in Rotorua, I proposed to Beth, and we announced it that very night at the Water Ski Club Dine and Dance in the Ritz Supper Room. Ten months later, we were married, with Bev as a bridesmaid, and the following week, we left for Australia. I repaid the compliment to Bev by introducing her to Bryan, the brother of a friend. They walked down the aisle two years later.

Setting up a life with a partner away from family and friends and all that was known meant forging a particular bond, a complete reliance on one another. Unconstrained by small town society, we created the life we wanted in Sydney, in London and in our Beetle.

During those early years, we didn't often articulate our feelings about marriage, but on our first wedding anniversary, I wrote to Beth's parents:

It is incredible to think that this is our first year of married life. The startling thing is that we are enjoying it more all the time, and I hardly thought that possible. I must congratulate you both on that daughter of yours. She really is one in a million!

I think that being away overseas together is a wonderful experience for both of us. It does give us so much more in common, and possibly teaches one to be more considerate and tolerant.

At times, we have both had to use our sense of humour but then, no doubt, we would have had to anyway, whether in New Zealand or in a youth hostel in Venice with Beth going to her room and me to mine.

We have had our share of thrills: driving with George, our Japanese friend, in Sydney; riding on the Swiss railway and taking in the grandeur of the Alps; looking for a hotel in the Latin Quarter of Paris at midnight. Beth and I feel how dull it would have been had we not been together.

Beth's mother, Joyce, was protective of her daughter and concerned about me dragging Beth off to foreign countries. Just before our second anniversary, Joyce sent me a thank-you note with a veiled threat: I would be in serious trouble if Beth were to fall into any strife on the overland journey.

My Dearest Ivan
This is a letter just for yourself. My main object is to tell you how much we appreciate your goodness to Beth and how lovely it is to know she is happy with you. You really have made her a first-class husband. I can hear Beth saying, 'What about me?' but we know her; you were the unknown quantity.

From your letters home, reading between the lines, I am expecting Beth to come home a much more poised woman, as you have supplied to her the self-confidence she needed. I don't have to tell you just what I do think of her. You always thought I spoilt her, and so I did, but I think 'indulged' might be nearer the mark.

Your letters have been wonderful and I feel as if I have almost been with you. It has made the time go very quickly. It's almost impossible to believe you start your homeward trek in a week's time. I suppose I am foolish to worry over parts of your return journey. It is only that things seem to change overnight and awkward situations come out of nothing. I know you will take every care and precaution.

Dot tells me Mr Hooper is very worried over Ngaire, as he hasn't heard from her in six weeks. I haven't heard from you for over a fortnight now, and we think some mail may have been burnt in the Wellington fire, as it was mostly incoming mail that went. Soon two years to your anniversary—I wonder where you will be for it and whether we will be able to reach you with congratulations.

With our love, Mum.

We were uncontactable for our second anniversary: in communist Yugoslavia. On the beach, by the Adriatic, we celebrated with a picnic lunch and a refreshing swim. Out at sea, a cluster of fishing boats worked for their daily catch and, at our feet, the tiny fish were weaving through the clear, sparkling water. It was perfect in its simplicity.

Over the years, as we moved from New Zealand to Australia to London and back again, I'd always felt our marriage was relatively smooth, with few ups and downs. Our personalities were a good balance. I was the impetuous, emotional one who charged headlong into things, while Beth tended to stand back and assess a situation before acting.

Beth was brought up in a strict Victorian household with proper etiquette. She was supposed to tolerate situations silently. In complete contrast, I would react loudly to everything. Early on in our relationship, I astounded her by shouting back at a boy in the park who had insulted us.

I found out, much later, that my own father had warned Beth against marrying me. 'He's too deep and too dark,' he had told Beth, referring to my previous relationship. I had acted terribly in that regard, breaking off an engagement by letter, too much of a coward to ever face the girl again. It was shameful, and I suspected my father feared I might behave badly to Beth as well.

When overseas, we shared everything. We did household chores together to give us more time to go out. Our Japanese friend, George, who lived in the flats below us in Sydney, thought our relationship strange because I would carry the washing basket out to the line. Beth never knew how George's wife managed to lug the heavy load of wet clothes up the basement stairs.

Beth always said that she couldn't understand why one partner should be relaxing while the other worked. Luckily, I'd been living away from home and knew how to cook and clean. It was never at the point where we took it in turns, but Beth did feel our domestic situation went against the social norms of the time. She would inform her mother: 'My husband is cooking dinner for me—he must think I'm a terrible wife!'

Now, on our second honeymoon, we both shopped for food at the markets. Beth would prepare lunch while I poured the drinks or cut up the fruit. And as for washing clothes, in Rhodes I managed to charm the maids into sneaking the pile through the hotel machine, for a small tip.

As we packed up the Beetle to leave Rhodes, Beth exclaimed, 'I can't remember when we've had such a complete holiday. No housework and no cooking for five days! Whenever was the last time we did that?'

We were going on to Marmaris in Turkey, leaving Europe for

the last time. Our VAT claims hadn't been stamped in Italy because the customs people didn't work on Saturday afternoons, so the Greek customs fellow kindly did them all.

The two-hour ferry was another large one, so I had no fears of the Beetle falling off. Five vehicles had been loaded on the boat and we were about to leave when, hooting and shouting, a lady appeared in a car on the dock. She was supposed to be on board but had been told the wrong departure time. It was impossible to unload and reload the cars, so the crew made us shuffle them around on board, creating space for the extra vehicle. It was a circus. This time the Beetle was in danger of being squashed, with only a blanket between it and the new arrival.

The Beetle did receive a little attention in Rhodes. The brakes and the clutch were adjusted, for no charge. The mechanic told us the shock absorber was broken, but it would take a few days to organise fixing it. He said we were okay to keep driving on it for a short while.

We landed in Marmaris, amongst the expensive yachts and charter boats. Back in Turkey, it was time to determine whether the trip could go ahead, on to Iran. On the ferry, I spoke with an American who had been living in Ankara for ten years. He said it shouldn't be a problem travelling through Kurdistan, as long as we covered it in daylight. During the night the PKK (Kurdistan Workers Party) soldiers would come down from the hills to attack the Turkish army camps.

A support vehicle to accompany us would lessen the chance of danger. I had faxed my contacts at Volkswagen and the Australian Embassy and asked if an escort were possible over part of the route—the most dangerous stretch—from Erzurum to Dogub-eyazit. A reply was yet to come.

Chapter 6

Friends and Foe on the Road to 'Dog Biscuit'

ISTANBUL—Situated on the southern extremity of the Bosphorus and formerly capital of the Eastern Roman Empire; after 1453, the centre of Ottoman rule up to the end of World War I, when the government was transferred to Ankara.
• Aya-Sofia (Mosque of St Sophia, 532–538) • Sultan Ahmet Mosque (Blue Mosque, 1609–16) • Basilica Cistern • Mosque of Suleyman the Magnificent (Mihrab Altar, 1556–1566) • Palace of Seraglio • Museum of Antiquities • Walled Pyramid of Constantine • Aqueduct of Valens • Obelisk of Theodosius.

AA Strip Map, 1961

Armed with the brief history and sightseeing notes in our 'guide-book' (the *AA Strip Map*) and visions of Oriental magnificence, we imagined Turkey to be a strange and other-worldly place. In school, we had learnt about the ANZACs at Gallipoli—a stale-mate of trench warfare against the Turks, a quarter of a million casualties on both sides. From an overland truck driver in London, we knew to beware of Turkish people throwing stones at cars.

As we crossed from Greece into Turkey, we had another tip, this time from a bus driver. 'Don't pay what they ask for petrol,' he advised. 'You have to bargain them down.'

Petrol was cheaper than in Greece, so we hadn't filled the tank before the border. Not long after driving into Turkey, we stopped at a garage, a collection of small sheds. Intent on following the bus driver's advice, we shook our heads and waved our arms when the price was requested. 'No, no, no,' we determinedly replied, attempting our first bargaining experience in Turkey.

Anger disfigured the attendant's face. He shouted heavy Turkish words, firing them at us. In horror, we watched as all of the mechanics and attendants lined up in the driveway, ready for battle, rocks in hands.

Quickly, we changed our minds, paid the full price and sped away from there. Later, we were to discover that petrol was a fixed price in Turkey, and there was no question of bargaining. Had we misunderstood the bus driver? Or was he playing a joke on us? Beth and I never worked that one out.

Istanbul is the only city in the world divided by two continents. From afar, the minarets were the most obvious difference from the European towns we had visited. Thin slivers cut through the sky, towering above the city. Massive domes, half-obscured by buildings, rose up to greet us. Ancient architectural styles, completely foreign to our Western eyes, lined up against one another, displaying Byzantine, Roman and Ottoman dominance. Alleyways twisted to and fro, weaving through the path of history.

Hordes of people rushed along the narrow streets, wardrobes and other wares strapped to their backs. Cars worked as minibuses, with passengers crowding in, their bodies squashing into cramped spaces.

Our stay in Istanbul was characterised by Turkish hospitality. After the incident in the garage, we were concerned about antagonism towards travellers. We soon realised the Turks were an inquisitive people, willing to provide assistance in return for a chat. On our first day in the city, we asked an army officer for directions and were invited to lunch, followed by a sightseeing tour! On the second day, a friendly fellow in a market insisted we join him for coffee.

On the third day, we met up with Dr Zhevket, an acquaintance of Bev's. He took us to a restaurant for a typical Turkish dinner. Over our tiny cups of sweet coffee, I interviewed him. Dr Zhevket went straight into the political situation. We knew that Adnan Menderes, the president, had been executed a few weeks ago, and that martial law existed at the moment.

'We passed ten years, very difficult, very hard in Turkey,' Dr Zhevket explained. 'After the war, every countries grow but no Turkey. Here there are many problems. Some people liked Menderes, but not every people.

'General Gursel has taken control, and all the country like him. All the Turkish men, all the women and soldiers very glad for the next month election. Before, soldiers not vote, now democratic, soldiers do,' he continued, as we tried to follow with our limited understanding of the politics.

With the fear of communism in our blood, I asked him if he thought Turkey would succumb. 'No,' he answered. 'I don't think anybody like the communism.

'Turkey is trying to educate the children,' he stated proudly. 'School compulsory and we must speak two languages, first perhaps English and second, French or German or Italian or Russian.'

Dr Zhevket showed us the Blue Mosque. It was the tiles inside which were blue; the outside was stone grey, with six minarets aspiring to heavenly heights. The architectural elegance of the external domes was surpassed by the beauty inside. The sun shimmered through the stained-glass windows, creating streams of colour and light in the mosque. In our stockinged feet, we examined the mosaic tiles decorating the walls and the rich carpets on the floor. Watching silently as a prayer service took place, we wondered about this religion, which required daily rituals as opposed to a church service once a week.

'The Mosque Blue shines in the heart of everybody,' Dr Zhevket whispered.

I was having my boots repaired just outside the covered markets when we were hailed with a 'How're you, digger?' These three New Zealand chaps were living in Istanbul and planning to go home on an overland journey next year. 'You're already halfway there,' we laughed, thinking of the distance we'd covered in the past seven weeks.

They led us through the covered markets, sharing their knowledge. The biggest bazaar in the world was a feast of sights, sounds and smells. The locals clamoured to buy and sell. Entire lanes of the markets were devoted to specific products: gold, leather, carpets. We bartered for a black-and-cream striped rug made from goat hair and felt we were able to get a jolly good buy. The rug would keep us warm on the cooler nights in the desert. The three Kiwi chaps invited us for Sunday lunch at their house on the Asian side of Istanbul. Apologising, we declined, planning to spend time on a beach by the Black Sea. The chaps rushed off to catch the Bosphorus ferry, the only link between the two sides of the city.

However, we did make time for afternoon tea with George's mother. She spoke no English, but it seemed our Greek-Turkish friend George had explained who we were on the tape he recorded in Athens. She was overwhelmed to hear her son's voice, and tears welled in her eyes as she clasped her hands tightly together. Sweet coffee and a vanilla lolly in water were served up to us. Nodding politely, we accepted and drank it, Beth and I exchanging furtive glances in our worry that the untreated water would make us sick.

It was in Istanbul that we met a number of other overlanders. There was a Danish couple who had lived in New Zealand for ten years. They had returned to Denmark for their wedding and were now making their way back to New Zealand overland. Dick, Pat, Sally and June were a group doing the journey in a Landrover. Their route was a little different from ours. We were going to Syria, Jordan and Lebanon and out through Iraq, whereas they planned to go straight across Turkey to Persia. We were all camping outside Istanbul, right by the airport. It was a new camping ground, free and very muddy, with the workmen still putting down lawns. Beth and I spied some cabins which hadn't yet been finished and we set up our camp beds in there.

At the British Embassy, we checked up on the political situation in Iraq. The staff said there should be no problems, but we had read in the newspaper that the Iraqi government was threatening to close the British Embassy in that country. We also heard on the grapevine there had been trouble in Syria, but it was only internal, between Nasser and the Syrian Government, so it shouldn't affect us New Zealanders.

Our visas for Iraq were arranged without any difficulty. In the Iraqi Embassy, we met two English girls and a Canadian chappie hitchhiking to Australia. Unfortunately, the girls were not the best diplomats, making loud, rude comments about the Iraqi service. I felt that one had to learn a certain amount of tolerance and patience when dealing with people like those at the Embassy.

But Iraq was not to be. Despite the reassurances from the British Embassy, our trip was suddenly smack in the middle of political upheaval, and our planned itinerary went to hell. The week before, Syria had broken away from its four-year-union with Egypt. Now, the revolutionary government ordered the immediate expulsion of all Egyptians from the country. In retaliation, Nasser was threatening Syria and had cut relations with Jordan and Turkey, who recognised the revolutionary government. Meanwhile, in Iraq, the government was suppressing separatist revolts by Kurdish tribesmen in the north. Down south, there was still tension after Iraq had tried to claim sovereignty over Kuwait and British troops were called in by the Kuwait government. The British Embassy suggested we go straight through to Iran.

I had wanted to tape the conversation at the Embassy but, after much discussion with higher levels, the staff refused. Instead, I relayed the information onto tape when leaving the Embassy.

The road border into Syria is officially closed, but the Embassy thinks there is a chance of a person getting through if they arrive on the border with valid visas. Well, that's not a chance we're going to take! We found out the road to Persia via the Black Sea is by far the better route. The journey through the centre goes through military zones and, if you're travelling with womenfolk, that presents a problem.

We were disappointed by the change in plans, but I didn't want to cause any unnecessary risks for us. The new itinerary meant missing five countries. Israel fascinated us, especially with the added intrigue of having to carry two passports each so that Israel could stamp one, while we showed the Arab countries the other. And we were interested in the significant religious sites. Iraq had promised the chance to get rich. We'd been told the country was desperate for foreign currency, and we'd hoped to use the black market to make extra money for our trip.

The new route by the Black Sea took us close to the border of Russia. There was talk of the Soviets flexing their nuclear power and detonating a bomb in their Arctic testing grounds. It was to be the largest man-made explosion in history. We were relieved that President Kennedy had recently announced the end of the US three-year moratorium on nuclear testing.

Now, we were following a path similar to the group in the Landrover. Travelling together put my mind at ease as we sailed across the Bosphorus, marking the end of Europe and the beginning of the unknown continent of Asia.

Beth recorded the moment.

Istanbul is a wonderful city, one of the most interesting cities we've been in. We're on the ferry which takes us over to Asia. The ferry vessels are very large for the small crossing. Looking around the skyline, there are many mosques—there must be hundreds—on both sides of the city.

Lots of holidaymakers are on the Bosphorus in small crafts. There is a tower on a tiny island. Apparently, the legend goes that a maiden was locked up there and was to be devoured by sea serpents. Lysander swam from the European side of the city and rescued her.

We've been drinking a lot of Turkish coffee. It's made in a small pot, a spoonful of coffee and a spoonful of sugar per person, with very little water. This is simmered, and it comes in a tiny cup with sediment on the bottom which you don't drink. It's rather sweet, but we like it very much. The tea is made in a traditional method, in a tall boiler with coals beneath it or sometimes in an electric one. A little teapot with a small amount of water and many tea leaves sits on top of the simmering boiler, and the tea stews. You have tiny waisted glasses, on china saucers, and you half fill them with tea from the pot and then water from the urn.

We assumed our parents knew little about the Middle East, so we hoped to share this exotic land with them. As we described what we saw, we had no idea what they would make of it all.

for love and a beetle

1961—Turkey

On Watch and Being Watched

Driving out from Istanbul, the Landrover ahead of us, we shot along on a wonderful, modern highway. Dr Zhevket had told us that President Menderes was nicknamed the Builder, and most of these roads were his doing.

Despite the modern road, we had a very close shave. Heavy vehicles seemed to have no concern for others at all. If they wanted to pass, they'd pass, regardless of any oncoming traffic. On the highway, which could be described as three lanes, I pulled out to overtake a slow truck on a downhill stretch. At the moment the Beetle was abreast of the truck, an oncoming bus pulled out to overtake a truck on the opposite side of the road. As we came to the bottom of the hill, we were on a collision course, with two trucks on the edge, the bus and the Beetle in the middle. It was a miracle that we avoided an accident. We veered sharply to the left, the truck slammed on its brakes, nearly losing its load, and the bus steamed on ahead. The incident gave us quite a turn.

The new road took us to Ankara, the capital of Turkey since 1923, a modern city boasting flats and new buildings. It wasn't as glorious as Istanbul, but it, too, had a long history, one which saw the town called Angora after the goats of that name.

Camping in a park on the outskirts, our main aim in Ankara was to visit the British Embassy, check that Syria was still impassable and obtain advice on the roads to Persia. When applying for maps in London, we'd requested routes via Syria, Jordan and Iraq, so we had no directions for driving through Turkey. By chance, the Press Attaché was from Wellington. He confirmed that the Black Sea Coast was the best way.

Feeling a little scruffy after two months on the road, I treated myself to a haircut. Unlike many other overlanders, I still managed to shave regularly, sitting on our camp stool, a mirror in one hand, razor in the other and a bowl of cold water at my feet. Beth and I were even more careful about our appearance now that we were in a Muslim country. We dressed neatly and washed our clothes as often as we could.

Ankara gave us the opportunity to learn about Ataturk, the wonderful man who created modern Turkey. With the group from the Landrover, we visited Ataturk's mausoleum, a grand monument with colonnades and paved courtyards. I was most interested by his official motorcars: two Lincolns, part of the display of his personal effects and memorabilia inside the memorial. We were the only foreigners there. The other visitors were Turks paying their respects to the national hero.

The events of the first night we spent in the countryside were to become typical, as we travelled along the Black Sea Coast. After following a bullock cart track off the road into the scrubby bush, we set up camp, the two tents and the two vehicles forming a protective square. Inside the square, we cooked our meals, sharing utensils and food among the six of us. It felt safer to be in a group, although safer from what, I wasn't really sure.

When we went to sleep that first night, we could hear one or two locals wandering around the camp. They'd watched us eat dinner, staring at our plates and saucepans, laughing at our camping stoves, and nodding as we clambered into our tents. It was terribly cold, so we slept in jumpers and long trousers.

A female scream woke us in the morning. June, deciding to get up early and have a wash, had stepped out of the tent to find fifty locals surrounding our camp, standing and squatting, waiting to see our movements.

We went about our morning tasks, cooking porridge, toast and eggs. All the while, one hundred eyes watched us. Jokingly, I called out, 'Is this better than TV?' The children were braver and came close to us, barefooted, dressed in tattered rags. I showed one boy an egg. He disappeared and re-appeared a little while later, cradling four eggs. I offered him a cigarette or some money; he took the cigarette.

Some older people arrived: the tribal elders, we presumed. A shrivelled, wrinkled man, wearing rags topped by a turban, stepped forward, coughed at us, indicated his throat and held out his hand. We guessed he was the chief, asking for medicine for his sore throat. All we had was our anti-malarial tablet, so we gave him one of those. Happily, he chewed on it, beaming at us, although we knew the tablet had a frightfully sour taste.

A mass of younger children came running, giggling and gaggling. Remembering the trick I'd mastered in the Australia Hotel in Sydney, I wiggled my teeth, pulled out my false dentures and held them in the air. Shocked silence turned into hysterical laughter. The kids tried to tug on their own teeth with no success.

I was pleased they had their own; mine had been yanked out when I was sixteen and replaced with dentures. My teeth had been black and rotting. Our German dentist said it was because I was never taught to clean my teeth. With my new dentures in place, I was no longer sensitive about grinning with my mouth open. At first the pain was terrible, but at least I had someone to share it with. My best friend, Russell, had his teeth taken out the following week. I never knew if he needed new teeth or if it was done in sympathy for me.

Newspaper was a popular commodity among the onlookers. We had some English papers, airmail copies which had been sent to Ankara, laid out underneath our drying saucepans. The lads eyed them up, beseeching us to hand them over. When we did, their value became apparent. The papers were for cigarettes, to be rolled up around tobacco and smoked. The thin airmail paper was an ideal weight for rollie cigarettes.

Tin cans were also sought after. After rinsing them out, we gave them away, imagining they would be used for storage or maybe even as a cooking pot on a fire.

As we were about to leave, a huge fellow lumbered up to us. He pointed to the photo he was holding. It was of him winning a wrestling championship. Shifting from foot to foot, in front of us, he mimed a fight. Dick, Pat and I looked at each other apprehensively. 'Oh no, he wants to wrestle,' Dick groaned.

'We'll just pretend,' I muttered and began to playfight with the muscular chap. Thankfully, he guffawed at my inept display and joined the silliness, pretending to wrestle with me, much to the amusement of the local audience.

There were only two women in the crowd, heavily veiled. Their clothes were torn, but not dirty. Beth and I both noticed the womenfolk in Turkey had a raw deal. In the country area, they walked several steps behind their husbands, carrying heavy loads on their backs, while the men carried nothing. Some of the loads were incredible. We saw men with more than one woman following them and assumed that polygamy was still practised among the peasant people. Shrouded in cloth, the women hid their faces when they saw the Beetle.

The friendly campsite receptions were a contrast to the behaviour during the daytime. The warning from the overland truck driver in London was right: Turks threw stones. As we approached each village or cluster of houses, groups of children and teenagers would line the road to pelt the Beetle with rocks. The danger factor worried us most. A broken window not only cost money, but could also cause injury to Beth or me. When the car windows were wide open, on the other hand, we risked the possibility of the missiles hitting us in the face or head.

We didn't understand the antagonism, but we did concoct a way of dealing with it. As we came close to a group of trouble-makers, Beth and I would shout from the car, squirting our spray bottle of water at them. Surprised by the role reversal, the kids would forget their stones for a moment, just long enough for us to pass by safely. They would shake their fists menacingly when they realised their moment had gone.

I had a rather unpleasant experience this morning, Beth spoke into the tape recorder when we stopped for lunch. *We were driving along a narrow street, five of us in the Landrover. I was sitting on the outside. A boy—I suppose he must have been about ten—spat fair at me, or at the car or both. Anyway, it landed on my cheek and just about turned my stomach. Pat and Dick jumped out of the Landrover, but one of the men in a nearby welding place clipped the boy over the ear, so I felt we had been avenged a little.*

We met up with Ivan, and I got into the Beetle, telling him about it. He said 'The next child who does anything against us is going to get a fair kick'. We're sick of these children throwing stones.

We'd gone no further than a mile or two down the road when a boy and a girl threw stones at the car and hit the rear window. Ivan stopped the Beetle with great flourish, hopped out and chased the kids up the street. The most humorous part was that the boy was only three or four years old and about two foot nothing. He was running flat out, as fast as he could go, and Ivan was striding after him. It looked so comical! Ivan smacked him on the tail when he caught him. A woman standing nearby thoroughly agreed that the boy deserved it, and she told him not to do it again.

Twice, the locals did have a valid reason for throwing stones at us. Coming through one of the villages, I accidentally ran over a chicken. I couldn't tell if it was dead or not. A man sprinted after the car, cursing us, his fist in the air. We decided not to stop.

The next animal accident could have been disastrous. It was on a dirt road with little traffic. As we came around a corner, a donkey and cart appeared in front of us, crossing the road. Slamming on the brakes, we skidded sideways, nicked the donkey, careened down a sand embankment and hit a lump of metal. The donkey, cart and driver were fine. We were lucky to escape with a small dent. Not in the least surprised by a blue Beetle crashing into his donkey, the cart driver slid down the embankment to check that we were okay. Shaken up, I began yelling at him until Beth calmed me down. The driver, unconcerned by the entire incident, helped us get the car back on the road and cheerfully waved us off.

While travelling with Dick, Pat, June and Sally, we continually swapped seats, taking it in turns to ride in the more comfortable Beetle seats or in the crowded Landrover, squashed against their pile of camping and car equipment. It was in London that the four of them had decided to do the overland trip together. The girls were pleased to have the security of travelling with two men— particularly Pat, a jackeroo, who could turn his hand to anything. Beth and I hadn't met a jackeroo before and we assumed his family must own at least half of northern Australia. Dick, the owner of the Landrover, was a dentist and an easygoing group leader.

One day, Beth was driving the Beetle with June as her passenger. We'd packed up camp early that morning, having put our clocks two hours forward so we had more daylight hours. It meant getting up at 5am but our clocks said 7am, so it felt a little later. I set off in the Landrover, the Beetle following.

Still driving along the Black Sea Coast, we were on our way to Trabzon, once an ancient harbour and now a town of forty thousand people. Dick was at the wheel as we passed through small villages and then stretches of countryside with no buildings in sight. We were reminiscing about our lives in London, recalling the songs from shows we'd all seen. There was a shallow river crossing which the Landrover managed with ease.

'Dick, I think we should stop here,' I said, after we forged through the water. 'The Beetle might have some problems coming across.'

In the shade, we waited for the Beetle to arrive. Often as we travelled, we would pull up by the roadside to look at the scenery or for a toilet break behind a tree. I wasn't worried that we hadn't seen the Beetle for a short while.

We had a drink of water, purified by our iodine tablets, and waited and waited and waited. Sally, usually the quietest one in the group, finally voiced our thoughts. 'Where are they?' she asked, her face crinkling with nervous tension.

'Let's go back,' Dick decided, preferring action to standing.

Five miles away, we spotted them. The Beetle was by the side of the road, flanked by another vehicle. From a distance, it appeared to be a police car. We approached cautiously, unsure what was happening.

'Hello,' Beth called out, putting my mind at rest immediately. 'We had a puncture. The first one since we bought the car. What's that? 24,000 miles or so? That's a pretty good record, isn't it?'

Far more practical than me, Beth had jacked up the car. As she and June had been trying to unscrew the bolts, a police car had come by and offered assistance. Beth proudly insisted to us that she and June could have done it by themselves but had agreed to let the policemen help.

The Beetle went in front when we set out again. Half an hour later, it was Beth and June who had to turn back and find the Landrover. This time, *we* had a puncture. Dick and Pat whipped off the tyre in minutes.

Trabzon took on a single aim for us: to have our tyres mended. At the first garage, the mechanics didn't even have a tyre iron and were jumping on the tyre to wrench it off. In disgust, we grabbed our tyres and went to find another place. The next chap managed to get the tyres off, but then had to send them back to the first shop to have them vulcanised. We were relieved when the two tyres were returned in one piece.

The Beetle was lucky—it had no more punctures all the way to India. Meanwhile, the Landrover was constantly hitting stones and we had to keep stopping to change the flat tyres.

From Trabzon we headed inland to Eastern Anatolia, an undeveloped region with traditional villages far apart. It was a lonely area, and Beth and I were pleased to be with the Landrover.

We were told that in the military areas we had to report to the police. They ordered us to camp in the police compounds: dusty spots of dirt surrounded by barbed wire. At night, the police locked us in. We didn't know if that was for our safety or theirs! Not that we minded our 'camp ground', apart from the toilets, which were large pits with two planks across. Taking turns to use the facilities, each one would exit from the wooden shed, white-faced, holding his or her nose. Squatting on the planks was dangerous. They were wet and slippery; the possibility of falling in was very real. All of us preferred the outback method of going behind a tree and burying it with a shovel.

The police were pleasant to us. The only tourists who made it to this part of the country were the overlanders. Curious about the vehicles and the equipment, the policemen would come and speak a few words of English while peering into the cars and tents.

In Erzurum, the police pointed us in the direction of the copper shops, where Beth bought three small round dishes. A crowd quickly gathered to watch us and, as we left, the shopkeeper began crying. We guessed that the money must have really meant something to him.

The local women were in *purdah*, their faces covered. Also inquisitive about us foreigners, they liked having their photos taken. But the men were protective of their womenfolk. As Pat and I were filming the complying women, two men suddenly stepped in front of our cameras and shouted 'No!'

Agri was the other place we camped with the police. There, we first had to chase out the geese and children before we could set up our tents on the uneven dirt ground. Just as the tea was boiling, a man from a house opposite the compound brought over a plate of hot, savoury pastries.

A police guard stayed on duty all night, keeping the children and adults back from the fence. We felt like animals in a zoo. The people watched intently as we cooked dinner: tomatoes fried with meat in breadcrumbs, and some potatoes.

Driving towards Dogubeyazit, we delighted in the sight of the snow-capped peak of Mt Ararat rising up from the brown land. The road forward took us to another border crossing: Iran. As we prepared ourselves for the next unfamiliar country, Beth and I realised that we had accepted the disappointment of missing the countries of Syria, Jordan, Israel, Lebanon and Iraq. Meandering through Turkey had been an eye-opener: different religion, food, culture. And we had made some great friends: Dick, Pat, Sally and June were good fun and excellent travelling companions.

September 1996

No Fear for the Tourists

The headlines in the *Turkish Daily News* of 16 September, 1996, said little about the PKK-Turkish fighting in the eastern part of the country. So we decided to push on, via Ankara, to check with the Australian Embassy once again, and to have the Beetle tuned by the Volkswagen dealer. Our biggest fear was breaking down in the midst of a war zone.

Changing our route meant we had to make up some time. On Monday, we relaxed on a day cruise around the Twelve Islands off Fethiye, and Tuesday was the long drive. The road took us through rugged mountains, clad in pines. It would dip down into green valleys decorated by fruit trees. Women in blue and green headscarves worked in the fields, almost obscured by the lush crops. Sheep grazed on succulent pastures, spoilt by Australian standards. We passed countless stone ruins, overgrown with grass and flowers, a gentle reminder of a long-distant past. After cutting inland for a few hours, we returned to the coast, curving along the sea cliffs, no guard rail to protect us from plunging downwards. Beneath us, the blue Mediterranean stretched out; white horses raced towards the shore.

Not only was the countryside picturesque, but the bus drivers weren't so crazy, and there were no trucks. This drive wasn't on the tourist route, which made it a pleasant journey but with fewer options for accommodation. Our guidebook mentioned some lodges at a place called Cirali, on the coast, close to the ancient city of Olympos.

At 6pm, we came to the turn-off for Cirali. It was a narrow road down a mountainside, and at the bottom we were 'there'.

A mud road, some shanty shops and no signs. Slightly concerned, we couldn't imagine any town or accommodation in this remote area. Following our noses, we drove down a lane to the sea, stopping suddenly when we saw a person.

'Hello!' we shouted. 'Can you tell us how to get to Olympos Lodge?'

The man, obviously a tourist, looked at us strangely. *He doesn't speak English*, we thought, and wondered what else we could say to make ourselves understood.

'Hotel?' Beth said, trying again, as the man stared at the Beetle, transfixed.

'Ja, ja,' he finally answered, pointing behind him to a rock wall covered in shrubs. A stream of German followed as he laughed and chattered excitedly to us.

Eventually we worked out that he 'knew' our Beetle. He'd read a story in a German newspaper about the car and recognised it immediately. Not only that, but Wolfgang actually worked at the Volkswagen factory in Wolfsburg and had heard about our visit there!

'Very nice car,' he repeated and went to find his wife and share the news of the Beetle.

After the tourist towns on the Aegean Coast, Cirali was an idyllic haven: a long empty beach; the lodge in a serene setting, sweet-smelling jasmine hanging from the patio and peacocks proudly strutting in the gardens. The following morning when we enjoyed an early swim, Beth and I were the only ones in the water. Further up the beach, where a stream entered the sea, was the site of the ancient town of Olympos. Ruins remained in the midst of a tranquil, wild garden; birds flitted between the flowering oleanders, their song the only sound to break the silence.

On we went through Side, a romantic rendezvous for Cleopatra and Mark Antony. Then, sad to leave the sea behind us, we aimed for Konya. Once again, we were treated to impressive country-side, going up and down treeless mountains and into fertile valleys. The fine wide road teased us with expectation but, as we began climbing upwards, it became a single winding lane through steep, rocky country.

Grain and apples grew in the fields, tended with tractors and other mechanical farm equipment. Beth commented that on our previous trip, the farmers were heavily dependent on animals, donkeys especially, along with hoes, scythes and the like. She was amused by the tractors. Most boasted a little seat and steel frame over the left back wheel for the women to sit upon.

Despite the lack of road signs and street names in the huge, modern town of Konya, we found our hotel. It was opposite the Mevlana Museum, once a place of worship for the followers of Mevlana, known as the Whirling Dervishes, an Islamic religious order established in the thirteenth century. Since being outlawed by Ataturk in 1925, the dervishes now only whirled at their annual festival in December and for tourists. We didn't have a chance to see the energetic, traditional ceremony.

While crossing the town square, we came across another Kiwi, Robin Brandt. A collector of Turkish carpets for many years, Robin had written a book on the subject and returned frequently on buying trips. He was keen for the industry to use New Zealand wool. It was better quality, he told us, because in Turkey crops were more profitable and the sheep were pushed up to higher ground, causing a decline in their fleeces.

After giving us some tips on carpet buying, Robin led the way to a nearby shop and introduced us to his acquaintance, Mehmet. The shop, appropriately named Silk Road, was piled high with carpets. The only clear space was for the low chairs on which customers sat while doing business. Mehmet explained that he sold antique carpets, as well as new kilims designed by himself and woven by an army of outworkers in the villages.

'Between farm working, a lady make six to twelve kilim a year,' he told Beth as I filmed the carpet lesson. 'Some mountain ladies, they like to make busy designs. The plains women, they like to make open, simple styles.'

'Many designs symbolic,' he continued. 'The colours and the wool quality—that's what important. I make my own dyes, not use synthetic. I am selling by square metre.'

Mehmet mostly sold to dealers, but he was happy for the tourist trade to enter his shop. During the discussion, Mehmet's two young assistants served apple tea from a silver tray. This traditional custom was incongruous with the mobile phone strapped to Mehmet's belt.

The two assistants glowered at the video camera, embarrassed to be on film. One's black hair was combed upwards in an Elvis style, and he was wearing a waistcoat and printed shirt. I guessed they were twelve or thirteen years old. At length, Mehmet made it clear that it wasn't like the Indian child slavery system. He was their mentor, teaching them the carpet trade, housing them and giving them health insurance and English language instruction.

Beth wanted to buy some carpets, and she liked one of Mehmet's. It was made by a weaver of Kurdish heritage from a village near Konya. With the media focus on the Kurdish fighting in the eastern part of the country, we hadn't realised there were Kurdish people living peacefully throughout Turkey.

After folding the carpet into squares, like a sheet, the assistant tied it with a red string and handed the small bundle to Beth. Mehmet shook hands and gave me his business card. The quote on the back contrasted with the wheeling and dealing of the carpet industry: *Let's meet where the love, art and the culture meets. Let's meet at the Silk Road.*

Leaving Konya on an excellent highway, we saw twenty sheep in a safe haven between four lanes of traffic, waiting patiently for a chance to cross. It was an amazing sight in a city of six hundred thousand people. The sheep were astonishingly well-behaved, with only a shepherd and no sheepdog to keep them under control.

Because we were in Ankara over the weekend, the Australian Embassy was closed. I was relieved, for it meant they couldn't give us any bad news. The last time I had phoned, they had said travel in eastern Turkey was safe, but only during daylight. They had suggested we keep a low profile, as any media might attract attention and encourage a kidnap/hostage incident.

It was a catch-22. I hoped for some assistance from Volkswagen: a check-up on the car; a contact name for a garage in Erzurum; and possibly an escort if we were to get into trouble. In return, I could offer them publicity. Beth and I talked it over.

'It's stupid,' she said. 'They've told us to keep a low profile, so let's avoid the media completely.'

'We can always get them to put an embargo on it,' I countered, 'and ask them not to run the story 'til we've crossed the border.'

Beth shook her head. 'Just don't get us killed,' she muttered, unconvinced by the idea.

Volkswagen arranged the media, and we spent the next morning with a photographer, three television cameras and some news-paper reporters. Beth baulked at the amount of interest—she had been hoping only one journalist would turn up. When we told them of the one-week embargo, one TV station, which had wanted to air the story that night, decided against filming and left.

The VW PR woman was unable to attend and sent her sister, Gamze, to look after us, instead. Gamze was wonderful, translating for everyone and organising the entire day. There were flowers for us and a facelift for the Beetle: new shock absorbers, brake pads, spark plugs. The slow-leaking puncture was mended, and the wheels changed around. Various parts of the engine were taken out, and a young boy diligently washed them in a bucket, piece by piece.

VW provided a lunch of kebabs and then packed us off by taxi to the Museum of Anatolian Civilisation, which provided a fascinating look into Turkish history. I was too nervous about the Beetle to really enjoy it. Beth compared me to a new father pacing at a baby's birth. Back at Volkswagen, we had to wait another hour, and I succumbed to the shoe-shine boy working outside the VW dealership. While he was cleaning my shoes, he gave me some sandals to wear—not the best footwear for the dusty streets. When I asked to film him, the boy performed like a movie star, grinning at the camera, slicking back his hair and making large, dramatic gestures.

Finally, the Beetle was returned to us, in perfect condition. The garage had also arranged for us to have the brakes checked at Erzurum.

The next morning, we stopped briefly by Ataturk's Memorial and, as in 1961, I still found it was the car display inside the memorial which interested me the most. But this time, we had a greater understanding of Ataturk and Turkish history in general. As the first President of the Turkish republic, Ataturk had propelled the country into its present form, introducing numerous social and political policies to transform Turkey into a modern secular state.

Route 260 was the worst road we had travelled in Turkey. For thirty kilometres, the road was dotted with potholes. These were no impediment, however, to the trucks and buses that roared along in the centre of the road. There was evidence of roadworks but, as far as we could see, nothing had happened yet. As we hit one particularly nasty pothole, we heard a hubcap ping off. It disappeared into the bushes, and it took us ten minutes to find it. During the search, we saw three other hubcaps that had suffered the same fate.

In a small village, we bought bread, spoke with the shopkeeper and watched a woman on the footpath teasing a fleece. Just outside the village, I filmed some women picking apples in an orchard. When I played back the video for them, they giggled and crowded in closely, astonished to see themselves on film. In delight, they presented us with a bag of newly picked apples.

We spotted an electrical shop in another village, and I dashed in to get a lead for our bulb. The lights in the hotels were so bad that we had brought our own 60 watt bulbs, but often we couldn't unscrew the lights to change them. With a lead, we could just plug the bulb in and then dangle it over the bed, making it possible to read at night. However, we did wonder if the frequent blackouts in our hotel rooms were related to our higher watt bulbs and computer usage.

The shop was stacked with all sorts of electrical equipment. A tiny path between piles of dusty motors, televisions and radios led to a back room where business was done. It took a while before I was understood. One chap worked on the electrical lead, while four others sat and watched the television. Beth had been waiting in the Beetle for twenty minutes, so I went to get her. The chaps were pleased to have female company and hospitably poured tea for her. It was a disgusting brew, but it would have been rude to refuse, so Beth forced it down.

We'd read much about the troglodyte dwellings in the Cappadocian Valleys and yet, their weird appearance was still unexpected: fairy chimneys, white rock pinnacles jutting up from the gentle slopes, adorned with windows and doors. There were triangular ones, pointing upwards; some clustered together as a bunch of mushrooms; others were shaped like giant phalluses. And in them all, people had once lived, carving out rooms inside the rock towers: houses, churches, complete cities.

The Valley of the Fairy Chimneys looked as if it were from the pages of a fairytale book. The windowed pinnacles were reminiscent of medieval towers; one could imagine Rapunzel imprisoned inside. Close up, the chimneys were much taller than I'd guessed, with ladders leading to the higher rooms. Some were twelve storeys high! As soon as we stepped into the rock rooms, the temperature dropped suddenly, the stifling heat of the day banished to the outside.

On the lower slopes, some of the dwellings were still used by people and animals. Camels rested in the shade inside one of the rock houses, and sheep with long tails wagging like dogs wandered around the edge.

The other type of rock house was the underground one. The Goreme Open Air Museum was a collection of cave houses and churches. Frescoes and paintings decorated the churches and, in one chamber, there was a refectory stone table with benches to seat forty to fifty people. During an Arab invasion in the seventh century, the Christians simply rolled large stones in front of the openings, protecting themselves from discovery and persecution.

Volcanoes caused the unearthly landscape, spreading an ash across the countryside which developed into a soft, porous stone. Sand and wind eroded the stone into the strange shapes. The early inhabitants found the rock easy to carve and created homes which could always be expanded with a little more digging. The underground cities were built when invaders crossed the lands and the locals needed a place to hide and survive.

A benefit of the underground dwellings was their natural air-conditioning. When we sought some shade for our picnic lunch, we discovered trees were few and far between. In the underground city of Kaymakli, the temperature was a cool sixteen degrees Celsius.

Tens of thousands had lived in Kaymakli, a maze of tunnels, houses and rooms. Numerous layers were carved deep down into the rock. We didn't go too far in, Beth preferring to stay close to the exit. Shelves and cookingware reinforced the underground lifestyle. I wondered if I could ever adjust to such a confined space away from the natural light.

We had three days exploring the underground houses and fairy chimneys of the region. It was our last sightseeing before we tackled the dangerous stretch. I decided to get the spare tyre mended in the town of Uchisar and went for a haircut while I was waiting. There were no other customers in the hairdresser's. Communicating by gestures, I indicated two inches—'That's how much I want cut off'. The barber nodded and his assistant put a towel around my shoulders. Smiling at me, he began cutting. After he'd finished one side, he brought a mirror over to show me.

'Oh God!' was all I could splutter. It was so short. I was a sixty-two-year-old grandfather with a punk haircut. 'Why did you do that?' I shouted pointlessly, unable to explain my anger. He stared at me, shocked. Obviously, he wasn't playing a joke on me. Shrugging his shoulders in confusion, he pointed to the door, demonstrating that he didn't expect to be paid because I was dissatisfied. Then it came to me. When I had indicated two inches off, he had taken it to mean I wanted my hair two inches long! Sighing, I waved at him to continue with the other side. If it had to be that short, it might as well be symmetrical.

Beth wanted to visit the Yellow Caravanserai, a Selkuk building from the thirteenth century which was an early hotel for travellers. I stayed in the Beetle as she went inside to look at the stone rooms catering for people and their animals. She returned to the car livid.

'The man at the gate said he saw me on TV this morning!' she announced.

It was a silent trip back to the hotel. I rang the PR woman at Volkswagen and she confirmed that one of the television stations had broken the embargo and aired the story that morning. She was almost as upset as we were and said she would try to arrange an escort from Erzincan.

There was no consoling Beth. She was incensed that I had put us in this dangerous position, which could so easily have been avoided.

'How dumb will we feel if we're kidnapped?' she snapped at me, referring to the low-profile advice from the Embassy. 'We can't expect them to help us out now. Why did you have to put us at risk for fifteen seconds of fame?'

'We can turn around and go back. We'll do it again next year.' I knew she would disagree; she wanted to keep going, too.

Despite the possible danger, I couldn't help feeling that we were untouchable. It was that arrogance of the tourist. We were Australians on holiday, uninvolved in Turkish-Kurdish politics. Nothing could happen to us. Later, after we had passed through the region, I realised how stupid I had been. By no means were tourists 'immortals' on their travels. In fact, they were more likely to be attacked—in the kurdish case, for the international publicity, but generally for their assumed wealth.

The Volkswagen woman rang back to say that a mechanic would escort us from Erzincan to Erzurum. Slightly relieved, we went to dine in the hotel restaurant, where a German fellow approached our table, having recognised us from a German newspaper. Beth glared at me.

That night we checked our emails. A message from a friend in Sydney told us she had been to a clairvoyant the day before. The clairvoyant had said she had friends who were travelling; they were in danger and should turn back. It was the last thing we needed to hear.

The next day it was impossible to stay worried as we drove through a stunning landscape of fairy chimneys and pink rock valleys, up into the mountains to Sivas. Each time a car tooted at us, Beth tensed, concerned that everyone had seen the television story. Usually, I beeped the Beetle's horn and waved to locals working in the fields, but today was not the day to draw any further attention to ourselves.

In Sivas, we met Marc, a French motorcyclist on his way to India. Middle-aged, he had recently grabbed at the chance to do what he had always wanted. Temporarily leaving behind his wife and his business, he was out on the road, enjoying a newly found freedom. In the tradition of the pioneers of flight, his friends had written their best wishes on a white silk scarf, which was draped elegantly around his neck.

Jolly Marc gave us some light relief. He was super-confident about travelling through the war zone. The only aspect he wasn't looking forward to was the ban on alcohol in Iran. He lifted our spirits, impressing us with his impeccable dress while living out of the back of a motorbike.

Into the War Zone

With the spectre of Kurdish-Turkish fighting hanging over our travels, we learnt more about the situation. Divided by national boundaries, the Kurdish separatists were struggling for a Kurdish homeland, using terrorist actions to bring world attention to their plight. During the eighties, the threat of a large Kurdish nation state had led the Turkish government to undertake a policy of assimilation, outlawing the Kurdish language and culture. After three million Iraqi Kurds fled to Turkey in the early 1990s, the international concern forced the Turkish government to ease off the restrictions, legalising Kurdish speech and songs.

It was in the south-east of the country that the struggle was focused, and the PKK headquarters was in that area. There was a Kurdish majority in the region, discontented by the poverty and lack of government services.

The latest incident had stemmed from a Turkish attack. While the world was diverted by the Iraqi scuffle with the USA, the Turkish army had struck at the PKK to dispossess them of land and military equipment. Attacks were made under the cover of darkness. In this most recent incident, the PKK hadn't yet taken any hostages. I was aware that international travellers had been prime targets in the past.

Police headquarters in Erzincan was the rendezvous for our escort. Three young fellows in a new Volkswagen Polo were delighted to have a day out driving. One was the mechanic, the other two were friends along for the ride. They gunned the engine and sped off, testing out the grunt of their car. We could see them waving in the mirror, pleased that our old Beetle could handle the pace.

Not far from Erzincan, we saw the first tank, perched high on a knoll overlooking the road. From then on, every intersection, bridge and hill was protected by a tank or foxhole. The road was the dividing line: one side was held by the Turkish Army, the other by the PKK. Well-established army camps would appear by the roadside, sudden bursts of equipment and technology in the dry, dusty emptiness. At one camp, we could even see several helicopters transferring troops.

The tense military presence made me realise how stupid I had been. The Embassy had been one hundred per cent right. This was indeed a war zone and we were at risk. Burnt-out buses and trucks littered the roadside. Tracks leading up to Kurdish territory were blocked. We knew we were being watched from atop the observation towers, where binoculars glinted in the sun.

At one point we came to a standstill. This is it, a PKK roadblock, I thought nervously, hoping our escort would somehow look after us. A long line of trucks and buses, interspersed by one or two cars, queued along the road. After twenty minutes, our escort took us to the front of the queue. It was no roadblock, but a nasty accident instead. A tanker had plunged into the river. We were waved through, and the Volkswagen Polo soon picked up its rally car speed again. The lads weaved in and out of the traffic, mostly trucks and buses, checking in the rear vision mirror occasionally to see if the Beetle was keeping up.

We felt a little safer with an escort, but still, it was a nervous day's drive. To while away the time, Beth marked each army camp on the map and then realised we might appear to be collecting military information. Afraid to stop for lunch, we ate in the car. Our escorts told us that even the locals didn't travel the road in the dark.

Erzurum, the army town where we'd camped in a police compound in 1961, was our resting point for the night. Our escort took us to the Volkswagen dealership. There, the brakes were checked, and we were provided with tea after our long drive. We thanked the Volkswagen people profusely, only wishing they could accompany us the following day as well.

On the one hundred and seventy miles to Dogubeyazit, there seemed to be an even greater military presence than the day before. Soldiers pulled us over at checkpoints to examine our passports and ask if we were carrying guns. More tanks, more helicopters, more camps. And amidst it all, the locals were going about their daily tasks. In one river bed, four women in full *purdah* were washing carpets, working in unison. Elsewhere, streams were lined with women wading in and out of the water, washing their clothes. Veiled women carried water back to their mud houses. Shepherds, with their sheep and goats guarded by fierce dogs, called out for cigarettes.

The raw poverty of the land, the villages and the people was sobering. Water, trees and crops were scarce in the dry, rocky landscape.

When Mt Ararat came into view, we stopped to take a photo. Shrouded in cloud, it appeared mystical, living up to the legend of being the resting place of Noah's Ark. Beth collected a few pebbles for her art class back in Sydney. They were making Arks for Christmas, filled with animals, to delight their various grandchildren. Beth had promised to bring back some authentic stones.

Late afternoon we arrived in Dogubeyazit, otherwise known as Dog Biscuit, thankful the dangerous stretch was now over. We'd forgotten that Dog Biscuit was a real frontier town: a main street of dirt, potholes and clay, lined with food shops and chemists.

At the hotel, we met up with Marc. He too had had no problems with the checkpoints. We all booked into the newest hotel, assuming it would be adequate. It was just six months old. On the surface, everything seemed fine, but nothing actually worked. The toilets didn't flush, water ran down the walls of the bathroom, the lift was broken, the banister wobbly—and we had a single sheet on our double bed. Laughing at the veneer of modernity, we had a cup-a-soup for dinner, washed down with the last of the Barcardi, which we couldn't take into Iran.

Before crossing the border the next day, we caught a cab with Marc to Isak Pasa Sarayi, the fortress overlooking the town. Many of the 366 rooms were intact, and our guide pointed out the harem, solarium, bathroom and long-drop toilet. Judging by the number of rooms in the harem, we figured the prince had had his pick of women! Set into the rock, the fortress was camouflaged, reflecting the reds, browns and yellows of the hill. Beth and I declined the walk up the tower, but Marc climbed to the top and waved his white silk scarf. Beth took a photo for his wife. The yellow and red stripes of brick encircling the tower gleamed against the deep blue sky.

It was time to move on, and we made our way back down the hill to our Beetle. After we had paid off the guide, Beth told me that he had probably rather enjoyed the morning's work.

'Every time we went up any stairs in the fortress, the guide was behind me, patting my bottom!' she revealed with a laugh.

'That's why I wouldn't climb the tower,' she added indignantly. 'I didn't want to be touched the whole way up!'

Chapter 7

Domes, Deserts and Dutch Cyclists

1961—Persia

Before the Revolution

In magazine pictures, the Shah looked terribly dashing and, according to the ladies, he was extraordinarily handsome. He conjured up romantic images of Persia: opulent palaces, exotic women and a luxurious lifestyle in the languid heat. Apart from the glamour of the high-profile Shah, we knew nothing about Persia except that we could expect deserts, nomads and camels. We were completely unaware of the rumblings of unrest and revolution in the country.

Our first day in Persia began with the sound of splashing water. Still with our friends from the Landrover, the six of us had camped by a river bed. In the early morning light we were treated to the sight of two dozen camels drinking. Amazed by the scene, Pat and I grabbed our movie cameras and began filming. Docile creatures, the camels allowed us to come right up close, and we could capture their hairy faces. When the two camel drivers had recovered from their surprise at finding tents and two vehicles by their watering hole, they were friendly. The chaps laughed in wonder at the noise of their own camels played back to them on my tape recorder.

Eight days we had to traverse the country; that was how long our visas were valid. We could have applied for an extension but hoped it wouldn't be necessary, as we hadn't included the extra cost in our budget. The time frame meant doing long distances every day, a minimum of two hundred miles.

After two incidents in the first few days, we were so terrified that we were determined to cross the country quickly.

The night before we were to arrive in Tehran, we planned to camp at a watering hole. As we began to set up our tents, a group of soldiers emerged from the bushes, their rifles pointing towards us. Uncertain of our offence, we froze, afraid that any false step would provoke gunfire. The soldiers watched us carefully and then waved their guns at the cars. Eventually, we understood. They wanted us to move—right now. This was a Bedouin watering hole; if we were to camp here, it would cause trouble.

The next episode frightened us even more. Beth explained the events of the evening to our parents, no doubt causing them concern:

I think it's the sixteenth of October. We had a bit of a fright two nights ago when we were looking for somewhere to camp. Down a road, we found what appeared to be a dilapidated and deserted mud village, so we backed the cars up to the wall of a house to get some warmth from it.

While we were cooking our dinner, these two soldiers came out of the darkness with their rifles trained right on us. They indicated that there were nomadic people around here who were inclined to cut people's throats.

Unfortunately, Dick had two punctures. One wheel was mended and the other was off the Landrover in pieces. Our little pump was not strong enough to pump it up. We packed the Beetle in record time, urged on by the thought of cut throats, tied the tyre from the Landrover on top and headed to Tehran.

By this time, it was midnight and everything was closed up. Two policemen were in a little hut, so Ivan stopped to ask if they had a pump. In their yard, there was a whole series of stolen cars, but not one had a pump. The policemen took Ivan down to a shop where a man was sleeping on the bench and he produced a bicycle pump without a valve. So that was no good. They woke up another chap, and he offered us the same sort of thing. Eventually, the policemen hailed a taxi driver, who went and found us a pump. We pumped up the tyre and drove back to the others. During this time, a camel train of thirteen camels went past us on its way into Tehran.

When we got back, the soldiers were still there, presumably guarding the others with their rifles well loaded. After driving down the road for half an hour, we came to a truck place where people stop for drinks and sleeps. We parked within sight of that, and slept in the car.

The two incidents had shaken up all of us. Unused to both soldiers and guns, we were stunned to be in the sights of a rifle, even if the soldiers were promising to protect us.

We passed briefly through Tehran and headed for Isfahan, which we had heard was one of the oldest cities in Persia, with many tourist attractions. The town was full of beautiful mosques, all domed and some tiled in blue. The large square had two mosques one at each end. One was for the public and had four minarets for calling the people to prayer. The other one, smaller and domed, was used only by the Shah and didn't require the minarets, because it was a personal mosque.

In the villages, the women wore *chadors*, huge black pieces of material covering everything except their faces. We spotted fewer *chadors* in the towns, most people wearing Western-style clothing. To make sure she didn't offend the Muslim religion, Beth changed from the shorts she wore in the Beetle in a skirt before we entered the towns.

We saw a few other overlanders, including a Kombi van flying an American flag. Travelling with the Landrover was sometimes slow, but we managed to give them a hurry-along. Often we'd pack up camp early, at 6am or 7am, and do a hundred miles before stopping to cook breakfast. After leaving Isfahan, we camped the night in a garden with fountains, a virtual oasis in the desert. Another night, we came across a soft drink factory—we guessed it was Pepsi—which had grass all the way around it, another oasis in the never-ending dry dirt.

Persia was so different from anything we'd ever seen, with its desert scenery, mud buildings and mosques. The towns spoke of an opulence from another age, while in the water-less landscape, the villagers carved a life learnt from the traditions of centuries. We assumed the Shah and his glamorous palaces to be in other parts of the country or perhaps hidden in the sprawling city of Tehran.

At the town of Bam, we farewelled Pat, Dick, Sally and June. They were heading south towards Shiraz on roads marked as mere tracks on their map. As much as we wanted to accompany them, we couldn't take the risk, as the Beetle was low to the ground. None of us had any idea what sort of rugged roads they might encounter.

Extract from 1961 AA Strip Map—Tehran to Zahedan via Isfahan, Mileage 1,034

A little tar towards the end, but generally a sandy surface with risk of sand drifts between the Afghan Pass and Bam.

Miles

	ZAHEDAN
	Cross plain to
50	Garagheri
	Ascent of Gilubek Pass
25	Nasratabad-Sipi
	Ascent to the defile of Darwazek-Nadiri or Afghan Pass.
32	Gurg
36	Shurgaz
13	Mil-i-Nadari (tower). Later at Qal'eh-i-Chasemhr keep right at fork.

18	*(edge of) Iranshahr (Fahrej)*
17	*Vakilabad*
19	*BAM. Turn right and later left in town.*
13	*Drazin*
30	*Tahrud*
21	*Nabid*
36	*Mahun*
	Several wadis and often difficult.
20	*KERMAN*

The AA Strip Maps were misnamed really. They weren't maps at all, rather a set of directions telling us when to turn left or right. Occasionally, we turned too soon, taking a side road to the next village and then rejoining the main road. With so few roads, particularly in the desert, it was almost impossible for us to get lost. We always found our way back to the correct route.

Driving on gravel and dirt roads wasn't a problem for the Beetle, and it coped well with the sand drifts. We tried to avoid the wadies, old water beds often concealing pools of water. One time, we came over a rise and went straight into one, without any warning. Despite our concern, the Beetle powered through, and there was no damage. We could see that in winter it would be extremely difficult to navigate. The snow would make it hard to stay on the road, and dried wadies, filled with deep snow, would be an unseen danger.

20 October, 1961

10,979 miles from London

At first, the flat nothingness of the desert had terrified us. The brown dirt stretching away in every direction. *Barren, ugly,* we thought, comparing it unfavourably with recent images of the high sea cliffs on the Adriatic coast and the lush fields of Austria.

But then we began to see it. The minute changes. A tussock or four blades of yellowing grass breaking the flatness of the plain. Tiny piles of dirt, scraped together by an animal, a person or perhaps the lasting effects of a whirling sandstorm. Oddly shaped rocks and sudden volcanic outcrops, a lifeless moonscape offering narrow valleys of shade. Browns transformed into yellows, oranges and reds as the sun made its arc across the wide sky. The glow of our cooking fire and the sparkle of faraway stars were insignificant against the blackness of the night. It was as old sailors spoke of the sea: eternal movement in texture and colour.

Hazy figures moved on the horizon—nomads and their camels, we presumed. About once an hour, a car or truck would pass us, and we would rush to wind up the windows, as sand and dirt splattered across the windscreen. Staring through the churned-up dust, we determinedly kept sight of the road markers, the small white rocks which were the only indication that we weren't driving aimlessly in the desert.

We had stopped for an early lunch, intending to take some film. No vehicles had passed for nearly forty minutes, and Beth began driving up and down the road while I filmed. The little Beetle was a bright blue speck on the brown backdrop. I knew our families would be fascinated by this country and hoped for some good footage, especially for Mum. She would be pleased to see her 'new' car exploring foreign lands.

Thirty feet away, Beth was turning the Beetle around. I wanted one more shot with the sun now directly overhead. Brushing dust off the camera, the warm air drying my mouth, I suddenly became aware of the silence. There was no 'dak–dak–dak' from the Beetle. Beth had jumped out. All I could see was an arm waving frantically from the other side of the car, her head obscured by the luggage on the roofracks.

'The engine just cut out,' she yelled as I hurried towards her.

I switched the ignition and the engine chugged desultorily.

'Bloody hell!' I groaned. The Beetle was supposed to keep on going. It would never freeze or boil over, the advertisements promised. 'If you had to, you could drive a VW all day at top speed through a desert.' Perhaps they hadn't tried.

With my inept mechanical skills, there wasn't much I could do. *Check the most obvious first*, I decided, and pulled out the dipstick for the fuel tank.

'It can't be the petrol,' Beth said, analysing the possibilities. 'We should have enough for sixty miles. That's what we calculated on the map.'

The dipstick came out clean. The tank was empty. The reserve had five litres. It would take us about thirty miles, not as far as Kerman, the next town. With my long legs sticking out of the door, I folded in half to flick the reserve switch on the floor near the clutch.

Beth smoothed the map out on her bare legs. The AA Strip Map had marked all of the garages on our route. Nothing had changed since the last time we looked. The nearest fuel was still sixty miles away. We couldn't understand why the petrol had run out. Apart from driving up and down for the filming, we hadn't made any detours. Why hadn't this happened when we were in Athens surrounded by garages?

'There might be a leak, or maybe it was that poor quality petrol at the last place,' I suggested.

'Probably the heat makes it burn faster as well,' Beth added. 'It'll be okay, someone will come by. Anyway, we have enough food and water for a week.' Beth was reassuring herself, as much as me.

Part of me was confident we would be 'saved', but there was a niggling 'what if?' feeling. Neither Beth nor I could believe it. We were living out our biggest fear—breaking down in the desert. In London we had packed the car with sixteen bottles of fruit juice and a five-gallon can of water to stop us from dying of thirst. It was a fear of the unknown. We were used to the green grass of New Zealand. The only time we'd seen a desert was in Egypt on a side trip from the ship while it was passing through the Suez Canal.

Beth was fanning the map to create a breeze. It made little difference to the heatwave in the Beetle. The temperature was cooler in the desert air outside the car. Yesterday we had hit a bump and the heater on the driver's side had hummed into life. Now the darned thing wouldn't switch off! Sweat trickled underneath my collar and down my back, forming a wet, sticky seal with the plastic seat. We joked that the heater reminded us we were in the desert. The weather outside was, in fact, only slightly uncomfortable.

At this point, we couldn't do much but hope. Driving along, watching intently for another vehicle, we wondered where the Landrover was now and wished we were all still together.

Thirty minutes. Twenty-five miles. At a quarter to one, the Beetle chugged to a standstill, the reserve tank empty. We hadn't seen anyone for nearly two hours.

Drinking tepid fruit juice from our melamine camping mugs, we scanned the desert: a harsh landscape in which long-term survival was impossible. We could camp the night, a few nights if need be. Lately, we had been sleeping in the car, folding the seats down into single beds. The hard surface was lumpy and uncomfortable so we would push clothes into the holes and gaps. But it was safer than the tent. The soldiers had implanted an image we couldn't dislodge: nomads slitting our throats by moonlight.

Food wasn't a problem. Plenty of tins still lay under the seat: meat, soup and fruit. Twelve bottles of fruit juice remained, and the water can was nearly full. Our jerry can was, of course, empty. As we plotted our mileage on the map, it had seemed unnecessary.

'I can hear something!' Beth's cry spurred me into action. I leapt onto the Beetle's running board to get a better view of the road. Sure enough, there was a white vehicle going in the same direction as us. We'd only been 'stranded' for ten minutes.

The Volkswagen Kombi van pulled up behind the Beetle, and we quickly related our problem to the two scruffy German chaps. Glancing appraisingly at Beth's tight white shorts, they listened and nodded. Then they exploded.

'You ran out? Ran out of petrol? *Unglaubich!* No spare can? *Das ist ja mahnsims!* How could you do that? This is a desert, you know.'

Mumbling 'stupid, stupid', they led us around to the back of the Kombi, proudly overflowing with enough equipment to deal with any contingency. I tried for the usual camaraderie between overlanders and was rewarded with a humiliating lecture on 'Being Prepared'.

'Are you carrying water? Do you have enough food? And what about spare parts? No Volkswagen service out here, you know.'

Grateful for the petrol, I stayed quiet, bearing the tirade, knowing we were foolish. The Germans could spare ten litres. Not enough to make Kerman. At least, the next time we ran out, we would be closer to civilisation.

Back in the Beetle, we laughed, at ourselves and at them, slightly hysterical in our relief. 'We should have bought a Kombi, not a Beetle,' Beth remarked, 'and then we could carry as much gear as them!'

Beth estimated we would fall short about ten miles from

Kerman. We hoped that, closer to the town, there would be a better chance of hitchhiking in for fuel. Again, I drove at a steady speed, waiting for the moment when the engine would chug into silence.

And then a mirage.

Shimmering above the brown desert, a petrol dump in a one-tree, mud-house village. A new 'garage', unmarked on the maps from London! With comical hand signals, we tried to explain our joy as the chap pumped the petrol by hand into the jerry can. Bemused, he nodded and laughed along. The acrid fumes danced in the heat and tickled my nose. A piece of dirty cloth filtered the petrol as it was funnelled into the Beetle.

As we fumbled in counting out the *rials*, Beth grinned at me. We would make the next leg after all. To Kerman. To Pakistan and India, and just maybe, back home to New Zealand.

1996—Iran

The Wrong Expectations

Ayatollah Khomeini had led Iran to a cultural revolution in 1979, doing away with the corrupt opulence of the ruling class and the flow of petrodollars to Britain and America. The revolution also ended the Shah's attempts at modernising Iran through land reform and the establishment of a democratic government. The new Islamic Republic of Iran became a theocratic government based on the teachings of the Prophet Mohammed and his successors. With the implementation of a strict Muslim code and the impact of the long war against the American-backed Iraq, Iran took an anti-Western stance. We planned to make sure people knew immediately that we were Australians, not Americans.

It was difficult to determine how our presence would be received in Iran. The books and media reports by Western writers intimated that travellers in Iran faced enormous obstacles, danger and hostility. By contrast, the Iranian embassy and the one Iranian guidebook we were given stated that travellers were welcome and at no risk. Evaluating the propaganda from both sides, we imagined the truth to be somewhere in between.

Entering Iran will be problematic and time-consuming, we thought, anticipating officials who would demand to see the entire contents of the car to uncover 'contraband' items. We approached the border crossing with trepidation.

The difficulty, it turned out, was in leaving Turkey.

A Turkish official examined our passports and the carnet, grunting as he read them. He looked up at me, waved the carnet and announced, 'Serious problem.' Shaking his head, he added, 'Illegal,' for good measure. I didn't know if something was really wrong, or if he smelt the chance for extra income.

Remaining calm, I followed the man into a threadbare office; a few tables and chairs had been scattered about and there was very little in the way of technology. Two other officials came to join us and, thankfully, one spoke good English. He informed me that on our entry into Turkey, from the side trip to Rhodes, the carnet hadn't been stamped.

'We came in at Marmaris,' I explained. 'It was on a small ferry from Rhodes. We're driving this Volkswagen overland from England to India. It's our second honeymoon. We did it once before, in the same car, in 1961.'

The Beetle plans didn't impress them. The officials needed to contact Marmaris by fax and verify my story. With their communication network, it could take days.

Unlike the rest of the trip, which had a flexible itinerary, the

Iran leg was pre-booked and we were to be accompanied by a guide for our sixteen days in the country. Delays would cause problems and cost money.

Resorting to some heavy PR work, I began pulling out the supporting evidence. Photos of the car in Turkey in 1961. Pictures of the family and the Beetle in a recent New Zealand newspaper showing three generations: my father in the background, me, and Tahni on the bonnet. More photos of us leaving London in August. Media coverage from Germany. And the coup d'etat: a copy of the story which would appear in the Turkish media the following day. After all our worry about the broken embargo and a high profile in Eastern Turkey, the customs officials had never heard of us.

The officials smiled, talked among themselves and pointed at the car. I was beginning to feel slightly desperate. The discussion in Turkish continued. Finally they turned back to me.

'You have honest eyes,' the English-speaking official pronounced. But still I had to sign a statutory declaration to say the car had entered the country at Marmaris. And they insisted on a copy of the carnet.

'The photocopier does not work. You must go back to Dogub-eyazit and get copy.'

Luckily, we had followed the advice in the travel guides and carried extra copies of all our documents. I handed over a copy of the carnet and, finally, they waved me on to the next stage, wishing me well on the trip. It had taken two hours to get through Turkish customs; now we had the Iranian section to endure.

Beth was directed to a separate room behind a steel door. There were no windows or chairs. A mass of bus passengers were sitting on the floor, mostly well-shrouded women.

The carnet was stamped without a full inspection of the Beetle and its contents. The custom officials questioned whether I was carrying sexy magazines or liquor, and I had to write down the serial numbers of the mobile phone, video camera and laptop computer. They didn't want any Western products going astray on the black market. I was unprepared for the next request.

'Can I have your pen?'

Stupidly, I was using an expensive Waterman pen, which I kept in my top pocket. One would have thought I was a wiser traveller than that by now! I offered the man some cigarettes instead.

Beth returned and we only had the final checkpoint to go. Unfortunately, it wasn't a mere formality. We learnt later that our motorcyclist friend, Marc, was detained there for two hours. As we approached, we were met by our Iranian guide, Kianoush. He spoke to the officials, the Beetle was directed to the front of the queue and, in minutes, we were in the Islamic Republic of Iran.

Kianoush was driving a two-year-old white Hillman, a rental car hired specifically for this job. He couldn't fit in the back of the Beetle, not with our piles of travelling essentials. Anyway, it was enough of a change for us to have a guide, let alone one inside the car. Accustomed to being independent, we were concerned how we would adjust to being 'on tour'. But we had chosen the route and the cities we wanted to visit. The advice had been to book accommodation in advance, because there were so few hotels catering for tourists, but we had discovered that task to be an impossible one. Communications from Australia to Iran were unreliable and, in the end, we were happy to have accommodation organised through a tour group.

We'd decided on this method of travel for peace of mind, for ourselves and for our daughters. If we did get into strife, we would be at less risk with an interpreter. It also meant we were to receive an insight into the country. On our first trip, we had known so little about Persia. This time, we hoped to remedy that with a guide.

It was nearly three hundred kilometres to Tabriz, the closest town to the border with tourist accommodation. Following Kianoush, we weaved through the mountainous region of Azarbaijan, not far south of the border with the former Russian states of Azerbaijan and Armenia. Rising above us were bare, steep slopes, the browns and oranges of the rock bright under the deep blue sky. The hot midday sun accentuated the barrenness of the landscape. In the valleys, villages sprang up, the mud-brick houses built around courtyards.

In many places, the sealed road ran parallel to the old road, the one we had travelled along in 1961. Mostly, the road surface was good. The only traffic hazard was the buses thundering in both directions, taking passengers to and from the border.

As soon as we entered the outskirts of Tabriz, we understood why we'd read so many warnings about Iranian traffic. Three lanes of cars and buses crowded into a marked two-lane street. Pedestrians crossed busy roads, heedless of the cars, trusting their fate to Allah. It was a free-for-all in which traffic rules ceased to exist.

Tabriz, the capital of the province, was now a city of over one million. The massive growth surprised us, and we were pleased we had Kianoush to lead us through the jumble of streets. At the hotel, we relaxed with a cup of tea instead of the usual glass of wine, since alcohol was banned in the Islamic Republic. Marc arrived, sunburnt and exhausted from delays at the border and the long ride to Tabriz. Amidst the maze of Tabriz, he had paid a taxi driver to guide him to the hotel.

Kianoush was a history graduate and a linguist. The next morning, he was keen to show us the historical sights of Tabriz before the long drive to Zanjan. But first, we had an unusual request for our guide: we needed to organise third-party insurance on the car. The insurance from London had covered us as far as Turkey; insurance for Iran could only be purchased in the country. After asking the locals at the hotel desk, Kianoush took us to a local insurance agency, where we paid ten dollars for third-party insurance. Judging by the city traffic and the dents in every car, it seemed unlikely we would make it across the country without some kind of ding.

The sightseeing started with the Azarbaijan Museum, which chronicled the beginnings of the Iranian Constitutional Revolution, a 1908 uprising against Mohammad Ali Shah in Tabriz. Russian intervention helped quash the revolt. It was a sign of times to come. Russia occupied Tabriz a number of times, including during both World Wars.

Like much of the city, which echoed an era of former glory, the mosque was in a sad state of disrepair. Its grandeur of the fifteenth century had been destroyed by one of Tabriz's many earthquakes. Kianoush told us that Marco Polo had visited the mosque on his travels. Over the next two weeks, we were to discover Tabriz was indicative of many cities in Iran. The historical sites suffered from neglect, restoration having become a low priority during the recent years of war.

Knives. Our next town, Zanjan, was famous for them. Entire streets were lined with knife shops. Inside the shops and spilling out onto the road, knives were being made, sold or tested, touched against the finger to check their sharpness. In one shop, I filmed as Beth bought a penknife for her brother, Brian. The multitude of knives was astounding. From machetes to kitchen knives to flick knives, there was one for every occasion.

The shopkeeper, happy to demonstrate his wares for the camera, pulled down bundles from the shelves behind him. The knives were wrapped together in newspaper, tied with string and piled on top of each other—masses of paper bundles from floor to ceiling. Thousands in this one shop alone! Beth whispered to me, 'It makes me feel nervous. I've never seen so many knives in my life.' We couldn't understand the market for so many knives and assumed that Zanjan knives must be sold around the country.

When Beth went to pay for the knives, she did it correctly, according to custom. Unlike that morning. She had bought some sandals and offered the money to the shopkeeper. He had held up his palms in a negative gesture and shook his head. Confused, Beth thought she had offended the man. Perhaps he wasn't allowed to accept money from a woman. Without Kianoush or me there, she could do little but offer the money again. This time, he accepted. Later, Kianoush told us it was custom to refuse a present or service once or twice. He added that serious business was generally preceded by small talk and many cups of tea. It was all about Persian politeness.

A new highway, only opened the week before, sped us to Qazvin. Few vehicles were on the road and the Beetle hummed along at 60 miles per hour, a speed it hadn't achieved since the Italian autostradas.

Queues were forming outside a food shop in Qazvin. During the Iran-Iraq war, food shortages had led to the issuing of food coupons. Kianoush said these coupons were still used. Already, we'd seen another legacy of the war: a high number of people with missing limbs. Begging was against the law and the faith, explained Kianoush, although we had seen a few people asking for money. Donation boxes were placed around the cities, like post boxes, and this money was administered for the disabled and poor. The stability of Australia and New Zealand meant war was an alien concept to us. Of course, we had read media reports during the Iran-Iraq war, but once the bombing had stopped, its news value had ended. By contrast, the aftermath of a war—poverty, injury and rebuilding communities—continued in obscurity. While we knew the history of the war, we didn't expect to still be seeing the immediate effects.

Dress Codes: *Islamic dress codes are strictly enforced. In public, women must wear the minimum of a scarf covering their hair and neck, and a loose-fitting overcoat. They must also wear dark stockings or long socks. Basically they can only show their hands and face. Make-up is also frowned upon by some of the more devout Muslims. It is not uncommon for women, even foreign women, to be publicly berated for 'loose* hejab'. *The government recently enacted legislation that gives jail terms for women not wearing appropriate garb. Men, too, must be circumspect in their dress. Shorts cannot be worn in public and short-sleeved shirts are sometimes frowned upon.*

Advice from the Australian Embassy, Tehran

On meeting Kianoush at the border, Beth had automatically gone to shake his hand. Politely, Kianoush had extricated himself from the situation. Beth had suddenly realised she had to consider her every action. It was forbidden for men to touch women; the only public affection permitted was between members of the same sex.

Apologising for her mistake, Beth asked Kianoush to help her with these cultural points. She was wearing a long skirt, stockings, a light jacket to cover her bottom and a scarf over her hair. 'Your clothing is fine,' he said, 'and a little make-up would be okay, too.' Kianoush was upset with the comments regarding women in the *Lonely Planet Guidebook*. He told us the social codes were far more relaxed than the 1992 guidebook had stated.

We only saw one case of the law being imposed on clothing.

In our hotel, a female tourist in a fitted dress was walking out of the lobby when a Revolutionary Guard intercepted her. He requested she go back upstairs and change.

Some British women were complaining about having to wear so many clothes in the heat. Ignorantly, they had brought long, heavy gabardine coats with them instead of a lightweight material suitable for the climate. Beth noted that the Iranian women looked beautiful in their national dress, while the tourists appeared unstylish and uncomfortable.

Later, Kianoush remarked, 'The *chador* is worn so women do not tempt men.'

'It has failed,' Beth replied, 'because the women have such lovely eyes, and they certainly know how to put them to extraordinary use. Don't you think?'

Kianoush shook his head, and Beth said, 'Ask your wife.'

He appeared bewildered by the concept that the women could still be alluring despite the effort made in covering their bodies.

The dark *chador* gave the impression of a dull uniform, a black unfashionable tent. But underneath the *chador*, and away from the gaze of men, Iranian women dressed in stunning colours. In the villages, we saw women in layers of red, yellow and green, embroidered with a metallic gold and topped off by a multi-coloured headdress of rolled scarves. The fabric shops and markets boasted a lavish array of bright golds, pinks, reds, materials adorned with sequins and beading.

While we had read that women were second-class citizens in Iran, from what we saw, they were represented in all aspects of society. There were women on the streets, going to schools and universities, working in shops and offices, on television as announcers. Kianoush told us that a woman could also be an ayatollah, a religious and political leader. He added that at eighteen years of age, each person was expected to choose an ayatollah as a mentor. About one hundred ayatollahs currently practised in Iran, and each one had different strengths in the social, political or religious arena.

One crucial area we did notice as being inadequate for women was in regard to toilet facilities. We could find men's toilets everywhere, but women's didn't exist. 'I guess they just cross their legs,' Beth joked, having to rely on hotel toilets and the great outdoors. Sensitive to our needs, Kianoush would wait up ahead when we stopped by the roadside. Aware of the risk she was taking in 'exposing' herself, Beth sought secluded spots and put me on guard.

'Be very, very careful driving in Iran'

We hadn't planned on going to Tehran, but the tour company was hoping for some publicity, and we agreed. The Australian Embassy confirmed what we had read: tourism in Iran had dropped considerably since the Revolution. These days, the government was slowly encouraging tourism, but travellers were still a novelty, nevertheless, especially independent travellers like ourselves, as most people favoured the ease of an organised group tour.

The tour company had been excellent and we enjoyed having Kianoush as a guide. Dark-haired and sporting a moustache like most Iranian men, Kianoush was intelligent, funny and courteous. He had a vast knowledge of Persian history and knew much about the rest of the world, despite never having been outside the country. Echoing Imam Khomeini, Kianoush declared, 'It's not that we don't like Americans, we just don't like their politics.' Contrary to the Western idea of a 'closed' society, Kianoush answered all our questions and allowed us to go wherever we wanted. There was no sense in having any part of Iranian life hidden from us.

The side trip to meet with journalists in Tehran was our thanks to the company and Kianoush, and Beth would add, no doubt, a chance for my fifteen seconds of fame, this time in Iran.

We'd heard about the six-lane highway to Tehran, but nothing could have prepared us for it. Pure chaos. Every road marking was ignored. Cars whizzed through flashing lights, performed u-turns across six lanes of traffic, overtook on double white lines, and sped through pedestrian crossings. The six lanes were really ten, with cars and buses forcing their way forward, pushing into any gap whatsoever. All of the traffic was at a constant speed— fast! In the midst of it, we saw a cyslist riding the wrong way through the six lanes.

Beth compared it to stock car racing: battered old cars belting their way along a track, unconcerned about hitting one another. Most cars had dents and it seemed that, with such frequent accidents, they didn't bother to repair them. As much as possible, I stayed in the one lane, keeping Kianoush in sight and asking Beth to check whenever I needed to overtake. It was a stressful drive, and we were amazed to arrive in Tehran unscathed.

And all for one journalist.

The tour company had promises from a number of media organisations, but other news had taken precedence. Kianoush was slightly embarrassed about the non-show. We weren't concerned, simply exhausted from the car race. The journalist wanted our impressions of Iran. We were very positive, commenting on the incredible progress since our last trip. After the Revolution, Iran had attempted self-sufficiency, refusing to import from the West. The result had been massive industrial growth, generally in the country areas, where smaller towns had sprouted into economic centres. Along with the big towns had come a network of highways, linking all corners of the country to transport goods, food and probably weapons as well.

Beth added that the people of Iran were extremely polite and helpful. In Iranian books, we'd read paragraphs on the Iranian personality: 'Iranians are by nature hospitable people. The basic spontaneous features of the Persian character are sensitiveness, kindliness, and willingness to help. The desire to be friendly and helpful prompts Iranians never to say "no". It is their own way of being polite and tactful.'

We had expected Iran to be like any society, some people obliging, others not. Therefore, we were surprised that so many went out of their way to be of assistance. Between Kianoush's quest to show us the best sights and the friendliness of the locals, we felt we were treated to the very best of the Islamic Republic.

On our way to Kashan, we passed through Qum, a religious town, second only to the sacred city of Mashhad in Iran. The mosque in Qum was now one of the few places non-Muslims were not permitted. The town took on its religious significance in the ninth century with the burial of Fateme, the sister of Reza, the eighth of the Shi'ite emams. Beth shuddered at her memory of our visit here in 1961. She had worn a short-sleeved shirt in this holy city and had been asked by a policeman to cover her arms.

The arid landscape of Iran led the Persians to a fascination with gardens and water. The Bagh-e Shah Fin Gardens in the oasis town of Kashan was one of the best examples. Set inside the walls of the two-storey palace built by Shah Abbas I (1587–1629), the garden was fed by the Sulaimanieh Spring, which still provided part of the water supply for the town. This classical garden was at odds with the area north of Kashan, the Kevir Desert.

Gardens took pride of place in most towns and were elaborate affairs with waterways, bridges, fountains and trees. They provided a welcome respite from the dry heat and the hustle and bustle of Iranian city life.

The Pearls of Persia: Isfahan and Shiraz

Isfahan is half the world. The praise for Isfahan was well deserved. Sights from 1961 were ingrained in our memories: one of the world's largest squares (the *maidan*), and a magnificent mosque tiled in blue, palaces, gardens and arched bridges. In the sixteenth century, Shah Abbas had beautified the city, creating some of the most stunning examples of Islamic architecture. We were even staying in a piece of history, an old caravanserai converted into a hotel.

We had two nights and one full day in Isfahan which, of course, wasn't nearly enough. It made Kianoush all the more determined that we should see as much as possible. In the morning, a visit to a Volkswagen garage was essential, because the brakes needed readjusting. The garage absolutely refused payment, not just the standard custom of refusing twice, so we gave them one of our Australian gifts: a boomerang.

The other interruption to the sightseeing was a re-creation of the 1961 photo in the *maidan*. There was a problem, however. At some point in the past thirty-five years, the *maidan* had been closed to traffic. To our surprise, Kianoush decided it was okay to drive a little way into the square. Beth drove the Beetle, while Kianoush and I directed her into position. The scene was set; the only missing factor was a pushbike in the background. Encouraged by Kianoush, a cyclist was soon riding back and forth, and the photo appeared almost identical to the shot taken when we were just twenty-seven years old.

Stretching behind the Beetle in the photo was the *maidan*. Twice the size of Red Square in Moscow, it was built by Shah Abbas in 1612 as a polo field, and the original goal posts were still standing. Designed around the *maidan* was the Shah's palace, a two-storey building with arched windows and doors. A seven-storey section jutted up from the centre of the palace, a place of government and a pavilion to view the polo matches. Rows of shops now filled part of the old palace and, next to it, the never-ending bazaar, its entrance the opening to a mini-city maze, with mosques and courtyards inside.

The crowning glory of the *maidan* was the Masjed-e-Emam Mosque, adorned with four minarets and a blue-tiled dome, taller at this angle than the nearby mountains. From a distance, the mosque presented a solid blue exterior, but each step closer unveiled more detail. It was intricately tiled, inside and out, its patterns of blues threaded through with whites, golds and greens. Walking under the towering portals to the inner sanctuaries, we were overwhelmed by the splendour of the architecture and the richness of colour and design. Part of the dome had been brought down for repairs; lying the wrong way up on the floor, it looked like a giant skateboard ramp, a strange analogy in this holy place.

But we were not to linger there. Kianoush whisked us onwards to other sights: bridges, pavilions, mosques and of course, the tea houses, an integral part of Iranian life, where men socialised, drank tea, smoked cigarettes or the hubble-bubble, a water pipe stuffed with their preferred blend of tobacco. Many of the tea houses were set around the gardens, providing a tranquil meeting place.

That evening, we were relieved to rest our feet and sit down to dinner in the hotel restaurant. But before we'd even ordered, there was a phone call. Kianoush had noticed one of the tyres on the Beetle was flat. Postponing dinner, we unpacked the car, extracted the spare tyre and changed it, with the help of four hotel staff. They sent the flat tyre off to be mended for the grand price of fifty cents. At 9pm, we settled down to room service of soup and chicken schnitzel. Usually we enjoyed dining on Persian food: boiled eggs, hard bread and rose jam for breakfast; lamb kebabs, stews and delicious rice for lunch and dinner.

A 5:30am wake-up meant a good start for the 485 kilometre drive south-east to Shiraz. Most of the trip was on a new highway, still being constructed. It bypassed many of the villages, but we did spot nomad camps with traditional black Berber tents and the modern-day addition, a truck. Camels were not to be seen.

Shiraz was another place reflecting the former grandeur of Persian times. During the thirteenth and fourteenth centuries, it was one of the greatest cities in the Islamic empire. Its importance waned until 1750, when Karim Khan made Shiraz the national capital. Utilising 12,000 workers, he created a royal district with the finest bazaar in Iran, irrigation systems, a moat and city walls. In 1789, much of the city was destroyed by Agha Mohammed Khan, the ruler who transferred the nation's capital to Tehran.

After two weeks of on-the-go travelling, we were pleased to have five days in Shiraz. It was a chance for a more relaxing pace of sightseeing, plus some extra work on the Beetle. The horn, indispensable in the terrifying Iranian traffic, had finally died. I wasn't surprised, because it was the original from 1961, although I imagined that Mum had barely used it when driving around Levin. The garage came up with a new horn, not a Volkswagen one, and aligned the wheels. Once again, it was an insignificant bill of ten dollars.

Across Iran, it was costing two dollars to fill the tank. The price of food and souvenirs were cheap, too, by Western standards. Kianoush told us that many Iranians were struggling; the wage for a public servant was forty dollars a week, in the private sector wages were double that. The cost of our hotel rooms, at a tourist price ten times that paid by a local, must have seemed exorbitant. A set of new car tyres was the one item we considered expensive. Deciding we couldn't take the risk of crossing the desert into Pakistan with the punctured one as the spare, we bought a new pair, imported from Korea, for A$250.

Shiraz was brimming with beautiful buildings. We visited the oldest Jammu mosque, Masjed-e Jame-e Atigh, some parts of it dating back to 600 BC. Next stop was a theological centre, Madrase-ye Khan, founded in 1615. The study rooms surrounded a tranquil courtyard. We had a brief discussion on religion. Kianoush said Islam believed in the equal status of the sexes, but the two had different roles. Then, it was on to the 'Garden of Paradise', dotted with small ponds and great old cypress trees. The lovely two-storey palace in the centre of the gardens was now the Faculty of Law, just one of the departments in this university town.

Two poets were partly responsible for the revered status of Shiraz. Sa'di (1207–1291) and Hafez (1324–1389) contributed much to Persian poetry and literature. Both were honoured with elaborate shrines set among marvellous gardens, lakes and fountains. Each shrine had a tea house in its garden. At the mausoleum of Hafez, we sipped rose essence tea. The tea house at Sa'di's shrine was underground, creating an intensely peaceful atmosphere.

A good restaurant provided a nice dinner. But the next day Beth was cursing the temptation of the salad bar, an item we hadn't seen before in Iran. It was unusual for either of us to get sick and Beth didn't tell me until we were at Persepolis, nearly sixty

Morning tea in the desert, Eastern Iran. 1961.

The same desert, Eastern Iran. 1996. Picture taken from the opposite side of the road.

The Beetle, my sweater and a camel tower, Iran. 1961.

Same Beetle, same sweater and the same tower. October 1996.

Looking down on the Iranian countryside, 1996.

Revisiting Lahore YWCA in 1996 where we slept in the office in 1961.

Beetle finds a mate outside our hotel in Quetta, Pakistan. October 1996.

Works of art on Pakistani roads. October 1996.

Avoiding cars and bullocks on the final leg to Mumbai (Bombay). 21 November 1996.

At the gateway of India, Mumbai. 22 November 1996.

Pop and the Beetle – his favourite police car. Levin, New Zealand.

Ivan and Beth with the New Concept Beetle in Vienna. 1997.

kilometres from our hotel room. She soldiered on through the ruins, unwilling to let stomach cramps spoil her first visit to this once spectacular palace.

Persepolis was built by Darius I about 512 BC, during the period of the Achaemenians, who were also responsible for the construction of paved roads for the horse-drawn carts, and numerous caravanserai, the rest houses and stables for traders built at thirty kilometre intervals on the main routes. The ruins of the complex at Persepolis conveyed the image of a grand palace on an enormous scale. An impressive number of columns were still standing; soaring twenty metres, they dwarfed us. The seven-metre-high stone bulls at the entrance reinforced our sense of mortality and insignificance as we examined the ancient buildings.

Reliefs carved into the walls and stairways told of a lifestyle of another time: warriors and their weapons, animals, cypress and palm trees and twelve-petal flowers for the months of the year. The end for Persepolis came in 331 BC, when it was burnt to the ground, in revenge, by Alexander the Great.

Nearby were the remains of a more recent era: one of the world's biggest parties, held by the Shah in 1971 to celebrate 2,500 years of the Persian Empire. We could see some of the marquees which had housed the thousands of guests, a seventies *who's who* of the world. Kianoush was scornful of the money spent on the event, the guest list of Americans and the food and wine flown in from France. It was a memento of the frivolous lifestyle before the Revolution.

In Shiraz, we bumped into a British tour group we'd met earlier in Isfahan. These archaeology devotees, the youngest of whom was about eighty, were seeing the sites in an air-conditioned bus, accompanied by an English archaeology lecturer and an Iranian guide. Mostly women, they were dressed according to the custom, wearing headscarves and mackintosh raincoats over their skirts. One man, whom we guessed to be ninety, was immaculately dressed, always sporting a tie. In Isfahan, Shiraz and Bam, they stayed at the same hotels as us and seemed to be having an absolute ball. Beth and I admired their spirit and hoped that, twenty years on, we too would still be adventuring.

With Beth ill for a few days, Kianoush was forced to cut back on the rest of his sightseeing plans and only take in the museum, bazaar and palace buildings of Shiraz. On a diet of dry toast, Iranian pepsi (very popular with the locals, even for breakfast!) and vegemite mixed with bottled water, Beth began to recover.

A Modem Disaster

Away from the ancient sights of Shiraz, we were attempting to get back into twentieth-century technology. Told that it was impossible to send emails from Iran, we checked with a computer shop. The shop assistant sold us the right plug and even tested it to show us it worked.

In the hotels, we could only use the laptop at the front desk, because the phone lines were at reception, under the anti-American slogans and the arrows pointing to Mecca. The night clerk in Zanjan was happy for me to try to connect. I left the laptop with him while I ran upstairs to get the phone numbers. When I returned, the line was dead. In trying to be helpful, he had plugged the modem into the electricity, instead of the computer, and blown it up.

I was devastated.

Without a modem, our whole communication network went

down. Kianoush came to the rescue and had his tour company organise to send a modem from Tehran for us.

But it seemed 'hooking up' was not to be. The modem was supposed to arrive by bus in Shiraz. From 3am on Monday morning, Kianoush went back and forth to the bus station, checking to see if the package had appeared. There was no sign of the fellow who was bringing it or of the modem itself.

Agitated, Kianoush shot down there once again. In his hurry, he ran into the bumper of another car, causing further distress. We tried to calm him down, telling him the modem didn't matter, but we didn't realise what was at stake here. In addition to not presenting an efficient image of Iran for us, Kianoush was concerned about the cost of the accident in his hire car and the cost of the modem. If it didn't turn up, he was to be held responsible.

After his numerous phone calls to the tour company in Tehran, the office there finally said they would sort it out. The modem never did turn up. We faxed Keris to send a replacement to us in Pakistan. We didn't know that the next modem experience would be even more of a disaster.

Yazd, a walled desert town of muddy-brown clay buildings, was known for its Zoroastrian past, an ancient religion predating Islam. One of the first religions to worship an omnipotent god, Zoroastrians revered fire as a symbol of god and kept eternal flames. The one we visited in Yazd was reputed to have been alight for 1400 years.

Outside the town, two Towers of Silence stood ominously high on a hill. Believing in the purity of the earth, the air and the water, the Zoroastrians would not bury or burn their dead; instead, the corpses were left on top of the towers to be disposed of by vultures. Fifty years ago the Shah had outlawed the practice, and the dead were now buried in a cemetery nearby.

In Yazd, we finally managed to change money. For the past few days, we had been trying to get some local currency, but there was always a problem. We couldn't find a bank which handled foreign transactions; we were told the wrong closing time, the wrong opening time or the bank closed early for no reason. While the 'international' hotels advertised foreign exchange, they didn't actually offer this service. To our embarrassment and his, we resorted to borrowing money from Kianoush.

At 7:30am, we arrived at the bank in Yazd in plenty of time for this transaction, which we knew would be long and tedious. The huge number of people milling around the bank seemed to accept that any transaction took an eternity. One teller filled in forms for us, which we had to give to another teller in the international section. Here, they would fill in some more forms, take our American dollars, check their legality, then send us back down to the first teller. Because it was a special transaction, we were brought inside the bank office, behind the tellers. The first teller would check the forms and the calculations with a hand-held calculator, verify our passport, then take the forms to the cashier. The cashier would check the forms again, count out the money, check it again, look at our passport and, at last, put the rials into our hands.

The process could take anywhere from forty minutes to two hours. The first difficulty was in finding a bank that handled foreign exchange. If Iran really wanted to encourage the tourist dollar, it was obviously imperative to make money-changing easier. The black market was alive and well; we had many people offering to 'change dollar'. Knowing we would put ourselves and Kianoush at risk, we refused but, at one stage, it had appeared to be the only possibility in our state of financial desperation.

The other main problem for tourists was the communication

network. Telephoning and faxing caused enormous frustration and wasted time, as each international call had to be booked through Tehran, and there was an overload on the lines. We succeeded in making *one* phone call to Australia.

In most hotels, the fax machine was locked away in the manager's office and staff were reluctant to check it for incoming faxes or use it for outgoing ones. Moreover, with Persian politeness, they were unwilling to admit it if the fax couldn't be sent. Communication was essential for us; we had to keep the family informed of our whereabouts. A radio journalist from BBC Asia hoped to interview us by phone in Iran or Pakistan; the ABC Radio in Sydney wanted an update; and TVNZ was trying to set up a filming date in Pakistan for the next segment on *The Holmes Show*. Frustration was an understatement.

As we drove through the desert, we were stunned by the changes. In some places there were still the brown gravel plains of our memories and steep, ridged rocky outcrops bulging like monstrous camel humps. Elsewhere the bleakness had been conquered; patches of green grass and low shrubs hid the brown monotony; trees beckoned with their shade. The desert had been tamed.

His jet black hair glinting in the sun, Kianoush explained that the government had a policy for 'greening' the desert. In suitable regions, planes were conducting aerial seed sprayings to extend the 'livable' areas. Dates, potatoes, apples, corn, sunflowers and pistachio nuts survived with the assistance of *ghanats*, the underground water conduits. Yazd was famous for its *ghanat*-builders. Theirs was a dangerous trade involving boring a well and then digging a horizontal tunnel a long distance under the ground, just wide enough for a man.

With the greening of the desert came the new roads and the

development of the villages into regional centres. The sandy road outlined by white rocks in 1961 was now a two-to-three-lane highway, white dotted lines glowing on the hot black surface. No chance of straying from this road, with its platoons of electricity poles marching towards the nearest town. Traffic roared across the plain. Eating lunch by the road, we counted 150 trucks, 17 cars and two buses heading in one direction in half an hour. It was an area similar to where we'd seen just one car in 1961.

Our astonishment at how we had made the first journey grew as we drove further into the desert. Beth guessed rightly that I was boyishly disappointed by the new highway. Secretly, I had been hoping to test out the Beetle on an unsealed road.

As the present overprinted itself onto our memories, we tried not to romanticise the past. Development was necessary for survival. But still we were shocked by this redefining of the desert. On our entire journey, nothing before or after struck us quite so strongly.

The desert architecture remained, in a striking contrast to the modern asphalt road. Houses, insulated with a mixture of mud and chaff, were a shade lighter than the brown desert soil. *Bad givs*, chimneys designed to catch the wind, and domed roofs worked to cool the rooms, while the high mud village walls protected the houses from the ravages of sandstorms.

At the small town of Mahan, we met Mike and Phillip, two Englishmen planning the route for the 1997 Peking-to-Paris Motor Challenge. The vintage car rally, covering 16,000 kilometres, was to be the first one to cross Tibet and the Himalayas.

The night in the Mahan hotel with Mike and Phillip was one of chaotic camaraderie in adversity. Firstly, the hotel had overbooked. The two Iranian guides travelling with Mike ended up sleeping on mattresses in the prayer room. Next there was a blackout. In trying to fix it, one of the hotel staff badly burnt his arm and was rushed off by motorbike to a doctor.

We remembered our gas lamp, an item we had packed 'just in case'. With four people and two torches, we pulled it out of its box, read the instructions and got it working. Dinner was plain rice cooked on our camping primus and then, still with no lights, early to bed for everyone. Kianoush worried that he hadn't shown us enough sights that day, particularly the mausoleum in Mahan. We reassured him that it wasn't necessary that we see every single mosque and every historical sight in each town we visited. He wasn't convinced.

Sandcastles and a Desert Picnic

The Bam Citadel made up for any missed sightseeing. The Arge-Bam looked like an intricate sandcastle crafted by a giant in the middle of the desert. On a large hill, complete with fortified walls and a moat, the citadel was built in bricks moulded from the reddish brown clay of the desert. The walls, stretching for more than three kilometres around the citadel, were guarded by twenty-eight watchtowers overlooking the ancient trade route across Persia. The security remained; the only entrance to the citadel was a gate on the southern side. It was thought that the citadel was from the Safavid period (seventeenth century). Continuous repair and habitation over the next two centuries accounted for its well-preserved state.

Once inside the citadel, we found the town laid out in front of us. As we walked through the narrow lanes in the steadily increasing morning heat, Kianoush pointed out the bazaar, the mosque and the military barracks. A long, hot climb took us up to the king's quarters inside the fortified palace. Houses and mansions opened out onto squares, and we could identify the remains of the stables. The citadel even had a *caravanserai* for the more friendly visitors. From one of the towers, we enjoyed the same view as the guards of old, but ours was overlaid by a contemporary outlook as well. On the plain beneath us, we could see the modern city of Bam spreading out across the desert, hemmed in only by date and citrus orchards.

Other indications of the present were the signposts. Every so often, signs had been hammered into the ground. Instead of pointing the way around the citadel, as we might have expected, they were in praise of the Ayatollah Khomeini. 'Our revolution was an explosion of light,' one said, offering an English translation for the rare tourist. 'The way to improve a country is mainly through its culture,' proclaimed another, quoting from the Imam himself.

Still another declared, 'Khomeini is an everlasting reality'—a totally unnecessary reminder. There was no chance of forgetting the Ayatollah Khomeini in Iran! His picture was painted on city walls; streets, squares and mosques in every town had been renamed in his honour; the biggest monument in the country was being constructed outside Tehran.

In Bam, the quest for tourism was a reality. The following morning, a new airport was to be opened by the First Secretary. Recently, a conference/entertainment/tourist village had been built on the outskirts. In addition, the town was working towards opening all fourteen citadels in the region for tourists.

Much to Beth's dismay, I had packed a certain brown sweater in our luggage. In 1960, during those rainy nights in London, Beth had painstakingly knitted this sweater while enjoying our new TV set. It was the only one she ever made for me and, thirty-five years on, it had been worn by all of our daughters, as odd jobs clothing. Beth had laughed at my sentimentality as I resolutely placed the much-darned sweater into our 'absolute necessities' pile for packing.

It was to be worn just once on the trip. In 1961, Beth had photographed me, in cream cotton pants and my khaki sweater, under a camel tower in the desert by the road to Kerman.

Ninety kilometres from Bam, we saw it, rising up from the flat desert, an eighteenth-century lighthouse for traders during sandstorms. Hot in her Western-style *chador*, Beth felt the dress code equalled as I pulled the heavy jumper over my head. It was a tighter fit than it had been on my twenty-seven-year-old frame when I was nicknamed Slim and didn't boast a middle-aged paunch! My thick black hair had turned grey, but *at least my spirit of adventure hadn't grown old on me*, I thought. The three of us were here again: the Beetle, Beth and I. Back in the desert.

Before the desert gave way to mountain passes, we encountered a surreal scene: three Dutch cyclists picnicking on the sand. Nannike and Geert sat on a plastic sheet, eating lunch, their bicycles laid out beside them. They had met Peter in Tabriz, and he was riding with them at the moment. Carefully observing *hejab*, Nannike was wearing a long-sleeved shirt, trousers and a scarf underneath a peaked cap—a difficult outfit for cycling in the desert! Nannike and Geert were on their way to Nepal to work in the school of a Dutch/German project, the Himalayan Rescue Dog Squad. The couple had sought sponsorship for each kilometre and government support to provide money to the centre. They were enjoying their trip, mostly camping and receiving generous hospitality wherever they went. Beth and I were impressed by their selflessness and determination.

Nearly a year later, we were to hear from them again, but the news was horrific. After seven months cycling, Nannike and Geert had reached Nepal and were on the final leg to their destination.

Across ten countries, their worst experience had been Pakistani children throwing stones at them.

In a letter to us, Nannike described the moment which had destroyed their plans. It was on the fifth of December, just 160 kilometres short of reaching their goal of Kathmandu.

The rear of Geert's bike was nicked by a truck. In the impact, Geert lost control and was thrown in the air. His injuries were severe: brain damage, broken ribs, partial paralysis in his right leg and heavy bruising on his right shoulder and hip. Terrified he would die, Nannike had to focus on tackling the Nepalese medical system. In Mumbini, the nearest hospital, the doctor gave him a minor examination and announced they would have to wait seventy-two hours before any treatment. If Geert survived this period, the doctor said, only then would he spend time treating him!

Fortunately, when Nannike contacted the Himalayan Rescue Dog Squad project, they sent one of their volunteers, a European doctor. He examined Geert thoroughly, diagnosed the brain damage and insisted on a brain scan to determine the extent of injury. They moved Geert to Patan Hospital, only to discover it had no scanning equipment. Finally in Bir Hospital, Geert had the brain scan and was found to have an oedema, probably a fracture of the skull, plus damage to his lower back. He was also suffering double vision.

On Christmas Day of 1996, Nannike and Geert returned to Holland. Geert recuperated well but, five months later, when Nannike wrote the letter to us, he still had double vision and frequent fatigue. She said it would probably take a year for him to recover fully. In spite of everything, the pair were still hoping to fulfil their plans of volunteer work in the Himalayan Rescue Dog Squad project. However, this time, they said, they would arrive by plane.

Our last night in Iran was spent in Zahedan, close to the border with Pakistan. After an hour of frustration, I managed to send a fax to Keris and the family. It conveyed our delight in Iran:

All the concerns we had and those conveyed to us by others about the difficulty of travelling in this country have disappeared, and we are thoroughly enjoying our return to Iran. We have found it a most friendly country; people are very willing to help, and no anti-Western feeling has been apparent to us.

From a tourist point of view, this must be the best-value destination in the world. Last year, 500,000 tourists visited Iran, mostly Europeans, a few Japanese, a handful of Koreans and even fewer Australians and New Zealanders. It is planned to push tourism, with a target figure of 12 million. The earnings from tourism will become a major industry. They have a long way to go but also have a great deal going for them.

Iran has been such a huge surprise. We cannot believe that more people have not visited and enjoyed what we are experiencing.

So many warnings about Iran had made us slightly suspicious of the ease we encountered while travelling. Even the Australian Embassy had told us that we would be stopped at checkpoints on the roads and might be subject to harassment and possibly extortion by the military, the police and the radical Islamic militia. Instead, following Kianoush, we were waved through checkpoints and smiled at by the guards.

It all seemed to run just a little too smoothly.

Chapter 8

One Rung above a
Bullock Cart

1961—Pakistan

Cricket with the Customs Officers

Robert in Zahedan. The professional business card, displaying these three words, was placed in my hand. Robert smiled as widely as possible and asked, 'Money? Change?' We were crossing the Persian–Pakistan border that day, and our AA Strip Maps indicated there were no major facilities until the town of Quetta, nearly three days from the border.

'Okay,' I replied, pulling out five pounds, unsure of the exchange rate. We assumed Robert was a local entrepreneur, doing rather well for himself, accosting travellers from both directions, exchanging Pakistani rupees and Persian rials.

Not surprisingly, Robert couldn't produce the exact amount of rupees. I offered him a yellow sweater of mine and we called it square.

At the border, the customs officials were listening intently to the radio. The cricket was on: Pakistan versus the MCC (England) in Lahore. Inviting us to listen, they served us hot tea, the first decent cup since we'd crossed into Asia. Customs formalities and the cricket consumed a fair part of the day and, by then, it was too late to start the drive across Baluchistan, a no-man's land ruled by tribal forces. We camped on the border, setting up our tent on the dusty ground, watched over by the Pakistani border guards.

Baluchistan, we were to discover, was bigger than we'd imagined, with the town of Quetta a part of the region. Not far from the border, the road was blocked, piled with stones. A track led up to a mud hut. 'It's Baluchi customs,' I joked to Beth. Sure enough, it was! Three chaps greeted us, their long pyjama shirts and trousers filthy. One was wearing a balaclava, and another, in grey battle dress, had a rifle and cartridges slung over his shoulder. They came down to look at the Beetle, implying they needed our number plate details, but they didn't actually write anything down. They sauntered around the car laughing, a dog at their heels.

'Are you Baluch?' I asked, and they laughed some more, repeating, 'We Baluch! We Baluch!' Afterwards, Beth said to me, 'They looked so proud of themselves, they thought they were Christmas!'

The military town of Quetta, dwarfed by mountains, became an oasis in hot Baluchistan. Thanks to the hospitality of Dawn and John, we had a break from washing in a bucket and eating tinned meat. Dawn was the sister of a colleague in London. The couple, with their three-year-old twin daughters, had been posted to Quetta due to John's position in the British Army; he was a captain sent out to teach at a staff college.

Despite never having met us, Dawn insisted we stay. It was pure luxury. Exhausted from our 400 mile dusty drive, Beth and I were treated to refreshing baths, drawn by one of their five servants. As soon as I undid the laces, my shoes were whisked off to be cleaned. Our dirty clothes came back sparkling. The Beetle also had a bath; the servants gave it a washdown and scrubbed it inside and out. We ate delicious meals, prepared by the cook, who had been working for British people for over twenty years. It seemed a gracious life, and the womenfolk had a very social time of it all.

Dawn organised a picnic lunch by the lake and then drinks at the Pakistani Officers' Mess, so we could meet their local friends. One chap explained *purdah*, a cultural system whereby the women were forbidden to see any men outside the family. He told us that women could only come out of *purdah* if the husband or father agreed. It was odd to learn about this culture from these immaculately dressed officers who looked as if they had marched here straight from the Royal Military Academy at Sandhurst.

Two majors educated me on the tribal and Muslim way of life. The elders controlled how the family thought and acted. If a father requested a task, it had to be done, even if the son knew it was wrong. The following month, both of these men were to be wed in arranged marriages to girls they had never met. The girls were only fifteen or sixteen years old. To Beth and me, the concept was staggering.

Dr Holland and his wife ran the Mission Hospital, which had been founded in 1890 by his father. A marvellous, enthusiastic man working under difficult conditions, Dr Holland performed fifty cataract operations a day. It was hard for him to obtain medical equipment. He was forced to use the same knife blade for five operations, whereas a London specialist would probably use a blade just once. He said the blades were sent to Germany for sharpening but, on their return, the hospital had to pay customs duty and tax again.

Dr Holland and his wife were up against little things like that all the time, yet they remained devoted to their work. We gave them our scalpel blades, which we had been carrying in case of snake bite (although neither of us knew how we were supposed to cut out the venom!). Dr Holland's work made us feel ashamed that there wasn't more we could do for a mission hospital way out here in Pakistan.

The hospital wards were crammed, with mostly older people in the beds. When a patient came in, the whole family would move in, and the hospital had to feed them all. The staff tried to keep the premises clean, but they said it was an impossible task. Bedbugs infested the linen, and patients or their visitors would just go to the toilet against the wall.

Dak bungalows were resthouses set up in Pakistan and India during the rule of the British Raj for surveyors and travelling government officials. Usually they had two or three rooms for guests and a caretaker on hand to provide assistance and food. It was a relief to have this cheap accommodation (only three shillings), as it would have been impossible to camp. There were too many people everywhere to have a chance of finding a secluded spot for cooking dinner and sleeping.

Near Sibi, we found a *dak* bungalow for the night. But there was a problem. It was already occupied by a youngish chap. He insisted we stay also, but I didn't like his manner and said we would sleep in the car inside the bungalow compound. 'You must have dinner,' he said, and there was no choice but to concur. We were concerned about drinking the untreated water, but we had to be polite. I also disliked his politics. He was determined to slander the British Empire, and we didn't particularly appreciate his viewpoint. I related the evening to the folks at home:

This character was aged about twenty-three, just out of university and rather self-opinionated. We discussed the Kashmir problem and the reason he is anti-British. A big part of Kashmir is India, and they call it occupied land. They hope it will be free soon because ninety per cent of the population is Muslim, and they feel they should be attached to Pakistan.

He feels that Britain has flogged the wealth from India and not put anything back. We tried to point out what we thought Britain had given it: a foundation on which to work, something a lot of Muslim countries just don't seem to have.

We had curry and rice, a bottle of beer and green tea, and retired to our car about 11:30pm.

Unprepared for the roads in Pakistan, we found the driving demanding. In fact, *treacherous* was the only way to describe it. The central single lane was sealed, and on either side there was dust eight inches thick. When two vehicles met, they played a game of chicken, holding their course in the centre until the 'chicken' finally veered off into the dirt. There, the layers of dirt would grab the tyres, making steering heavy and creating clouds of swirling dust.

One time, we had a bus heading straight toward us. Veering off to the side into the dust blinded us, and we had no idea where the bus was aiming. 'Get out!' I yelled to Beth, and we both crawled from the passenger side, running a short distance from the road. Silence indicated there was no collision. When the dust cleared, we saw that the bus driver had also stopped. The two vehicles stood side by side on the road.

It wasn't a route for cars and buses only. There was much more to contend with: carts drawn by bullocks and donkeys, water buffalo, cyclists, pedestrians. Dead dogs littered the verge. A man's body lay atop a pile of stones; we presumed he too must have been killed by the dangerous road.

Alongside us wandered the nomadic tribes, their camels laden with possessions. Goats, donkeys and chickens were herded in the right direction by the colourfully clothed men, women and children.

The drive to Lahore brought us to the Indus Plains, the largest irrigated area in the world. The countryside was riddled with canals. Apparently, one of them was larger than both the Suez and Panama Canals. Green paddy fields and sugar cane contrasted with the dusty desert of Baluchistan. A large variety of birds hovered above us: crows, hawks, eagles, and parakeets, which were a beautiful green with long tails.

It was still hot in this part of Pakistan, so we travelled with the windows down. At one point, we had to stop at a railway crossing. Watching the train carriages pass by, we didn't notice him until it was too late. A young fellow had crept up to the car window and shoved his arm, a leprosy stump, towards Beth's face. Horrified, Beth pushed him away and abruptly rolled up the glass.

The begging appalled us. In the streets, people thrust their deformities at us, asking for money. We had never seen such disease, dirt and poverty. It was ugly and upsetting. Warned not to give money—which would 'encourage' the behaviour—we felt sorry for the beggars, but we did hear stories of mothers mutilating their children so they could beg. When beggars saw we were foreigners, they would encircle Beth and me, outnumbering us and pestering us for money. Apparently begging was against the law because, at the mention of 'police', the beggars disappeared.

We hadn't seen many beggars until Pakistan, although in Turkey, an Australian traveller was asking for money. I thought it irresponsible and rude to enter a foreign country and then survive on the charity of the local people.

Arriving in Lahore at 6pm was a mistake. There were no *dak* bungalows in the city, only expensive hotels. No camp grounds either. We had just one option: the YWCA and the YMCA. It meant spending the night apart in different areas of the city. The woman at the YWCA kindly helped us out. After we showed her our wedding certificate, she let us put up our camp beds in the office for the night. And then, in the morning, she refused payment.

When we collected our mail from the British Consulate in Lahore, we met up with the passengers from the three overland buses which had been stranded in Turkey. It was a half-day public holiday, but the Consulate staff had a lot to sort out and wouldn't be leaving for many hours.

From Lahore, a short drive took us to the border with India. I was a little edgy about our money declarations. I felt the authorities would be suspicious about our having driven right across Pakistan without spending more than two pounds on petrol and living expenses. Really it was seven, but our declaration didn't include the extra five pounds we had exchanged on the black market with Robert in Iran. However, the customs officers didn't see any problems and waved us on to India. Our speedometer reading was 12,393 miles from London.

1996—Pakistan

Communication Problems in the 'Old Folks' Wagon'

Iran–Pakistan border, 1996. This time, there were no delays, no cups of tea, no listening to the cricket. It was all done within an hour.

Taftan, the first village across the border, was rather rudely known as the 'asshole of the world'. The village was aptly named. Square mud huts, the same sandy colour as the dry ground, were ringed with garbage—tyres, car parts, food scraps, burnt cardboard boxes, rags, steel drums, metal and plastic bags. As the stench filled the Beetle, we noticed children and goats playing among the rubbish. This arid settlement had no grass, trees or bushes, just dirt and gravel. Tracks led off in all directions—personal roads taking the villagers wherever they wanted to go.

We were lucky. The border crossing was so quick we didn't have to spend the night in Taftan and could head on to Dalbandin, a slightly better village. But first, we had to fill the tank for the 350 kilometre drive. The petrol station was an assortment of steel drums next to a hessian humpy. Dressed in a typical *shalwar qamiz* (a knee-length smock over matching pants) the garage attendant pumped the petrol from a drum into a plastic container and then funnelled it, through a rag, into our tank. As usual, three or four men gathered to watch, interested in us and the novelty of a petrol tank in the front of a car.

Baluchistan was still under tribal rule. Roadblocks, inter-tribal rivalry and breakdowns in the desert were all dangers. We had hoped to put the car on a train from the border to Quetta, but the service only operated twice a week and it was too difficult to co-ordinate. Instead, we hired a local guide to deal with the roadblocks and provide a security blanket if we were to become stranded.

Six racial and tribal groups were scattered across Baluchistan. Flags and painted rocks by the roadside identified the different tribal areas. The road, although sealed all the way, was under repair, with rough sidetracks for detours. Bordering the sealed road was a nasty ledge, which had to be carefully mounted at each detour. The roadblocks were a primitive affair, just a rope along the ground which was suddenly pulled up for every car. The cost of our guide covered the fees demanded at the roadblocks. Despite the display of rifles and gun belts, there was no threat of violence towards us.

The desert scenery was similar to Iran, but here there were wild camels roving across the flat plains. In the distance rose the mountains of Afghanistan, hazy slopes on the horizon. In places, the desert was that of the picture books, with the yellow sand bare but for hardy tufts of yellowy grass and the scruffy brown camels. Small villages appeared wherever there was a hint of water, their mud huts almost camouflaged against the desert background. Only the men were evident. On seeing a camera, they would stop and pose for a photo, assuming stilted stances copied from Hollywood films.

A *dak* bungalow in Dalbandin offered rest for the night, but little in the way of comfort. Grotty and basic, the bungalow had no water and only occasional moments of electricity. Using our own supply of water, Beth and I took turns spraying each other with our squirter in the dry shower recess. Dinner was by candle-light, herb soup and baked beans done on our gas cooker, with fruit and lemonade. Outside, we could hear cars tooting through the night, so we chocked a chair against the door and quietly worried about the Beetle being robbed or stolen.

Beth laughed at my happy stoicism. 'Have your realised that the grimmer our living conditions become, the cheerier you get? Is it a brave face to support me or a love of adventure?' she asked.

'A bit of both,' I answered diplomatically.

The next night we reached Quetta, still the capital of Baluchi-stan and a frontier town boasting one luxury hotel, run by a son of the Aga Khan. While we did enjoy the oasis of the hotel with its lovely gardens and swimming pool, it was in obscene contrast to other parts of the town, to the dry, dusty shanties littered with garbage, a refugee camp on the outskirts.

14 October 1996—Quetta

Beth's Diary

We woke to Tara McCarthy's call from 2BL at 7am and then lazed in bed, watching TV. I guess we had missed it. Ivan has missed bacon and I miss brown bread, but neither of us has really missed alcohol.

Breakfast in the coffee shop and then we were informed that a gentleman from the Pakistan Tourist Department was in the lobby. We had a chat and he arranged a 4pm meeting with the press. Relaxed till then. At 4pm, sixteen members of the press turned up and the interviews lasted about an hour. Journalists all very nice.

The men here are particularly handsome. The women wear lovely long coats or tunics over the bloused trousers, always with a long scarf that is sometimes the size of a single bed sheet. It is appreciated if Western women cover their hair in the streets.

About 5pm, we decided to brave the city. The traffic is well-controlled, with a number of smartly dressed officers on each corner and one on the podium in the centre of the intersection. As yet, I cannot detect road names, so we were flying blind. Found Jinnah St, the main road, parked and walked to one of the bazaars and bought some fruit.

The pavements are bad, and we have to watch out for spitting, or we'll catch one on us. The covering over the sewer ditch is frequently broken, so the air is ripe. However, the city is pretty well organised, and we saw several supermarkets. At one, we thought we didn't have enough money for some drinks, and the fellow said, 'Pay tomorrow.'

So now that we are a little orientated, we will attack the bazaar tomorrow after the bank. Back at the hotel, we watched the news and had a pleasant Chinese meal. The staff are very charming—only women at Reception.

The Beetle found a mate at the hotel. The sales manager owned a green Volkswagen and was proud to park it next to ours, commenting, 'One has been all around the world, the other has not been out of Quetta'.

Four days in the city gave us the chance to do some Beetle repairs. After the rough ride from the border, we were concerned the suspension had been damaged. The garage replaced the rubbers, saying the shock absorbers were fine, and fixed the windscreen wipers, which broke during a surprise shower in the desert.

While I was in the garage, a photographer arrived at our hotel room. He told Beth he had read about us in the newspaper that day and noted we were here in 1961. Producing some 1957 photos of Australian travellers in Quetta, he asked Beth if she might recognise the people pictured. The photos were taken by his father, who had set up the photography business at ten years of age. Obviously, Beth couldn't identify the people but later, we did visit his dusty little shop in a street full of shoe shops and cobblers. He wanted to take some photos of the 1996 Australian travellers.

The photographer had seen the following item in *The Baluchistan Times* on 15 October, 1996. It appeared between 'APHC presents new wave of terror in Held Kashmir', a story about a campaign of terror by Indian forces in Occupied Kashmir, and 'Qazi urges Islamic forces of Afghanistan to unite'. We guessed that 'battle' in the article meant 'Beetle', but we weren't too sure if it was our age or our pronunciation which led the journalist to coin the phrase 'old folks' wagon'.

Journey from London to Bombay on Antique Car

QUETTA: An adventurist couple Beth and Ivan Hodge on board Volkswagen beetle and antique German car is scheduled to complete their second trip of a lifetime from London to Bombay by November this year.

On arrival, the couple told Press conference here Monday that out of their one hundred and twenty days London to Bombay journey, they had completed seventy days. They would resume their onward journey to Bombay from Quetta in a couple of days to complete ten thousands miles onboard ancient battle.

From Quetta, the couple basically Newzealanders but presently residing in Sydney, would go to Bombay by road through provincial cities and towns touching Lahore, Amritsar and New Delhi.

Telling tale of their first trip of a lifetime undertaken thirty five years back on the same old folks wagon beetle, the couple told newsmen that they were making the second trip of a lifetime as a second honeymoon.

They maintained road changes from Iran border to Quetta, Pakistan have changed remarkably, the new road from Taftan to Dalbandin is a joy and reflects great credit on Baluchistan. Road improvement should encourage other independent travellers, the speed breakers are a hazard for unsuspecting drivers. This results in restricting the driving distance in a day.

They maintained it is too early to make comments on the many changes in Pakistan. But what is so obvious is the growth and important of Quetta. A hotel of distinction like the Serena was not available on the first visit. Mind you, as young travellers we were happy to camp and stay in rest houses.

Replying to a question, couple said Pakistan has considerable tourist potential internationally, this needs to be encouraged by the authorities organisations.

Although the Volkswagen beetle may be old, Beth and Ivan Hodge are carrying with them the most uptodate communication with a lap top computer, email communications, portable phone and printer. This enables them to maintain communication with their apartment service business in Sydney, Australia.

Concluding, old couple said we cannot plan to be back in another 35 years but we hope our grandson in Australia will drive the reliable beetle when he is old enough from Bombay to London, he is just two at the moment.

Taking the same route as thirty-five years before, we drove towards Sukkur, crossing the Central Brahui Range at the Bolan Pass. For many centuries, the pass was a popular route between Central Asia and India for nomads, traders and invading armies. Curving through the mountains, we admired the dramatic scenery and the determination of the road and railway builders. The British had achieved an incredible engineering feat in constructing a railway line through these rugged mountains.

Beneath the rocky cliffs, the road clung to the banks of the dry river bed, occasionally tunnelling through the solid rock. The river bed was a road of its own, catering to nomadic tribes and shepherds. It was now the time for the nomads to come down from the mountains and spend the winter on the slightly warmer plains. They travelled in groups with their camels, donkeys, dogs and sheep. Armed with guns, the men rode the camels, while the women walked behind. Their possessions, wrapped in sacks strapped on either side of the camel, were two extra humps pointing in the wrong direction. When I went to film them, the men shook their fists and raised their rifles.

Closer to Sibi, we came upon a wedding party, a boisterous, colourful group walking by the road. Other guests travelled by trailer, standing confidently balanced as the tractor pulled it along. In the midst of it all, a woman in a brilliant yellow sari and bright pink scarf was dancing to the rhythm of a drum. As the woman moved to the music, her long hair, earrings and white beads swaying, I realised she was, in fact, a man.

Road repairs were undertaken manually. Workmen broke up the large rocks with hammers, cutting them down to size as needed. Drums of tar were hooked onto wooden poles, hoisted between the shoulders of two men and carried to the relevant spot. Donkeys lugged other materials, either by cart or in pouches slung over their backs. The men camped by the side of the road, moving their tents as they worked their way along.

Police checkpoints greeted us as we entered the province of Sind and neared Jacobabad. We weren't stopped and drove on, wondering the reason for the latest roadblocks. Our out-of-date guidebook mentioned the *dacoits*, organised bandits waging a reign of terror by kidnapping, rape, blackmail and murder. Unsure if they were the reason for the police presence, we continued on our way, wary of any suspicious behaviour.

On the Indus Plains, the traffic suddenly became worse. Our days in the desert had hidden the reality of a teeming Pakistan, the ninth most populous country in the world. There was no escaping that fact on the journey from Sukkur to Multan. Beth described the day in a fax to my father and her mother in their respective nursing homes in New Zealand:

Due to the standard of the villages we had passed, we decided to drive the 400 kilometres to Multan. The road was flat and barely two lanes, but the problem was twofold: heavy truck traffic and a road under constant repair. *Large lengths had been dug up and it was full of potholes and bulldust. Usually the road went along the main street of every village, meaning that we had to cope with animals, carts, pedestrians, bikes, buses and pick-up buses, as well as the trucks. In fact, there are few cars on the road, so I guess that anyone who has to travel and has money, flies.*

Luckily the trucks travel at a sedate pace and are quite happy to be passed. Not so the passenger pick-up or bus. They have the right of the road and hurtle along, stopping wherever they are hailed. Passengers are all over the roof and hanging on to the back by a toenail.

As if all this were not enough, we suddenly came to a line of trucks stopped, we think, because of a breakdown. We estimated, quite conservatively, that there were eight hundred trucks lining the road. The only thing we could do was cross to the other side of the road and travel in the bulldust to pass the long queue. So much for now driving on the left hand side of the road after being on the right for so long! Ivan dodged the camels, people, goats, and carts like a veteran. At one time, we followed a bus which was tearing through the dust, but he was too fast for us. The passengers were getting the ride of their lives!

We were relieved to clear all this and could not believe our luck to strike a second long hold-up an hour later. We arrived at Multan about 6pm, very tired. The countryside was lush and green, with mangos, bananas, corn and cotton. I can only get on to the computer to write this because Ivan is watching Zimbabwe play Pakistan on the television.

Due to the difficulties of communication in Iran, we weren't able to phone Beth's mum, Joyce, until we had reached Pakistan. After our reassuring call to Joyce, Beth's brother, Brian, faxed us to relay Joyce's relief, as well as details of his new grand-daughter:

Mum is one hundred per cent at the moment. She was becoming very agitated regarding your safety, certain you were heading straight into troubles. Nothing I said would sway her belief, and your phone call the other day was perfect. She made great play of somehow 'knowing' you were calling and was poised with her hand on the phone when you rang. She telephoned us three times to share the joy and is now telling everyone: 'I knew Ivan wouldn't take her into any trouble spot'.

I felt twenty-seven years old again with the looming fear of Mrs Mudge's wrath if I were to endanger Beth. Like my mum, Joyce had always wanted to travel. When we returned to London in 1985, she had hoped to visit us there but became too sick to make the trip.

She did come to Australia, though; it was while we lived in Adelaide. We drove her north to show her the mines of Burra, where she pushed Britta under the fence to fetch a piece of malachite for her collection.

For Joyce was a rock hound.

She'd climb a mountain and come back down with a sack of rocks strapped to her back. Beth's very traditional father had discouraged his wife from working, and so her passion for rocks became a full-time affair. Through the local rock club, she learnt to cut and polish. Her husband made the equipment for her, creating a cutting and polishing studio in the garage. Later, she did a jewellery course so that she could set the stones herself.

Wherever we travelled, we collected rocks for Joyce: mica and tiger eye from India in 1961; a lapis lazuli necklace from Pakistan in 1996, the stones were from the hills in Afghanistan. Joyce said she remembered the origin of every rock in her collection. When she moved into the nursing home, she donated her rocks to the rock club. They needed trailers to cart away the huge collection.

The rock legacy was handed on. Beth collected rocks, and our three girls wouldn't go near a beach without bringing home buckets of pebbles and shells. It wasn't a knowledgeable collection like Joyce's, more of a pleasure in their appearance and shape, regardless of worth.

Joyce and Beth were very close and, until we married in 1959, Beth was living at home. It was a wrench for both women when Beth and I went travelling overseas. Despite my having taken her daughter away, Joyce liked me, 'adored me', Beth once said. Curly, my nickname for her, has stuck to the present day, and her independent will was still asserting itself, even with the nursing home rules. Suffering from spondylitis, swelling in the vertebrae, Joyce was now in a mobile chair. The nurses had set the wheelchair controls at a sedate pace, but Joyce was having none of that. She would turn the controls up and shoot around the corridors like a rocket.

Joyce had been pleased for us to set off on a second Beetle honeymoon. It gave her some news to boast about to her two sisters—both over eighty; one, an artist, was still teaching, the other had just given up tennis, but remained keen on tenpin bowls. When Beth and I were unable to phone, Keris would ring Joyce or send a fax to stop her from worrying about us.

The clothes of Pakistan were a kaleidoscope of colour. Both men and women wore lilac, fuschia, turquoise, yellow and lime. In Multan, many ladies were in *burqah*, a full body covering, eyes peering out from delicately embroidered eyepieces.

The colourful clothes were matched by the colourful trucks and buses. These were no ordinary Bedfords, but amazing works of art in brilliant colours, glinting in the hot sun. In fact, the trucks and buses were painted and decorated almost beyond recognition. It wasn't simply a matter of coating the entire vehicle in red or yellow or blue. Mascots, baubles, badges, tassels and streamers were affixed front, back and side. On some trucks, the only undecorated space was a peephole on the windscreen for the driver to see out.

The loads carried by these moving artworks were incredible. Filled to the brim, they often had yet more freight balanced on top. Sometimes even a car was tied on precariously. A few passengers would be squashed into the empty corners, with one or two extra clinging to the front bumper bar.

Resigned to the lengthy delays, the truck drivers would settle down to camp by the roadside. As far as we could tell, the traffic jams were caused by the road repairs. There were narrow sections where two trucks coming in opposite directions would meet and be unable to pass. Due to the build-up of traffic behind them, the trucks couldn't back up into a wider section and move aside. It looked as though the traffic jams would take days to clear. As we weaved our way forward along the edges of the road and between the trucks, the drivers all waved cheerfully and indicated the best way to go. Mini-buses and government cars were the only other vehicles pushing their way through. At least they had authority. We understood the pecking order on the road: the bullock cart was the lowest denominator and our Beetle was just one rung above that.

On our way to Lahore, four policemen pulled us up. *Time to pay 'road fees'*, I thought. But it seemed that extortion was not on their minds. 'We welcome you to Pakistan,' they said smiling, 'and wish you a very good trip.' The unexpected hospitality came as a pleasant surprise.

With our sketchy map, Beth found navigating in Lahore impossible. Asking directions was nearly as difficult; everyone was anxious to please and give suggestions despite not knowing the answer! Finally, a young man on a scooter led us through this city of seven million people to our hotel.

The general manager of the Holiday Inn was so delighted with the Beetle that he insisted we park it out the front and then he placed signs on it: 'Beetle around the World'. Over the next few days, handwritten notes of congratulations appeared under the windscreen wipers. A Mr Javed wrote: 'Congratulation. I wanted that you travelling again and again for enjoy of life'. The security guard had added his wishes: 'In Respect of Mr and Mrs, Congratulation. You are great and your car is great. I wish you long life.' The one which affected us most was from a doctor at the Mayo Hospital. 'Congratulations,' it said simply, 'I envy this kind of lifestyle.'

Two Tired TV Stars

The travel company which had arranged the guide from the border to Quetta was keen to link some publicity with our trip. Mr Walji organised a press conference with about twelve journalists from newspaper, radio and television. Two days later, it was media time again—many long, tiring hours.

The Holmes Show in New Zealand wanted an update of our travels and sent a freelance reporter to interview us. The reporter had been recently reporting for CNN on the Taliban side of the war in Afghanistan. 'I can take you up there,' he said. It was an interesting offer, we had missed seeing the country on both trips. 'They'll blow up your car though,' he added, rapidly making the decision for us.

The reporter was accompanied by two cameramen. We were also being shadowed by a film crew from Pakistan TV. As they followed us around the city, filming us looking at the sights and careening through the traffic, Beth and I decided stardom was overrated and really quite exhausting. However, we did learn a little about filming, a lot about Lahore and, in the end, we had fun.

Our first stop was the YWCA where we had camped in the office thirty-five years before. It was now a school, as well as a hostel, and accommodated both women and men. A number of overlanders were staying there: Dutch, South African, English and Kiwi. Harry and Maryke, a Dutch couple in their twenties, were on their way to Australia by motorbike.

The following year, after our return to Australia, Harry and Maryke came to stay with us in Sydney. Still on the BMW motorbike, the couple seemed to have caught the travel bug, and they had no intentions of remaining in one place for very long—let alone, going home.

Jacqueline, the manager of the YWCA, was curious about our previous visit. She had started working there only a few months after we'd passed through! Intent on repaying the kindness displayed on our first visit, we made a donation to the hostel. Jacqueline gave us a tour of the hostel and then presented us with gifts made by village women. She told us that the craftwork was part of a scheme to help the women become literate and employed. The state of women was in flux, with the Islamic tradition of *purdah* fading, due to a poor economy and the campaign for women's rights.

The filming continued with us taking in the sights. The cultural and artistic Lahore had a long history under various rulers. The centre of the Moghul Empire, it had been capital of the Punjab for the last thousand years. The Moghuls constructed many impressive buildings and gardens, some of which were destroyed under the later Sikh rule. In 1846, the British took Lahore, imposing their own distinctive style of architecture.

The current structure of Lahore Fort dated from 1566, when

the third Moghul emperor, Emperor Akbar, based his head-quarters in Lahore. The fort was on the World Heritage List and it was much larger than either Beth or I had expected, incorporating numerous buildings, palaces, a mosque, pavilion and tombs. The Palace of Mirrors was like being inside a gemstone; the walls and ceiling a myriad of delicate shimmering glass mirrors, reflecting and refracting the light in every direction. The Palace of Mirrors had been designed to protect the Empress and her court from inquisitive outsiders.

Opposite the fort was the Badshahi Mosque, one of the largest mosques in the world. In red sandstone, itself looking much like a fort with massive gateways, its appearance upheld the claim that the courtyard could hold 60,000 people. We read in our *Lonely Planet Guidebook* that the mosque was the scene of an international outcry in 1991, when hardline *mullahs* complained about Princess Diana's visit: her skirt was too short and, as a non-Muslim, she shouldn't have been given a copy of the Koran.

Domes, minarets and towers dotted the city, and the call to prayer floated through the air. Boys and teenagers played cricket on any available patch; one park had about twenty games going at once. In the bazaar, we joined the throng of locals shopping. Barrow boys sold nuts, dates and hot kumera. Sugar cane drink was a specialty; the whole sugar cane was pulped through a machine and poured into a cup at the other end. A stall of books overflowed, spilling under the tables, all over the ground. Jewellers displayed the enormous gold rings and elaborate long earrings worn by the women. Glitzy, gaudy bright fabrics beckoned from the material shops. Men carried rolled-up carpets through the streets, balancing them on their shoulders.

After Pakistan TV had finished, we went to the Central Post Office, accompanied by the freelance reporter. We were hoping the television cameras might pull some weight in the matter of one missing modem.

The day before, we had collected a parcel from Keris. With great excitement, I opened it, to find a letter, photos and some sweets, but no modem. Keris had definitely put it in, someone else had definitely taken it out.

'We'll be able to trace it,' the supervisor had assured us but, by now, we had learnt that people said whatever they thought we wanted to hear.

At the Central Post Office, we were passed from person to person. The senior customs officer wasn't responsible for the missing modem, we had to see the person who had recorded the arrival of the package. That chap said four parcels had come in with ours. All were damaged, so they had to be opened. It was a massive manual system, and I was surprised they could even locate the paper which listed the arrival of the package. We had to fill in forms, write a complaint, ring the post office in Karachi—in short, a string of post office procedures which would get us no closer to our goal.

'You'll never see it again,' one of the cameramen whispered as we followed all the instructions. Struggling through the red tape and paper warfare, unable to get a straight answer from anyone, I became angrier and angrier. It made no difference. Nothing did in this huge bureaucratic entity. An hour later, the post office staff was still saying, 'Yes, we can help. We will get it back.' But in actual fact, no-one could do anything. The modem had been stolen and couldn't be traced.

I was upset for Keris, who had gone to the trouble of buying a new one and sending it to us. And I was devastated that we would no longer have email contact. It had been such a joy to me, checking the email messages, writing to family and friends, as well as interested strangers. It had brought us closer to home. The girls would tell us of their social events, news of the growing Tahni, wedding plans and details of life at the office. I suddenly felt isolated from my world.

We arrived early at the border to India, hoping to cross quickly and drive on to Amritsar. It was 9am, the usual opening border time, but the officials didn't appear until half an hour later. Having seen us on the television news the night before, they were extremely friendly, studying the photos from 1961 and plying us with tea. One official offered to change some money for us, saying Indian banks wouldn't be open on a Saturday. We changed a small amount, and then he promptly told us to hide it because it was illegal to 'import' rupees into India. Beth guiltily folded the banknotes into her maps and sat upon them. At 10am, they let us go, farewelling us with best wishes for the final leg of our journey.

The pleasant half hour at the Pakistani border control lulled us into thoughts of an easy border crossing, so we were unprepared for the next six hours spent on the Indian side.

We knew there was 'bad blood' between India and Pakistan still stemming from the effects of Partition in 1947. India had been pushing towards independence from Britain since the early 1900s, but it wasn't until the 1930s that it started to become a reality. Around this time, the Muslim minority realised an independent India would be dominated by Hindus, so they demanded a separate Muslim nation. Muhammad Ali Jinnah, the leader of the Muslim League and later Pakistan's first governor-general, stated, 'I will have India divided or India destroyed.' Mahatma Gandhi was against Partition, foreseeing chaos in the impossible task of dividing the land into separate Muslim and Hindu regions.

In 1946, the country was thrown into conflict. Riots in Calcutta resulted in 4,000 dead, and the killings continued unabated across the country. The new British viceroy, Lord Louis Mountbatten, hurried a solution, concluding Partition was unavoidable. With his policy of passive resistance and hunger strikes, Gandhi was still urging a unified India. When the division came, it was littered with more civil unrest, yet more killings and the mass movement of around ten million people across the newly defined borders of India and Pakistan. Massacres, conducted by both sides, claimed the lives of hundreds of thousands.

From the beginning, Pakistan faced massive problems, the most obvious being that the new country was in two separate parts on either side of India. Twenty-five years later, East Pakistan seceded and became Bangladesh. Meanwhile, Kashmir was a princely state and hoped to stay independent from both countries. When a band of Pakistani tribesmen attempted to annex Kashmir, both the Pakistani and Indian armies became involved, prompting the first India–Pakistan war. The UN stepped in, drew a temporary border through the country and ordered India and Pakistan to hold a plebiscite. The vote never took place and the temporary border remained, leaving the ownership of Kashmir unresolved to this day.

And now the Kashmir problem was affecting us as we crossed the border. India suspected Pakistan of supplying arms to Kashmiri militants over the border in India. Both countries were using propaganda to discredit the other. The few vehicles which did try to enter India were stripped down in search of concealed weapons. It was a hostile atmosphere; the Indian officials determined to catch the Pakistanis out. Two buses had been held there for three days now. Every nook and cranny was being investigated. The Indian officials had even rigged up a pit so they could examine the undercarriage of the vehicles. Always nearby, the bus drivers were watching the inspections closely, concerned about their buses being returned in working order.

Other vehicles arrived at the border but didn't actually go through. Instead their goods were unloaded and brought to no-man's land. There, they would be picked up by workers from the other side of the border and reloaded on to a new truck. It was the same scenario for an Indian diplomat. Like us, he was coming from Pakistan to India. He and his family had to walk across the border while their bags were deposited in the middle, before being collected by Hindi bearers and carried to an Indian car.

I decided on my usual approach and produced photos of the same border crossing thirty-five years before. Despite the interest, there were still bribes to be paid. 'Visas no good,' one official told us, 'they're in English, not Hindi.' He said he would try to get them stamped, adding that cigarettes or perfume would make the process easier. We passed through arrivals and then it was on to customs. I didn't mind unpacking the car, but having the door panels stripped from our little Beetle would be terrible.

Aware of the stories about officials planting guns and drugs in vehicles, Beth sat resolutely in the Beetle, refusing to leave the passenger seat. We heard that guns had recently been hidden on an overland bus. The driver and backpackers were astonished to discover themselves in strife for 'smuggling'.

In the midst of the proceedings, it was time for lunch, and the whole office closed down for an hour. At 3pm, I finally had some success. The senior official became interested in our 'antique' car and organised an inspection. We unpacked most of our gear and they poked through it. Clambering inside the car, they examined under the seats and inside the glovebox but, thankfully, they decided it wasn't necessary to start stripping bits off, so our Beetle remained intact. Just after 4pm, the customs officials shook my hand and allowed us into India, the last border crossing on our 15,000 kilometre trip.

Chapter 9

From Houseboats to a Moving Palace

November 1961—Kashmir

Tape Recording

Ivan: *Once across the border, we drove to Amritsar, the holy city of the Sikhs in the district of Punjab. We only had three gallons of petrol in the car and needed some Indian rupees, but the bank was closed. On the way from the border, we were accompanied by a customs officer who wanted a lift. Amritsar is a town of narrow streets and small shops, with people sitting cross-legged on the steps outside.*

The next day, it took exactly one hour to cash four pounds! The State Bank of India was a shambles, a maze of papers and books. I wouldn't have a clue how they trade or do transactions. Everyone was looking at our travellers cheques as though they'd never seen them before, which was likely. One guy examined my passport, commenting on the pretty visas, so I told him what I thought of that!

The road has improved five hundred per cent since Pakistan—it's now two lanes. Today we're driving in Kashmir, heading up to Jammu and then to Srinagar. The countryside is very green. As yet, we haven't passed any animal-drawn vehicles, which is a real pleasure. Petrol has also improved a hundred per cent since Pakistan; the car was pinging badly there. Here's Beth to talk about the women.

Beth: *Some of the women in Pakistan and India are very beautiful. Lovely oval faces and lovely eyes. I think their beauty comes from their serenity in a way: their wonderful carriage; they walk very straight and proud. At the other end of the scale are the peasant women, who wear filthy rags but display a tremendous amount of silver and gold jewellery. They wear the old-fashioned amulets on their arms and a piece of gold, the size of a shilling, in the sides of their noses, even children of four years! I've seen a woman sweeping cow and horse manure off the streets while wearing two of these huge amulets up her arms and more bracelets on her wrists. I think whatever money they have is put into this jewellery as a show of wealth. Of course, the well-bred women do wear magnificent saris. I was inquiring into them yesterday at the markets.*

With its snow-capped mountains and vales of green, clear lakes, the Kashmir Valley was considered one of the most beautiful places on earth, and Beth and I were inclined to agree. It had taken us three days to drive up to Srinagar, the solid rain turning into snow at the top of the pass leading to the Kashmir Valley. Even the dismal weather couldn't obscure the beauty of this flat valley, eighty miles long and twenty-five miles wide, encircled by the eastern Himalayas.

The thing to do was to stay on a houseboat in Srinagar. The hundreds of moored houseboats had been built during the British rule. It was their answer to the decree by Kashmir's princely ruler that Brits could not own land in the province. Kashmir offered a cool retreat from the summer heat of the Indian plains.

We met Felix and Maxine the night before we arrived in Srinagar. They were staying in the same *dak* bungalow as us, and also drove a Volkswagen, a campervan. Beth and I found we had a lot in common with this Austrian couple and became instant friends, deciding to travel on together.

On the approach to Lake Dal, our cars were mobbed by the houseboat owners. It was a quiet time, many boats were empty and the owners were desperate for business. Fighting off the others, we chose to look at two and drove down to the lake. There, we were bundled into a *shikara* (a small gondola), which the chap poled out to the houseboats. As we left the shore, the other owners tried to clamber aboard but were repelled with the large poles. Too late, we discovered why. We were on the wrong *shikara* and were being taken to see a different houseboat. Finally, we sorted it out, won our choice of houseboat and settled on ten rupees per night, a discount of twenty rupees because we insisted on doing our own cooking. Between the four of us, it was very cheap.

The *Cherrystone*, an A-Class houseboat, became our home for four days. With its very British interior, we almost felt we were back in London again. There were two bedrooms, two bathrooms and a comfortable lounge area. The old-fashioned furnace came into its own during the cold mornings and nights. It was tended by the two servants. The guide's duty lay in taking us back and forth to the shore in the *shikara*.

While the rain continued, we spent our days in the shops, lured by the reputation of Kashmiri and Tibetan handcrafts. Felix splurged on some antique brassware made in Tibet. We kept within our budget, buying a small cherrywood carved wooden box and a 'Nehru' hat favoured by most of the men. Shopping for food could be done without leaving the boat because vegetable and flower sellers paddled around the lake, peddling their goods from dug-out canoes.

On the third day, the skies cleared and we surveyed the scene, awed by the majestic peaks and massive lake dotted with islands. A *shikara*, poled by two men, took us down the lake to the ancient gardens created during the Mughal reign. We could see that, in the past, these gardens had been grand and luxurious works of art with water features, but now they appeared old, tired and unkempt. Still, it was a lovely day to be out on the water, watching the daily life of the lake: women washing clothes and fetching water for cooking, children playing in the reeds.

We had thought we were used to it by now, but the sight of people publicly squatting for toilet purposes still shocked us. Much human waste was deposited into Lake Dal, and yet the water looked surprisingly clean.

The stunning scenery was an invitation to photograph. We could film the mountains and lakes easily, but the people were more difficult. Whereas the men enjoyed stepping in front of a camera, they carefully safeguarded their women from our lenses. I was thwarted in my attempts to take a single photo of these exceptionally beautiful women. Due to a combination of superstition, protective husbands and the Muslim religion, it was impossible.

Our four-day rest on the houseboat could have lasted four months, but we had to push on. We needed to board a ship before Christmas, and Felix had to be in Chittagong, East Pakistan, for his Austrian engineering firm. For our last night in Kashmir, we went even higher into the mountains. The detour to Pahalgam took us past fields of saffron and purple crocuses. The town itself, below a panorama of fir trees and sparkling snowy peaks, was dissected by two rivers. We rugged up against the chilly evening air, bundling ourselves to bed early. The following morning, the road back down to India took us via a mountain tunnel, an impressive structure blasted through the rock face.

After the peace of Lake Dal, we were once again horrified by the chaos down on the plain. There were few cars, but millions of cyclists, who had no traffic sense and rode right across our path. An old detergent bottle came in handy as a water pistol. Maxine resorted to buying a hooter to get their Kombi van through the traffic. Along with the irrational cyclists, there were pedestrians and holy cows wandering across the road, seemingly deaf to the sound of oncoming vehicles. The dead or wounded stood no chance as scores of vultures circled above, waiting for the next tragedy to provide a meal.

Disliking the hustle and bustle of Delhi, we stayed the shortest time possible, collecting our mail from the American Express office, stocking up on food and visiting the Red Fort built in 1648 by the Mughal Emperor, Shah Jahan. Driving in the city was exhausting, and we felt the fatigue building up, increased by the dirtiness of Old Delhi.

Beth and Maxine both bought saris and had a lesson in wearing them from the Indian women in the YWCA, where we were staying in the married quarters. Beth had admired the women's saris, so they re-dressed both her and Maxine in their own bright clothes. The girls spent the entire afternoon with the women, laughing most of the time.

Maxine was terrified that if she walked, her sari would fall to the floor. Beth felt that Westerners just couldn't carry off the style and said she and Maxine looked like two huge cart-horses, a striking contrast to the elegant local women. Wearing a sari was a skill learnt from infancy. The sari was one big piece of material, wound round the body with no fastenings of any kind. Felix and I took photos of the girls. Beth was right: they looked nothing like the local Indian women.

The Taj Mahal

That first image of the famed mausoleum—we knew we would carry it with us forever. Its impact was astounding: the grandeur and symmetry, the tranquillity and radiance; the starkness of the white shimmering against the dark green trees and water, and against the brown grimy background of the Indian towns. In its reflection in the long pool, the Taj Mahal seemed pure and unspoiled, otherworldly in the clamour that was India.

The love story behind the Taj Mahal was of epic proportions. A Mughal emperor, Shah Jahan, began construction of the mausoleum in 1631 when Mumtaz Mahal, his wife of seventeen years, died. Workers, architects and other experts were brought from faraway regions, including France, Italy, Iran and central Asia. Twenty-two years and 20,000 workmen later, the monument was completed. Every aspect of the building was a masterpiece, from the central dome to the marble screens to the carved designs gracing the walls.

Camping behind the Taj Mahal by the river gave us a different view of the mausoleum. As the sun went down, we watched the white marble transform into blue and purple hues until it was merely a dark shadow. Moonlight would have been remarkable, but our timing was not good. There was no moon. In the morning, we woke early to see the building by sunrise. It was worth every early morning minute.

A Procession of the Dead

The roads to Benares were demanding, but we had some pleasant views: a family of monkeys playing in the trees and our first elephant, a huge one with magnificent tusks tipped with gold. In the villages, we bought bananas, keeping up our diet of twelve a day between the four of us.

In a letter home, I explained a little about the city:

Benares is a holy city in India where all the Hindus wash away their sins in the Ganges River. We toured by boat, looking at the ghats (bathing places) and temples along the banks. Photos were strictly out. We also saw the unpleasant sight of bodies being cremated (as they do) and the ashes being thrown in the river. Benares is the dirtiest city we have seen. In fact, there are many dead bodies lying around, waiting for their turn in the hot box.

That was a sanitised version. For miles outside the city, there was a procession of people carrying dead relatives wrapped in white cloth on litters across their shoulders. Unaccustomed to seeing the dead, we found it revolting. Among the masses were the *sadhus*, pilgrims on a spiritual search, dressed only in loincloths and sporting long, wild hair. We found their appearance frightening and their behaviour unpredictable. Beggars and lepers crammed the streets and riverbanks, demanding money from locals and tourists alike.

Benares terrified us with its hordes of pilgrims, strange religious ceremonies and casual way of dealing with the dead. Moreover, we hadn't realised it was *Diwali*, one of the main Hindu festivals, which meant even more people crowding into the city. To celebrate *Diwali*, candles and lamps were lit, some floating upon the river. We saw the preparations for the evening and, apprehensive of the mobs, we decided to camp a long way from the city.

Beth had been looking forward to the famous silk brocades of Benares. The little open-fronted shops were stacked high with silks of every colour and pattern. Beth chose two lots: one in purple and gold, the other in stripes of yellow and green. Our visit to the government shop ended in an argument with the shopkeeper.

Maxine wanted a piece of beautiful gold brocade and Felix, a hard bargainer, discussed the price with the shopkeeper. Once the piece had been cut, Felix examined it again and found the stripes to be uneven. He complained that it was of inferior quality and refused to pay. The shopkeeper offered a discount, but Felix simply walked out.

The man yelled after him, hysteria breaking his voice. 'I can't sell this now. No-one buy it already cut.' Felix kept on walking.

Beth and I were upset by the incident. We felt Felix had been too harsh, especially as the material was cheap by our standards, while for the shopkeeper, it was his only means of survival.

The following morning, we separated from our travel companions. Felix and Maxine were going north to East Pakistan, while our destination was Calcutta, further south. We were sad to leave them; we had enjoyed each other's company very much, despite Felix's unfair bargaining. And we were sad to be on the last leg of our trip, just three hundred and fifty miles from Calcutta, the city where we had to organise berths on a ship home for the Beetle, Beth and I.

November 1996—India

A Wealth of Religion and History

India was rich in religion. The birthplace of Hinduism and Buddhism, it now flourished with a grab bag of the world's religions: Sikhism, Islam, Christianity, Judaism, Jainism and Zoroastrianism, one of the oldest religions, which we had glimpsed in Iran. Unfortunately, it hasn't always been a tolerant mix; conflict has never been far from the surface. In 1996, the first place we visited in India was the site of unrest, and it characterised the difficulties in this melting pot of religion.

Last time, we had missed the Golden Temple in Amritsar, from lack of either knowledge or time. Now, we gazed upon it in wonder.

The town had been named for the lake surrounding the Golden Temple; *amritsar* meaning Pool of Nectar. The Sikhs looked to the town as the centre of their religion and to the temple as their most holy shrine.

At sunset, the Golden Temple was in its full glory. A soft golden sheen emanated from the walls and domes; a reflection glinted in the pool and the sun was a pinky-orange spreading across the water. Coloured yellow lights hung from the temple, creating yet another layer of gold. The temple was in the middle of a man-made lake, only accessible by a bridge. Encircling the water were magnificent marble walkways while an attractive white building provided the backdrop.

To enter the temple complex, we had to remove our shoes and cover our heads. While Beth looked rather appealing draped in her brown and black Florentine scarf, I felt ridiculous in the pink and gold material wrapped tightly around my head.

In a regal ceremony, the Sikhs, with their large turbans holding up their long hair, marched together, swords in the air. The deep orange and yellow robes blended with the ceiling of dangling gold streamers. Throughout the temple complex, there was an explosion of colour. Wedding groups, people bathing, a Sikh trumpeting—they were all brightly dressed, celebrating their belief. Happiness illuminated the faces, and their joy was shared by us. Our spirits soared with these exuberant people in the stunning setting of the temple. The colourful, festive atmosphere was in lively contrast to the uniform dark clothes we'd seen in Iran.

Partition had separated Lahore and Amritsar, the two main cities of the Punjab. Creating a border in 1947 had been difficult, as Hindus, Muslims and Sikhs lived together across the state. The result was horrendous. Riots, religious massacres and a mass exodus took place. Muslims went to Pakistan and Hindus and Sikhs to India. In the 1980s, trouble again flared in Amritsar, with Sikh extremists occupying the Golden Temple, demanding a Sikh homeland. Prime Minister Indira Gandhi used the Indian Army to remove the Sikhs in 1984, leading to bloodshed and her own assassination by her Sikh bodyguards. Two years later, the extremists once again occupied the temple. Again, the Indian Army was called in and tanks fired into the holy temple. While most of the damage was repaired, a certain distrust remained, and the issue of Sikh independence was unresolved.

Amritsar was a teeming city of more than half a million. It was a festive Saturday evening with people out on the streets. The rickshaw which took us to the Golden Temple battled its way through the fumes, pedestrians, cyclists, buses and other rickshaws. The fellow pedalled furiously, making me even more concerned for our safety, and his. Afraid of the rickshaw tipping over, Beth and I gripped each other and leaned towards the centre. While we were in the temple, our rickshaw waited and then returned us, miraculously unharmed, to our guesthouse, Mrs Bhandari's.

Inside the guesthouse, we stepped back into the 1950s. Dinner was served in the very formal, wood-panelled dining room adorned with an eclectic collection of expensive china, crystal and silver. The ninety-one-year-old Mrs Bhandari had set up the guesthouse in 1955 and recently passed the management on to her daughters. In the backyard, along with the vegetable patch, tethered bullocks and roaming peacocks, there were some old cars up on chocks, lost in a time warp, waiting for work to be finished.

Never commit any evil deeds, accumulate a wealth of merits, completely tame one's own mind. This is the teaching of the Buddha.
Sign in Buddhist Temple, McLeod Ganj

A spectacular drive along a narrow, winding mountain road took us to the heart of another religion. Dharmsala was the home-in-exile of the Dalai Lama and the government of Tibet, who sought refuge here during the Chinese invasion of Tibet. Like all of India, it was a combination of past and present cultures: Indian, British and Tibetan.

In Dharmsala and the upper part of the town, McLeod Ganj, we suddenly felt 'mature'. Most of the travellers were younger people in grungy, ballooning Indian-style trousers, either trekking through the Himalayas or seeking enlightenment through Buddhism. Monks, young and old, male and female, Asian and Anglo, walked the streets in their deep maroon robes, their hair shaven or short. The Dalai Lama himself was not in residence, currently on an international tour. The monastery, temple, meditation and study centres all provided the chance to learn more about Buddhism and Tibetan history and culture.

An enormous prayer wheel held pride of place in the centre of McLeod Ganj. It gave the town a spiritual atmosphere, enhanced by the narrow lanes and lack of vehicles. Cows meandered along the streets, unhindered by humans. The cafés offered a meeting of minds, where locals and travellers gathered for discussions. Prayers drifted through the crisp air. The tranquillity crept into our minds and bodies, and we felt restored and refreshed.

But even in the ethereal Dharmsala, we could find a mechanic who worked on European cars and 'knew' a Beetle. The Nepalese mechanic investigated the petrol smell in the car and replaced a section of the fuel pipe. He was extremely apologetic at having to charge extra for the piece of hose.

In this clear weather, with snow sprinkled over the alps, we could understand why the Tibetans had adopted Dharmsala as their home. It was a magical place. Steep mountains clad in pine forests, fresh air, pristine water, villages clinging to the slopes. The sunshine painted a pretty picture of the Dhauladhar mountain range, but I imagined it to be a harsh climate in winter, with heavy snowfalls and impenetrable roads.

Our guesthouse was one of the many buildings balanced on the mountain's edge, the land dropping away at the bottom of the garden. Eagle views stretched out before us. The first evening we dined by candlelight, a blackout hastening us to find our torches, candles and gas lantern. Once again, we relied on our gas cooker for dinner, a spread of baked beans, eggs and noodles. We were lucky to have such provisions, and I wondered how others coped when the electricity went down for two days.

The guesthouse was a remnant of the British rule, a charming ninety-year-old homestead with terraced gardens, ivy and stone fences. We visited another British relic, the Church of St John in the Wilderness, a little Anglican stone church secluded in the depths of a dense pine forest.

Five decades on from independence, the 'Britishness' of the guesthouse remained. In the formal dining room, we had silver service meals, and each morning, there were fresh eggs for breakfast. During our stay, we had a telephone interview with Elizabeth Heath of ABC Radio in Sydney. Relaxed and happy, seduced by the beauty of the place, we could have waxed lyrical for hours on the mystical Dharmsala. It was far easier than the telephone interview we had had in Iran; then it was difficult to find a balance in speaking about the good and bad experiences, but here in the mountains, every experience had been positive.

The Buddhist monastery and nearby craft centre surprised us with the simplistic beauty of its buildings. A golden roof rested on a painted temple. Surrounding it was a serene garden; a series of courtyards were interspersed by fountains, cool water flowing down dark steps. The craft centre aimed to be self-supporting, providing money for the monastery. Europeans, Tibetans and Indians worked together, sharing skills and ideas.

We met numerous Westerners, all in the region for a reason. Off the beaten track, Dharmsala wasn't the sort of place travellers passed through. In the craft centre, there was a young American chap who'd come to India to do voluntary work. A middle-aged Kiwi couple planned to spend a year in Dharmsala. The husband would study Buddhism, while the wife taught at a local school. This couple defied the image of religious 'drop-outs', for they were ordinary people with children back home in New Zealand. As Buddhists, they wanted to learn more about their religion and make a contribution to the community.

Beth was enchanted by the arts and crafts of Dharmsala: jewellery, pottery, metalwork, painted wood, woven rugs, cashmere shawls and silver antiques from British times. We bought two 'singing bowls', brass bowls which emitted a gentle hum when rubbed with the gong. Then we had to make space in the Beetle for eighty small lacquered wooden boxes, presents for the guests at Liza's wedding.

Again and again, we returned to the same shop in McLeod Ganj run by a young Tibetan fellow. He had been managing the shop since his father retired to do further study and meditation. It was a pattern of working to a certain age and then devoting time to Buddhism. The son now had to support the father.

The placid confidence of the Tibetans struck us. They had an unshakable belief that Tibet would become free. It was merely a matter of time. Faith and optimism carried them through.

Reluctant to head straight back down to the hot, dense air of the Indian plains, we drove on to Simla, another hill station, along a narrow way carved out of the mountainside. Colonies of monkeys scampered by the edge of the road and over the roofs in the village. In the forest, two playful youngsters were jumping upon a sign which read:

To commemorate the 60th birthday of HH Dalai Lama. 1,000 trees planted on 6/7/95. Save trees to save lives.

Some of the roads were unsealed, so my dirt-driving skills were put to the test. I enjoyed the challenge, but Beth, suffering from food poisoning again, wished for smooth tarmac.

The mountain atmosphere evoked memories of our visit to Kashmir in 1961. With its refreshing climate and majestic scenery, I could well understand the Brits' attraction to the mountain region. Simla, the most well-known of the hill stations, was the summer capital during much of the British regime. To avoid the suffocating heat of the plains, the British government would be transported from Delhi to Simla by train, along with the wives, children and a glittering social scene. Set high on a ridge, Simla was a close reproduction of a stately English town, with traditional houses and British names. The Mall, the main street of the town, was for pedestrians but English ones only. Indians were forbidden there until earlier this century.

Despite the similar scenery, Simla had a very different feel from Dharmsala. It was a tourist centre, popular with Indian honeymooners, families and travellers. The streets were lined with hotels and tourist shops. Statues of the two unrelated Gandhis, Mahatma and Indira, graced the town. We found ourselves in the midst of what we guessed was a political rally rather than a religious parade. Men and women marched with loud speakers, banners, drums and an instrument we'd never seen before: long curved horns stretching up above their heads. It was a procession of colour: purple, red, blue and yellow saris among men with patterned hats and flags.

Our hotel was not a part of the colonial past. Built in 1938 by Raja Rana Sir Bhagat Chandra, the ruler of Jubbal princely state, the hotel was still under family ownership. Its claim to fame was as a setting for the movie, *Jewel in the Crown*, a colonial love story between an English woman and an Indian man. The formal gardens, pictured in the film, enveloped the building, creating a private island of tranquillity.

At breakfast, we met six Australian women, dental workers on their way to Tibetan hill stations. Over the past few years, they had been coming to the region for three or four weeks, checking teeth and training local nurses. It made me realise just how many volunteers were making positive contributions to other countries, unbeknown to the general public back home in Australia.

The tourism in Simla had little effect on the banks; it was difficult and time-consuming to change money. The bank could cash foreign currency, but not Australian dollars, no small American notes and none printed before 1990. As usual, there were forms to fill in and the conversion was a manual process. Our reward was a two-inch-high wad of Indian rupees stapled together. Holes in the notes were acceptable, but a tear made the money invalid. Rather than ripping the notes apart ourselves, we asked the bank to do it. They produced a pair of heavy pliers and yanked out the thick staple, leaving two round holes in every note.

Frustrations and Friendships

The Grand Trunk Road had been the main route across the sub-continent for centuries. It chronicled the history of the land, paving the way for invading armies, new religions, languages and culture. During the Mughal rule, *serais* (rest houses like the *caravanserai* of Persia) and trees provided comfort for travellers along the road. Traders and pilgrims traversed its length, while the local villagers utilised smaller sections every day, collecting water and food or herding stock.

We had experienced the Grand Trunk Road in 1961 and, even then, the traffic had been heavy. Now, it was a slow-moving car park, with trucks and buses billowing black fumes. The continuous sound of horns mixed with the revving of motorbikes and scooters, and the chugging of tractors. When we joined the Grand Trunk Road at Ambala, our average speed fell to forty-seven kilometres an hour. Apparently, this was faster than usual because it was a Sunday and the traffic was lighter.

In one hundred kilometres, we saw thirty trucks broken down by the road. The fully laden trucks had either careened off the tarmac during an accident or had a blow-out. Often the vehicles stayed on the road, separated from the passing traffic only by a circle of rocks and tree branches. Repairs were being carried out on the injured beasts right there! Mobile mechanics from the nearest town would set up makeshift garages by the roadside, undertaking full-scale repairs. Towing the trucks to the garage was out of the question—no doubt too expensive and too difficult. Instead, as with so many other aspects of Indian society, everyday life was conducted on the edge of the Grand Trunk Road.

With only a road map of the Indian subcontinent, Beth feared becoming lost in Delhi, but it was easier than she expected. The

Grand Trunk Road brought us close to Old Delhi, and from there we made our way to a guesthouse. Our accommodation was booked for us by Annemieke, an extroverted Dutch woman we had met in Dharmsala. Annemieke, her Indian husband, John, and their two teenage children regularly holidayed in the hill stations to escape the Delhi heat and to learn more about Buddhism. As so often happened, it was the Beetle which introduced us. Annemieke and John saw the car with its New Zealand sticker and wanted to meet these Kiwis who had braved the narrow mountain roads to Dharmsala in a Beetle, when they could have caught the train.

We had three days in Delhi before we were to board the Palace on Wheels. It was a time for organisation: washing clothes; finding information on shipping companies; getting maintenance done on the car; and, of course, shopping.

By chance, there was a telecommunications trade fair near our guesthouse. With my usual stubbornness, I was determined to make my email work and bought a modem chip for our mobile phone. Despite the assurances of the salesman that I would be able to connect to the internet service provider in India, I just couldn't get it to work. That evening I spent hours on the phone company helpline, with no success. It transpired that the chip was designed for local calls only. The following day, I attempted to return it to the shop but had little luck there as well. The company refused to take it back and sent me on a wild-goose chase to stores all over Delhi. Finally, we received a partial refund.

Frustration was building from other angles, too. At the end of each futile phone call, I wondered if foreigners ever adjusted to the Indian system. I was trying to discover dates and costs of the various shipping lines from Bombay to Sydney. My enquiries were passed from person to person, each one claiming no knowledge.

Eventually, I made an appointment at our guesthouse with a shipping agent. The fellow never turned up.

More difficulties came with our booking for the Palace on Wheels. Keris had organised it from Australia, but still there were difficulties: first in locating their office and then with checking our reservation. As I tried to learn which station our train departed from, I saw an enormous rat scurrying across the back of the office. It filled me with dread at the thought of the week aboard the train. I decided not to mention it to Beth.

Just as my frustration reached boiling point, my appreciation of India was restored. We had stopped for lunch at the Imperial Hotel when we were approached by a tall fellow. Introducing himself as the vice-president of the hotel, he said he loved our Beetle and invited us to stay at a reduced rate. We accepted for the following week when we would be back in Delhi for a few nights. I then tried to pay the bill for lunch, only to be politely informed by the waiters that it was 'on the house'.

The Beetle had given us a message. In the mountains, the speedometer had stopped ticking over at 169,400 miles. Some minor repairs (but no new speedo cable) ensured the Beetle would conquer the final leg to Mumbai. The mechanic changed the oil, adjusted the brakes and repaired a puncture. He, too, investigated the petrol smell and found a small leak. At another workshop, new glass replaced the window broken in Turkey. The first repair had been with normal glass and I had been concerned that it might smash easily on Indian roads or during shipping.

Queues of people were sitting in the lane near the garage, staring at a window. Intrigued, I went to see what was happening, and a middle-aged lady in a bright sari stood aside to let me in. Through broken English and large gestures, I began to understand that these people were lining up for lottery tickets. As we approached the window, the woman ordered hers and I paid for it. Everyone was friendly, laughing and watching my every move, trying to communicate with this awfully tall foreigner in their midst. I assumed the winning numbers of the lottery were posted above the window. I didn't know what prizes were on offer, but I imagined it would involve a bookcase full of Indian rupees stapled together in wads!

Meanwhile, Beth was shopping, buying more items for Liza's wedding. She had forty silk handkerchiefs made, one for each male guest and bought some jewellery for Liza. With just one month to go now, the wedding plans were in full swing, faxes flying back and forth regarding the guest list, menu, outfits, flowers, transport. Despite the distance, we felt involved in the planning. If we had been in Australia, the wedding would have been the focus for months on end but, while overseas, we could give our input while retaining our own plans. Now only three weeks from the end of our trip, Beth and I were looking forward to the wedding, knowing we would be home in plenty of time.

Annemieke and John had invited us for a drink at their apartment and then dinner with their close friends, the Ambassador for the Netherlands and his wife. Having travelled in the same clothes for nearly three months, we were at the point where some older items were facing the garbage bin rather than the washing machine. I searched through the Beetle for respectable outfits, while Beth washed her hair and did her nails.

The gracious parks and tree-lined streets made driving through New Delhi a delight. Like most embassies, the Dutch Embassy was in the suburb of Chanakyapuri. With its massive domed entrance hall, this stately white building was reputed to be one of the most gracious homes in Delhi. Once the residence of President Jinnah, Pakistan's first governor-general, its study had seen many dicussions on partition with influential leaders, including Gandhi and Nehru.

It was kind of the Ambassador and his wife, Joop and Els, to extend their hospitality to us, and I had the feeling they were pleased to entertain on a purely social level for a change. The dinner turned into a family evening with the arrival of their daughter and her friends. We enjoyed the interlude from our gas cooker dinners and local restaurants. It was family, friends and conversation, along with a delicious meal dished out by servants in white gloves.

Joop and Els had the same passion as Beth and I—driving. When working in the Middle East, they had travelled home to the Netherlands by car, taking the opportunity to see more of Europe. Fascinated by our trip, they insisted we leave the Beetle in their patrolled grounds while we were on the train. I was relieved by their generosity. We had planned to keep the Beetle at the hotel, but as it still contained most of our possessions, I had had some concerns.

Two days later, we drove the car into the eight-acre grounds of the Embassy and confidently handed over the key. Els packed us into her Mercedes and instructed her driver to deposit us at the train station for the Palace on Wheels.

Regal Rajasthan

Rajasthan was quite different from other parts of India. Ruled by Rajput warrior clans for over a thousand years, Rajasthan had developed its own distinct society and culture. Even during British colonisation, the Rajputs retained control over their regions, in exchange for an economic alliance. Divided by infighting, the Rajput clans were never able to unite their famed fighting skills against a common enemy. Their downfall came under the British, when the ruling class squandered its wealth, creating poor living conditions for its people.

During Partition, the Indian government promised the Rajputs the security of their titles, property and a yearly stipend. In 1971, the government annulled the deal, ending the stipend and decreasing the Rajput property rights. Now, Rajasthan was a mixture of extremes: farmers eking out an existence on the dry land; nomads and shepherds in the desert; grand palaces and forts luring the tourists; women struggling to bring up their children in the towns; former Rajput *maharajas* (rulers) surviving by converting their historic buildings into hotels.

The Palace on Wheels took us on a seven-day tour of Rajasthan in a train furnished to match the luxurious carriages of past *maharajas*. The plush surroundings and air-conditioning were a step up from the Beetle. This was a chance to enjoy yet another great train ride and to see more; the train travelled at night, covering distances as we slumbered. Having the same home for a week, a spacious cabin, was a pleasant change, and we were soon to discover we needed a good rest to keep up with the demanding daily schedule. Each carriage had four cabins, with their own bathrooms and a lounge area for breakfast. There were two dining carriages, containing a restaurant and bar. One afternoon, I was able to count twenty carriages. I guessed that we never even spotted half of the passengers.

Our arrival in Jaipur on the first morning was greeted with fanfare. Garlands of marigolds were placed around our necks, as two painted elephants watched us curiously. The elephants were sumptuously decorated with coloured markings, bright material and gold tassels. Snake charmers in turbans squatted by their baskets, cajoling pythons. It was an interesting display, which showed aspects of Rajasthani culture, but by the seventh morning of such greetings, we felt it resembled a movie set, the director calling, 'Action!' as we stepped from the door of the train. However, I assumed the performers were being paid, which was reason enough for the show to go on.

Jaipur, the capital of Rajasthan, was founded in 1727 by Maharaja Jai Singh II. It was a city crammed with historical sites, mostly painted pink, the colour of Rajput hospitality. Jai Singh was known for his Rajput fighting prowess, but he also studied astronomy and built five observatories across India. Jantar Mantar, the one in Jaipur, was a collection of bizarre sculptures and machinery, massive structures which could tell the time within two seconds. The old city with its wide boulevards also boasted the Palace of the Winds and the City Palace, now partly museum and partly a home for the former *maharaja*.

Lunch was in another palace of the *maharaja* which had evolved into the Ram Bagh Hotel, a marble edifice surrounded by tranquil gardens. Our fourth palace of the day was at Amber, once the capital of Jaipur state. It was more of a fort set high on the hillside. Elephants, saddled with bright coverings, lumbered loads of tourists up the steep slope to the palace. Through the narrow walls we went, terribly slowly. Since all the other elephants passed us by, Beth decided our animal was either very young or very old. Elephants were expensive to feed, we learnt, and hence a perfect gift for a person the *maharaja* wanted to destroy!

An extensive tour of the palace was a window into a previous time. There were quarters for the multiple wives, secluded from all others; a white marble temple; and the hall of victory, overlooking the lake, reflecting every movement in its mirrored ceiling.

17.00 hrs. Return to POW for evening tea and Fresh-n-up.

The wording of the Palace on Wheels itinerary amused me and highlighted our regimentalised day. We still had dinner to go, which involved a bus trip to Nahargarh Fort, where we had a display of dancing and fire-eating, with the standard curry and rice meal. It had been a long day for Beth and me, two travellers unaccustomed to seeing sights at this fast tourist pace.

As we slept, the train rocketed south to Chitorgarh. The remains of the imposing fort signified a far more prosperous age than the present. The Rajput warriors and guards had been replaced by children selling necklaces and postcards they had coloured themselves. At Chitorgarh Fort, the Rajputs had suffered three massive defeats. Their culture, dictating honour above death, favoured *jauhar*, the ritual of Rajput warriors entering a losing battle to go to their deaths, while the women and children burnt themselves on funeral pyres. There was no question of surrender; Rajput men and women would die before putting themselves in the hands of their enemies.

In the defeat of 1535, it was estimated that 32,000 Rajput warriors rode out to their deaths, while 13,000 women killed themselves. This medieval concept of 'upholding' the honour of the people was difficult to contemplate in our modern-day society, where the individual is more important than the group. I wondered what outcome history would have presented had these powerful warriors not practised mass suicide.

It was a three-hour bus trip to Udaipur; the train remained at Chitorgarh, its new broad gauge carriages too wide for the older metre gauge track. The old city of Udaipur conjured up images from fairytale books of palaces floating on lakes encircled by low hills. The Lake Palace did indeed appear as a romantic illusion shimmering in the centre of Lake Pichola. Built on Jagniwas Island in 1754, the palace was now a luxury hotel, which apparently discouraged casual sightseers. We were fortunate, for our tour included lunch there, and we were ferried across in a small, red-roofed motor boat.

It was cooler out on the lake, making the island an obvious choice for a summer palace. The arches, windows and courtyards were designed to catch the wind and distribute a refreshing breeze through the palace interior. Gardens and fountains splashed colour against the cool white marble walls.

The Lake Palace wasn't the only spectacle on the water. Further into the lake was another fairytale castle, the Jagmandir Palace, also a hotel. It was said that this palace had inspired Shah Jahan to build the Taj Mahal.

Back on land, there was no shortage of stunning sights bordering the lake. The City Palace was a massive complex of domed build-ings, extended over the centuries by different rulers. Now it was part museum, part home for the *maharani* and part hotel. Twisting corridors and tiny doorways, the right size for Beth but forcing me to bend in half, had been constructed as a defence to thwart attackers. Balconies and windows provided a lookout over the water, decreasing the element of surprise. For us, they offered wonderful views of the two palaces on the lake, with the backdrop of mountains.

Our first dinner on the train indicated the popularity of the Palace on Wheels trip. The two dining cars had two sittings, run with military precision. My calculations suggested one hundred and twenty guests, with probably an equivalent number of staff. The cost of the trip meant that the passengers were mature and were mostly experienced, adventurous travellers. It was an inter-national mix: Swiss, American, Canadian, Middle Eastern, Pakistani, English and an Indian woman who had been living in the USA. We traded travel tales and life stories.

We hadn't visited a national park in India and were looking forward to Ranthambhore, once a hunting area for the *maharajas*. Now it was a protected wildlife park, sheltering some of India's declining tiger population. However, we were told we were unlikely to spot a tiger. Three years before, park officials had been assisting poachers in their hunting and, since then, the tiger population in the park had halved. Despite the non-appearance of the tigers, it was a beautiful early morning visit. Set in an enclosed valley with a tranquil lake and imposing ancient fort, the park was an isolated patch of wilderness in an India teeming with people. From an open-sided truck, we watched deer and wild boar grazing in the long grass; monkeys chattering in the trees; and crocodiles by the lake. There were numerous species of birds, some balancing on waterlilies while peacocks strutted nearby.

While the other groups lunched on the train at Sawai Madhopur Station, Beth and I picked our way around the rubbish and cows, past the open sewer drain, and headed for the main street of the town. Away from the tourist group, the guides and the tourist markets, we could do the sort of local shopping we enjoyed. We felt more comfortable by ourselves, able to stop at any shop and talk to the locals, rather than being herded along as part of a group. The town was dressing up for *Diwali*, lights and tinsel decorating the street. As usual, Beth was interested in the local fabrics and designs and headed straight for the material shop, where she chose some cotton scarves and silk saris.

We noticed the men using three-tier stainless steel lunch containers, and we bought some. Their price was determined by weight. The three separate containers, held together by a handle, would be perfect for picnics on Balmoral Beach. In Bombay, they were the standard lunch containers for businessmen. Each day, after the husbands set off for work, their wives or cooks would prepare the midday meal of curry, rice and bread, put it into the cylindrical stainless steel container and take it to a pick-up point. All of the colour-coded containers for the suburb were bundled together and transported into the city stations, to join the thousands of other lunch containers. Miraculously, the colour-coded containers would then be correctly delivered by an army of workers on foot and bicycle to the right office and the right businessman!

For most of the day, the Palace on Wheels sped through the countryside towards Jaisalmer in the western part of Rajasthan. From air-conditioned comfort, we could see workers toiling in the fields under the hot sun. When we stopped at the stations, people would press their faces against the dark windows, wondering about this special train, not realising we were watching from inside. It was certainly a different way for us to travel, aloof from real life, protected from the everyday poverty of India.

Jaisalmer was over run with tourists, and for good reason. This desert town, with its majestic fortress and matching stone buildings, was nicknamed the Golden City because of the glow of the sandstone walls at sunset. On the way to the fort, we saw *havelis*, the ancient mansions of rich merchants. These homes were designed around inner courtyards which offered cool respite from the desert heat. Every inch of the courtyard walls was covered in murals and carvings, mostly depicting elephants and peacocks, the favoured bird of Rajasthan.

The art wasn't confined to the walls. In the shops and markets, there was a wealth of local fabrics for Beth to examine (and buy!)—printed, woven, embroidered and appliquéd.

The sandstone walls of the fort blended into the rocky outcrop upon which it stood, making the citadel seem even larger. The fort itself was still in use, a humming, vibrant mini-city of shops, eating places, hotels and temples. Narrow lanes buzzed with humanity without the additional mayhem of traffic, as vehicles were forbidden. Women sold necklaces, rugs and fabrics, all created by local craftsmen.

In one lane, a four- or five-year-old boy was dancing to a drum. His yellow, green and red turban bobbed this way and that as he struck each dance pose. The sound of the drum was accompanied by the jangling of his necklaces and murmured song. His silver waistcoat and watch glittered in the midday heat, and we laughed at his childish sophistication as he winked at us. Everywhere we walked, children yelled 'hello'. Shoes were lined up outside the Jain temples, underneath a sign that read:

Important Notice—Entrance of ladies during monthly course period is strictly prohibited. They are requested to maintain the sanctity of the temples.

A thirty-minute drive from Jaisalmer took us into the Thar Desert, just fifty kilometres from Pakistan. The town's proximity to the border explained the existence of soldiers and an army base. Out in the Sam sand dunes, our expectations of a peaceful camel ride at sunset rapidly evaporated. To our astonishment, we discovered hundreds of tourists, hundreds of camels and hundreds of camel drivers. In this barren desert, there were people as far as the eye could see.

Camel drivers and children heaved the fat tourists onto the back of the animals. It was two per camel on a rough seat of padded material tied under the animal's belly. Laughing, Beth and I recalled our first camel ride at the pyramids in Egypt in 1960. Dudley, our friend from the ship, had told us two important facts about camels: they spat and they had venereal disease. Believing this to be true, we were wary of the animals, afraid of catching germs. Later, we realised that we had naively fallen for another of Dudley's stories. He had been in Egypt during World War II, when it had suited the soldiers to spread rumours of the camels passing on VD to people. Despite the slanderous untruth, Dudley had put us off the animals for life and, in our minds, we always connected the two—VD and camels.

Still, we clambered aboard 'our' camel and set off on a short safari with hundreds of others. The camels were gentle, and it was easy to settle into the long-legged gait as we followed a path among the low dunes. As the sun dropped in the sky, the colours of the desert changed. The sand became a deep gold sea, fragmented by the long dark shadows of camels and people. The setting sun glossed over the reality of rubbish left in the dunes and the poverty of thatched mud huts. Life was exotically picturesque but harsh in this arid region.

Having become slightly blasé about Rajasthan's rich palaces and grand forts, we didn't anticipate the impact of Jodhpur. Perched on the hilltop, the Meherangarh Fort commanded attention from every point in the town below. It was a long, hot journey up to the fort, the path having been laid out with many right angle turns, to deter a rapid attack on elephant-back. As we rounded each corner, a troubadour struck up a performance, dancing or playing music for the tourists, hoping for a tip in return.

As we climbed higher, houses came into view below, giving us a brief insight into town life. Immediately beneath us, the yards backed onto the fortress walls. A sari-clad grandmother squatted by an open fire, feeding it dung fuel while cooking *chapatis*. The dung made up one pile, her dough the other. On the roof and walls of the house, more dung was laid out to dry. Five young children, the boys in shorts and the girls in saris, waved up to us, yelling 'hellohellohello'. We tossed them five pens, and they laughed delightedly, comparing each one. The small dirt yard housed goats, chooks and white rabbits.

From the fort's dominating position, we had a view over the whole town and the surrounding countryside. In one direction, a blue landscape stretched out before us: blue-painted houses, those of the Brahmans, the highest caste in the Hindu system. In the distance, the sun picked up the colours of the low red rocky hills and, further away still, we could make out the silhouette of yet another palace.

High above the land, the fortress, with its rows of cannons, appeared invincible. For many years, it was. The Rathores, a fierce Rajput clan, ruled the region in true warrior fashion, so that it became known as Marwar, the Land of Death. The Rathore warriors were assisted by their horses, a breed they designed for agility in battle and survival in the desert. Presumably, it was in their quest for excellent horsemanship that they developed the riding breeches, jodhpurs.

We were excited to be returning to the Taj Mahal after thirty-five years. But first, we had a morning visit to the Keoladeo Ghana Bird Sanctuary. Seeing the park by cycle-rickshaw gave us a quiet hour and the chance to spot more birds. The grass and wetlands were dotted with a great many species; the park had recorded over four hundred. Beth and I were pleased to have enjoyed a gentle morning before the hullabaloo of the Taj Mahal.

The building was as majestic as in our memories; the surrounds were not. Camera fees were collected, and hordes of tourists vied for the best photo opportunity. Beth described the scene in her diary:

The hawkers outside are the most aggressive we have encountered and hold their goods right in front of you, barring your progress. It is fatal to hesitate

for love and a beetle

or give eye contact. They come around the bus and bang on the windows. As usual, we had to pay a camera fee and then went through a bag check. Video cameras can only be used from the first flight of steps and still cameras from the central platform. Little fellows dash around, assuring you they know the perfect angle for the reflections and are happy to use your camera to take the photo—for a tip. We had photos taken at the same spot as thirty-five years ago. It certainly is an impressive building, with great patterns done in semi-precious stones. There were many Indian tourists, the women in vibrant coloured saris. It made a lively scene.

We had a better view of the Taj Mahal than in 1961. Before, scaffolding had obscured parts of the mausoleum. I joked that now the tourists were obscuring the building! In fact, the multitudes were causing damage, with regular paths wearing down the marble of the floor in numerous places.

The changes in thirty-five years were suddenly apparent to us. Travel was a leisure activity now available to most Westerners. India, in particular, offered good value for the dollar and, like Turkey, it had been inundated with tourists. The overland trail was less popular, but affordable airfares deposited travellers wherever they wanted to go. And all of these tourists were far more knowledgeable than we had been at twenty-seven. Guidebooks, novels, documentaries and movies filtered the information through. Even those who knew little about Partition had been exposed to the blockbuster film *Gandhi*.

It was not only the volume of foreign tourists that had increased. Many more Indian tourists were enjoying their national sights. In addition to the relatively new popularity and affordability of tourism, there was the population boom to consider: India had more than doubled its population since its 1961 figure of 439 million people.

We returned to Delhi train station the following morning. I had enjoyed the Palace on Wheels tour with its vast array of sights, meeting other travellers and relaxing in luxury. We had learnt much about the Rajput princes and their culture and history. But I knew that I couldn't endure such a tour for any longer than seven days. Tours involved waiting around for the whole group to be ready and then descending, en masse, to a site, village or shop. I felt it an imposition to turn up as a regimented group of thirty people. Probably, Beth and I were too accustomed to independent travelling, choosing our own itineraries, pace and destination. I was looking forward to getting back behind the wheel of the Beetle.

Chapter 10

The Last Days
of Freedom

November 1961

Calcutta Culture

Driving towards Calcutta, we noticed a change in the people. They were darker-skinned than the Indians of the west, and some of the children wore Western clothes. We'd seen the symbol of the Red Cross and wondered whether the charity organisation had been distributing clothes, or if these people were wealthier and could afford foreign garments. The countryside was more prosperous, with thatched-roof villages and dense, almost jungle-like bush. As we approached the city, the green gave way to industrialisation: huge factories, steelworks, gasworks and coal mines. The structures of houses and shops appeared more permanent, and the road wider and well sealed.

We also noticed a change in ourselves. Talk of the fascinating sights around us was frequently interrupted now by discussions of finding jobs and a house back home. The truth was that neither of us wanted to return, but it was the right thing to do. I liked to imagine us driving on in the Beetle, negotiating the political problems in Burma and continuing on to China, up through Russia and back to London. A fantastic dream. Reality consisted of ever-diminishing funds and the expectations of society, those of our families in particular. Get a job, build a career, buy a house and have children. It was all mapped out—we had just managed to detour off the map for a short time.

After we had found a place to stay in Calcutta, I recorded the momentous day on tape:

We reached Calcutta today on the thirteenth of November, 1961. That's one day ahead of our scheduled arrival. I think it's pretty good going to drive for three months, almost 15,000 miles, and arrive a few hours ahead of schedule. It has been a wonderful journey and I can recommend it to anyone.

It took us an hour and a half to come the last twenty miles. Calcutta has a population of about seven million, all congested into a small area. I would prefer to drive a thousand miles in the desert in Iran than twenty miles into Calcutta through the local hazards.

By luck, we were camping in an oasis in the very heart of the city. A chap at the men's hostel had sent us to St Paul's Cathedral, where the vicar recommended us to St John's Church. At last, we could use that letter we had carried all the way from London:

The Vicarage, Billingshurst, West Sussex
To whom it may concern,
This is to certify that to the best of my knowledge and belief Mr Ivan John Hodge and Mrs Elizabeth Jane Wendy Hodge are practising members of the Church of England.
Rev. R. Evan Hopkins

Probably, we would have been allowed in regardless, but we were glad to have the evidence. The Reverend E. E. Joseph kindly agreed to accommodate us in the beautiful grounds of St John's Church. We parked the Beetle in a secluded spot against the stone wall, away from the church entrance and close to the back of the Reverend's home. An outside toilet and running water meant we were quite comfortable, sleeping in the car and cooking on our camp stove.

One evening, the Reverend's servant came running over to us with a typed note. A policeman had seen us camping and wondered who we were. It seemed we were supposed to register with the Police Office. Immediately, we rushed to the Reverend's house, where he was still on the telephone. Once we had given our passport and car registration details to the police officer in charge, I apologised to the Reverend for causing him any upset. Both he and his charming wife weren't in the least perturbed.

St John's Church was a bastion from the British Empire. An Englishman, Job Charnock, had founded the city of Calcutta in 1686, and it was to remain the capital of British India until 1911. The cemetery of St John's Church housed the mausoleum of Job Charnock and the graves of other prominent British figures. The monument symbolising the 'Black Hole of Calcutta' was also in the graveyard. After Partition, it had been moved from its rightful position near Dalhousie Square; there it had signified the place where British residents were killed in 1756. During an invasion by the Nawab of Murshidabad, on the night of 20 June, more than one hundred Brits had been crammed into a twenty-foot-square cell in Fort William. The majority had died from suffocation before sunrise.

We'd heard that Calcutta was the dirtiest city in the world. We didn't agree; perhaps we were now accustomed to Indian town life. It was an exciting and surprising city, overflowing with people, and there was something to see on every corner. Our biggest shock came on the first day. A girl of about twenty-five, naked but for a strip of material which covered nothing, stood on a street corner, scratching furiously between her legs. Embarrassed by the sight, we assumed she must have some kind of disease. An hour later, we saw a naked man walking along, not a stitch of clothing on his body. No-one took any notice. Later, we discovered he might have been in the Jain religion. Some of their followers wore no clothes.

Jimmy was a market boy who lugged goods back and forth for customers and traders through the hectic paths of the market place. We were buying fruit and vegetables when he attached himself to us. There seemed to be no way to rid ourselves of him, so we accepted our new shadow. He helped us barter for food and then carried it for us. It was difficult to determine how old he was. Despite the term 'market boy', he was probably just a few years younger than me.

Over the two weeks we stayed in Calcutta, we got to know and like Jimmy. We learned he had a wife and child living in a village near Benares. Not only was Jimmy working to support his wife, but he also had to pay off a dowry debt for his family. One day, he took us to his living quarters: a bed in a minute room, which he shared with members of his extended family. The room opened straight out onto the street. Other houses had courtyards, with the men's rooms on the outside of the building while the women, in *purdah*, were hidden inside. But still, there were many women living on the street. Proudly displaying his street knowledge, Jimmy led us down a lane of prostitutes, young and old, commenting on the price of each one. 'Cheaper for the older ones,' he told me, watching my reaction, then adding, 'if that's what you like.'

The worldly Jimmy knew how to make a buck in the city. Anything we wanted, he could find for us, he boasted. It was time to get some more money changed, and Jimmy said he'd organise it for us. At first, we didn't quite trust him and gave him one pound to test him out. He told us an acceptable rate, took our money and disappeared. Ten minutes later, he re-appeared with our Indian rupees.

The next time, we passed him five pounds to exchange. I was anxious. If he cheated us this time, we wouldn't be able to eat for the next week. Smiling as usual, Jimmy pocketed the money and pointed to a shop over the road. 'I'll change it over there,' he informed us and then dashed through the traffic. We watched him, sauntering along. He came to the door of the shop and kept walking. My stomach lurched. I didn't know whether to sprint after him or wait, in case he'd spotted a policeman inside the shop. In the distance he was striding along the footpath, never looking behind him to see if we were watching or following. Suddenly, he stopped, spun around and headed back towards the shop. Eventually, he returned with our rupees. We didn't ask him what had happened.

When it came to boarding the ship for New Zealand, we couldn't take all our possessions with us. Having seen Jimmy's home, we decided to give everything to him: our camping table, stools, pots, pans, primus stove and sleeping bags. Jimmy was thrilled. It didn't matter to us if he kept the items or sold them, as long as they were a help to him and his family.

At the Customs House Cricket Club, I interviewed Mr Leslie Claudius, the captain of the Indian hockey team. Bruce Turner had given me an introduction. At home, I had played sport with Bruce, who later became the captain of the New Zealand hockey team. While still captaining India, Mr Claudius was also working as a customs officer and dabbling in cricket as a hobby. He invited me along to the cricket club, where I managed to tape a few words as he padded up to be wicket-keeper.

'Hockey is supposed to be the national game of India, but it is not so popular as it was before,' he told me sadly. 'Football has taken its place and then cricket.' Mr Claudius was passionate about his hockey. It was a sport in which India had dominated the world for three decades, and he had won three Olympic gold medals and one silver.

He explained how hockey had shown him the world. 'I've been in various Olympic Games, and I've been to practically all the countries in the Far East: Singapore, Japan, Hong Kong and British East Africa. We went to the continent and then in 1955, to Australia and New Zealand. That was one of my best trips. The players will never forget the hospitality the New Zealanders gave us—the Kiwis, as you call them.' I'd seen India play New Zealand on that tour and was impressed by their skill and determination.

In contrast to the well-travelled Indians, few teams had actually toured India. New Zealand was now coming on its first official tour but, as they weren't visiting Calcutta, Mr Claudius wouldn't be playing. 'There haven't been any tours—only from Japan in 1950, '51 and '52. But now there are a lot of countries participating for the first time in India: Germany, Great Britain, Holland, even Belgium, and maybe we will be inviting East Africa.'

The Indo–Pakistani rivalry was in full swing on the hockey field. In the Olympic Games the previous year in Rome, Pakistan had defeated India one-nil in the final. 'They were a good side,' Mr Claudius conceded. 'Pakistan has never been to India on a tour, only for tournaments.' Mr Claudius said he was retiring at the end of the year. He was disappointed to be finishing his international hockey career, but there seemed no doubt he would keep playing cricket for fun.

Sea Legs for the Beetle

Rumours abounded of cheap tickets to Australia and New Zealand. 'You can easily get a working passage on a ship,' we were told. Beth decided that I could work and she could 'passage'. But one look at the conditions turned us off. And it was unlikely we would be offered a position, anyway. The wharves were swarming with people hoping for a job. One traveller we met had been duped by a sailor. In exchange for a five-pound bribe, the sailor had promised to speak with his captain and arrange a job on the ship. The silly chap handed over the five pounds and never saw the sailor again.

A passage to New Zealand was more expensive and more difficult to obtain than we had anticipated. Despite being a major shipping port, Calcutta had few freight ships and hardly any passenger liners heading for Australia, New Zealand or even Singapore.

We weren't the only ones concerned about raising the fare and finding a ship. In the Amex Office, there was a group of five who had travelled overland in a VW Kombi. None of them had enough money for the passage. A New Zealand fellow had cabled his mother to ask her to pay his airfare of £180. He was already in debt to her for £300 and would be arriving home at Christmas with not one present to give. Some were flying to Singapore and then hoping to arrange a ship from there. One Kiwi couple had split up; the wife was on a ship from Calcutta to Australia, and the husband had gone by train to Ceylon, hoping to find a working passage and earn enough to pay for his fare and the freight of their car.

The shipping agents blamed the government for the problems. They said the government had closed down the smaller individual shipping companies, nationalised everything and standardised the charges. Amongst the shambles, it came down to two options for us: a more expensive fare on a New Zealand cargo ship that would take us all the way to Auckland, or a cheaper ticket on an Indian line to Sydney. We were planning to sign on for the Indian ship when we realised it might end up costing more and taking longer. The ticket would pay the way to Perth and then it would be an additional £1 a day for food on the remainder of the trip to Sydney, which would probably take about two weeks. Once in Sydney, we would have to find another ship to get home to New Zealand.

At the big shipping company of MacKinnon, MacKenzie & Co. we pencilled our names down for the *Wairata* from Calcutta to Auckland. Freight of the Beetle cost £100, plus loading charges. The prices astonished us. It was only £90 to ship the car all the way from London to New Zealand. Our passage was £147 each, plus the price of food if we were delayed in port. We had budgeted for an economy fare, but we were now paying first class. The cargo ships had between five and ten passenger cabins, which were spacious and equipped with their own bathrooms, and hence were all considered to be of first-class standard.

The British fellow at MacKinnon, MacKenzie & Co. told us the cost of loading the Beetle would be £30. Beth and I were becoming increasingly worried about money. Our careful budgeting had been blown out by the high cost of this sea passage. We didn't like to cable our parents for money; mine had already paid half the cost of the car. Asking around the docks about loading charges for the Beetle, we were relieved when a local chap quoted us £12.

Before transferring the Beetle from shore to ship, we gave it a good spring cleaning. We were both pleased at its condition: only a few scratches and stone marks, but no dents. Hopefully Mum and Pop would be happy to receive their well-cared-for, not-so-new, plush European car.

Down at the wharves, a mass of barges were lined up for business. Ours was a fair way out, so we assumed the chap would bring it in next to the shore. He didn't. Instead, the Beetle was pushed from barge to barge across wooden planks! Beth and I shared nervous glances while the numerous helpers reassured us with comments like: 'No cars fall in the river yet, but was close.'

Once the Beetle had made it to the chap's barge, we puttered out to the deeper water where the *Wairata* was moored. This was even more terrifying than rolling it across the planks. Ropes were strapped underneath the Beetle and it was hoisted up in the air. Dangling there, it swung this way and that. I was afraid, not only that the Beetle might fall in the river, but that it might drop on top of us!

Slowly, the car was heaved up to the deck of the massive *Wairata* and placed in the more capable hands of the crew.

The *Wairata* had only eight passenger berths, and Beth and I would share a cabin to Singapore; after that, we were to be parted. Individuals were joining the ship, so separate male and female cabins would be necessary. It was to be a different experience from the social whirl of our cruise ship over to Europe. The *Wairata* didn't even have a doctor on board.

Captain Keyworth preferred to meet his passengers before the journey began and we agreed to come aboard on a Saturday evening. The sight of New Zealand meat, bacon and bright yellow butter evoked memories of home. I was in heaven with my first glass of DB brown ale for nearly two years; it certainly had been a while between cold beers.

Our last week in Calcutta was full of fun and friends. While we were camping in St John's, an Australian couple, Jim and Aina, had asked if we would like to share their room to cut costs. We moved into their large bedsit with an attached bathroom and one single bed, for 15 shillings a night. Two days before we left, Felix and Maxine arrived, having driven non-stop to catch us. While we were pouring coffee for them, there was another knock on the door. This time, it was our Australian friend, Dick. The Landrover had blown up in Agra. Leaving the others to guard the vehicle, Dick had packed half of the engine in his bag and brought it to Calcutta for repairs.

The bedsit was just big enough for all seven of us to cram in. We shared rowdy mealtimes, the food cooked upon our camping stoves.

The whole gang came to farewell us at the wharf. Maxine gave us a bunch of roses, and I had a posy of flowers delivered to our cabin for Beth. We were sad to be leaving our travelling comrades, these like-minded people who were such a part of our overland experiences. Beth and I would have liked to spend months touring India, living cheaply, but it was time to settle down. Bittersweet feelings engulfed me. The thought of seeing our families and friends again filled us with joy.

It was the 27 November when we set sail from Calcutta, down the river and out to the Bay of Bengal. There were to be numerous calls at ports: Ceylon, Malaysia and Singapore, which meant our arrival in Auckland would be in the new year, 6 January, 1962.

Watching Calcutta fade into a haze, I wondered what the future would hold. In the local market, a fortune-teller had asked to read my palm before insulting Beth by calling her 'snake eyes'. Beth's blue eyes were a shock to the brown-eyed Indians. The fortune-teller was dressed respectably in a sari, and she spoke good English. As we stood on the pavement, she made obvious comments about us going on a long journey. After that, it became more interesting. 'There is a white P,' she said, 'and behind that much blue. You live in a big house on a hill and three children will come. You be successful,' she told me and then added, 'and when you come again to India, you pay more money.'

Thirty-five years later, all of her predictions had come true. She had seen the logo of Prudential, the company I worked with, our first house, our three daughters and the 1996 'second honeymoon' to India.

November 1996—Delhi
Beth's Birthday

Back on solid ground in Delhi, after our week rocketing along in the Palace on Wheels, Beth and I gave ourselves another treat, a Kerala-style massage. It was suggested to us by Annemieke, who often went to this particular health centre.

Reading the brochure while waiting for our appointment, we got the impression that this six-hundred-year-old tradition claimed to cure everything:

> *The Ayurveda Kendra specialises in Ayurvedic Treatment of the ancient medicinal heritage of Kerala for all rheumatic ailments, including Paralysis, Arthritis, Gout, Sciatica, Slip-disc, Polio and Spondilitis. It is also found to be the most effective form of treatment for Sinusitis, Migraine, Histeria, Insomnia, Insanity and Psychosomatic Diseases.*

Treatments were offered for almost every ailment: earaches, deafness, dryness of the mouth, fever, depression, speech impediments, chest congestion, sleeplessness, senility, hallucinations and even infertility.

We were undergoing a Pizhichil massage, 'effective for health promotion, relaxation from stress and strain, good for muscles and nerves, and an almost sure cure for all rheumatic ailments'. After dressing in a muslin nappy, I lay down in a shallow trough and basins of warm oil were poured over my body for two hours. Three men surrounded me, one on either side swishing and massaging the oil into my skin, while the third was collecting the oil and re-heating it. It was an incredible sensation all over—the scent of the medicinal oils, the warmth on my skin and the massage relaxing my muscles.

The masseurs identified the sore spots, my arthritic knees and elbows, and focussed on rubbing more of the oil into these. Another concoction was poured over me and then hot towels wiped away the greasy oil. On leaving the health centre, Beth and I felt light-headed and light-limbed, our bodies so relaxed they were drifting away from the footpath.

We would be on the road for Beth's sixty-first birthday, so we celebrated before we left Delhi. One evening we bumped into Don and Geri, an American couple from the Palace on Wheels. It was Don's birthday as well, and they insisted we join them at a French restaurant. The delicately flavoured food was a refreshing change from our usual curry and rice dinner. On the following night, we invited Annemieke, John, Els and Joop to dinner in the restaurant at our hotel. Annemieke presented me with some prayer beads and gave Beth an iron wall hanger for burning oil. When Els realised it was Beth's birthday, she sent her driver home for a very special gift from the Himalayas: a beautiful quartz rock encrusted with crystals.

It was a pleasant interlude before the drive down to Bombay. The Beetle was to be shipped on the 28 November, and we had to arrive by the twenty-second for freighting and customs formalities. At least four straight days of driving were ahead of us.

We didn't suspect that the last week of our overland trip would be the worst.

From Delhi, the first day's drive was two hundred kilometres, at a slow forty kilometres an hour, to Gwalior, an ancient city in Madhya Pradesh, India's largest state. It was Beth's birthday; she had a cold and felt sick and exhausted. The slow drive in the congested, polluted traffic didn't help. We wondered how the flocks of sheep and goats managed to breathe as they were herded along the main road through the billowing trucks.

Beth had an interest in the region around Gwalior after reading the book *India's Bandit Queen*. In the 1970s and '80s, the area had been terrorised by *dacoits*, bandits attacking and robbing villagers and truck drivers. Some *dacoit* gangs stole from the rich to give to the poor, but they were also involved in caste conflicts, murdering for disputes over land and honour. Surviving in the inhospitable ravines, most *dacoits* escaped capture. Police crackdowns in 1982–3 saw many innocent people threatened and killed. In a bid to restore peace to the region, the *dacoits* were encouraged to surrender.

One of the most famous *dacoits* was India's Bandit Queen, Phoolan Devi. Born a poor village girl, she was married at eleven years old to a man more than three times her age, who raped her and then took another wife. Phoolan Devi had tradition and circumstance against her at every step. In a country where land meant life, her family were embroiled in a property dispute which eventually saw the dishonoured Phoolan kidnapped by *dacoits* on the orders of her uncle. Soon after her capture, the gang leader was shot in a struggle for power, and the new leader took Phoolan as his possession.

The new leader and Phoolan became lovers and together they set up their own band of *dacoits*. The romance didn't last long, however. Her lover was killed by another *dacoit* band, who subsequently spent several days gang-raping Phoolan. She managed to escape and then went about creating her own band of *dacoits*. National notoriety came with the massacre of twenty-two upper caste Hindi men in the village of Behmai. The men were killed in revenge for their association with the murder of her lover and the rape and torture perpetrated against Phoolan.

In 1983, after five years of living as a bandit on the run, Phoolan surrendered. She agreed to eight years' imprisonment, in line with the sentences of male *dacoits* who had surrendered. But while other *dacoits* were freed after eight years, Phoolan was still in jail ten years later.

Beth discovered the end of the story in our *Lonely Planet Guidebook*. Phoolan Devi was released in 1994 and now lived in Delhi, working as an activist on social and prison reform. Once despised by the public for her crimes and for breaking traditional female boundaries, Phoolan had become a national celebrity, of great media interest and the subject of films and books.

Her life story was a reminder of the status of women in India. Despite the push for feminism in the cities, women in villages still suffered enormously, burdened with the highest workload and subject to the complete dominance of their husbands and male family members. As divorce was a disgrace, there were many cases of women burning to death in mysterious kitchen fires. Officials labelled it suicide, but it was often murder.

Speed Humps and Potholes

Our map of the Indian subcontinent showed the main roads, but there was no way of guessing their condition or the volume of traffic we might encounter. Twice, navigator Beth decided to check with the tourist officers at the hotels. Both times the tourist officers promised the route selected would be good, and both times they were wrong.

Part of the way from Gwalior to Bhopal was the worst road we'd come across in our three-month trip. To avoid the trucks, we had taken a secondary road. 'It's a good dual highway,' the tourist officer mistakenly informed us. It was more like one and a half lanes wide; each oncoming vehicle sent us into the dirt. We were crawling along at ten miles an hour, the Beetle rattling with every pothole, our bones jarring with the bouncing. A somewhat unnecessary row of speed humps flanked each village; high and unexpected, they came in lots of three, forcing us down into first gear.

Our slow process through the villages was accompanied by the joyful sight of laughing children. When we stopped to chat, the children seriously examined my tall frame and burst into yet another fit of giggles. At garages, the attendants assessed my height, then glanced, perplexed, from me to the Beetle, wondering why a giant would be driving such a small car.

Clothes strung out to dry flapped from every available space; ropes were rigged from the thatched roofs to the verandahs of whitewashed houses. Women dressed in bright yellow, green and red saris carried water from the wells, balancing the full buckets and pots on their dark hair. *Diwali* was in full celebration. Tractors were draped with tinsel and even the animals sported decorations. The heads and horns of goats, buffalo and oxen were painted blue, red or green; sometimes the artist had attempted an intricate tri-colour stripe. We wondered how they had made the animals stand still long enough.

The scenery was interesting, although a little desolate. Accustomed to seeing people everywhere, we became concerned about breaking down in this lonely scrub, the thoughts of bandits still in our minds. At one point, we even managed a toilet stop without a person in sight. We reached Bhopal in daylight, glad not to be driving in the dusk.

We didn't believe the road could become even more diabolical until the following day. Once again, we had hoped to avoid the truck traffic by taking a secondary route.

18 November 1996

Beth's Diary

Early rise at 6:30am after a restless night—thank goodness, my cold is better. We had decided to travel on 'yellow' roads (highways, not motorways) as we were more likely to find accommodation, and the 500km to Nasik on the Grand Trunk Road was too ambitious. It was a wonderfully interesting drive, but the roads were a disaster. Never have we travelled on their equal: the usual types of traffic on one sealed lane, which was deeply potholed and corrugated; there was just no way to pick a route through the holes without jarring the car. Came close to hitting a cyclist, who made a right-hand turn as we were passing him.

We had booked a hotel at Jalgaon, but at 4:30pm were still 90km short of this and averaging 30 km/h. Night falls quickly at 6pm, and it is very dangerous to drive in the dark. There was a town marked on the map, but I had no idea if it would offer accommodation. We were very relieved to come across a Rest House in Burhanpur and have collapsed here.

Our room is large and plain, with 1950s furniture, but clean, $3 for the night. The bathroom has a handbasin, a squat toilet and a tiled square base to stand in, with a jug of water to throw over oneself. Many mosquitoes! I have sprayed the room, sprayed myself and plugged in our mosquito repellant. We're using the sheets Judy screenpainted for us and my mother's duvets. For dinner, it looks like packet soup and cracker biscuits, plus one mandarin and one banana. The fellow who runs the Rest House served us tea in old china cups, in the rattan chairs on the patio.

Today we decided not to ask locals their opinion of the road and distances between towns any more; every answer has been completely wrong. Anyway, we're here now, safe, comfortable and grateful to have a bed. Tomorrow we will face the road again. Back to the Grand Trunk Road and then we stay at Nasik, where we will decide whether to go to Pune or Bombay.

On the Grand Trunk Road, we had the trucks to contend with. Despite a truck speed limit of 40 kilometres an hour, the 'kings of the road' were hurtling along, overtaking buses and missing oncoming vehicles by inches. We calculated there was a truck accident or breakdown every five kilometres, bringing the traffic to a halt as the vehicles stayed on the tarmac. The newspaper reported on a government crackdown on truck pollution. We laughed, considering it impossible. Often the fumes of the trucks were so thick we couldn't see to overtake.

By the sides of the road, we saw tree painters at work: three men painting white and red rings at a certain height around the tree trunks. Presumably, the rings were like the reflectors on Australian highways, marking the edge of the road to assist with night-time driving.

Rudyard Kipling had described the Grand Trunk Road as a 'river of life' and, indeed, there was much to see as we stopped and started our way along. The environment had changed to fields of dense crops of hay, corn, grapevines, mustard and cotton. Scarlet chilli was laid out to dry in the sun and purple onions were being harvested, all hands helping to pile and husk the onions, then bag and transport them. Eight bullock-drawn wagons were pulling several families and their possessions. Gypsies? Nomads?

Pilgrims? We didn't know. Dressed in rags, the children were playful and had lovely faces, but we could see the ravages of the hard life on the older members. Their weather-beaten faces were tired, far more lined than others their age.

In Nasik, we decided to approach Bombay from Pune. Although this way appeared a longer route on the map, we heard that the Grand Trunk Road was extremely slow from Nasik to Bombay, the 176 kilometres taking six to seven hours. This time, our information was correct. The road to Pune was good, and the Beetle accelerated to sixty kilometres an hour.

Pune, our last day of sightseeing on the trip, characterised what we felt about India as a land of contrasts and contradictions. By chance, we stopped in front of the famous German bakery, and I ordered cappuccinos and cake while Beth sent a fax to her mother at the nearby international phone booth. Falling into conversation with two German ladies, I discovered they were in Pune to attend the Osho Commune.

The Commune was set up by Bhagwan Shree Rajneesh, an Indian guru who had moved to America, attracted numerous followers and spent the proceeds on several Rolls Royces. After being deported from the USA, the Bhagwan unsuccessfully tried to organise ashrams in various countries, before returning to the commune in Pune. Although he had died six years before, the Bhagwan's teachings were still popular. They were based on a combination of different religions and alternative ideas.

The two German women offered to show us around the outside of the Commune. It wasn't visiting time, so we could only peer through the gates, glimpsing black buildings and lovely grounds. An intricately designed fountain was like a maze on a wall; with no starting or finishing point, it reminded Beth of an Escher drawing. One of the Germans had been coming to this ashram for ten years, staying a month each year. Most of the visitors were Europeans escaping from real life for a short while.

Walking through the Osho Teerth, a serene garden for meditation, we asked exactly what happened inside the walls of the Commune. The women explained they went to classes each day—meditation, awareness and so forth—and also spent time relaxing in the pool and massage parlour. After our last massage, I was keen for another and suggested to Beth that we check in just for the massage.

Free love had been associated with the Bhagwan, and he was nicknamed 'the sex guru' by the Indian media. I wanted to find out if the Commune members were stripping off their maroon robes and undertaking sex as a means to enlightenment. Unfortunately, the women divulged little, only saying that any person who entered the Commune had to undergo an AIDS test. Beth quashed my suspicions, noting the Commune appeared subdued and tranquil, an unlikely environment for rampant free love.

From the commune of this guru, we moved on to the museum of a true leader. The Gandhi National Memorial was set in a poignant building: the Aga Khan's palace, where Gandhi and his group had been under house arrest for two years. During this time, Gandhi's wife and a friend had died.

There were few people in the museum, mostly Indian tourists. It was a restful place, honouring Gandhi and impressing on us his strength and determination. The ashes of his wife, Kasturbali, had been placed in a memorial in the garden. One of the many signs listed the events which occurred in the palace.

Some milestones in Mahatmaji's Life at the Agakhan Palace:
Gandhi and his wife Kasturbali were interned in this place in 1942 after the declaration of the 'Quit India' resolution. He was

accompanied by Miraben Shri Pyarelal Nayar, Smt Sarolini Maell, Dr Sushla Mayar and his personal secretary Shri Mahadevbhai Desai.

10 August 1942 Gandhi and his colleagues were brought here from Bombay.

15 August 1942 Shri Mahadevbhai Desai died of heart attack.

19 March 1943 Sarolini Najdi released because of ill-health. Gandhi's last fast.

26 January 1943 Gandhi hoisted the congress flag at these premises.

26 January 1944 Gandhi hoisted the congress flag at these premises.

22 February 1944 Mahashytratra Kasturbali breathed her last after a prolonged illness.

6 May 1944 Gandhi and his colleagues were released from Agakhan Palace.

Like so many others before us, we wondered at Gandhi's achievements in the push for independence from Britain, and whether he could have made a difference to India's future had he not been assassinated in 1948. When Partition was decided upon, Gandhi was still calling for a peaceful, united India. Perhaps his policy of passive resistance was too idealistic for the realities of the sprawling, turbulent subcontinent. Gandhi had been a great man, an enigma to world leaders accustomed to the tools of violent protest, battle and war. The Gandhian concepts of non-materialism and passive resistance were outside their experience and understanding.

1996—Bombay

The End of a Long Drive

A hundred and ten miles took us from Pune to Bombay, our final destination. As we drove down the steep hills, the vast expanse of Bombay stretched out below us, half hidden by a haze of pollution. We were having a bet, twenty rupees for the first to spot the ocean. While I was concentrating on the road, the bends and the trucks, Beth shouted delightedly, 'I can see the sea!' It was a refreshing sight. We both suddenly realised how much we had missed it.

As Beth directed me to the hotel, I felt inordinately proud. The three of us had made it. We weren't twenty-seven-year-old spring chickens, but we still had that adventuring spirit, the guts and the flexibility to survive three months on the road in the Beetle. And the most incredible thing was that I felt exactly the same as last time: I could turn the car around and do it all over again.

The grin on Beth's face grew wider and wider. She knew what I was thinking. 'Perhaps we should go to the wedding first, Ivan,' she reminded me, 'and then we can start planning the next trip.'

I was wrong—we still *were* twenty-seven years old. The enthusiasm, the fun and the love were all still there; we just had more responsibilities added to our relationship.

In the midst of our euphoria, I decided that we must have been blessed with a guardian angel. On both trips, the biggest problem with the Beetle had been a flat tyre. While our daughters were worried about the dangerous situations, like the Turkish-Kurdish war zone, the real threat lay in the everyday—a car accident.

Now that we were safely in Bombay, I could laugh at the Indian road rules in the *Lonely Planet Guidebook*:

Drive on the Left—Theoretically, vehicles keep to the left in India; in practice most vehicles keep to the middle of the road on the basis that there are fewer potholes in the middle . . . Overtaking—In India, it is not necessary to ascertain that there is space to complete the overtaking manoeuvre before pulling out. Overtaking can be attempted on blind corners, on the way up steep hills or in the face of oncoming traffic . . . Use of Horn—Although vehicles can be driven with bald tyres or non-existent brakes, it is imperative that the horn be in superb working order.

Four days in the city were enough to organise freighting the Beetle and our flights home. Bombay had become our final destination because the port in Calcutta was silting up and receiving fewer cargo ships.

Despite having arranged the shipping two weeks before, we discovered it was not all as we had thought. The Beetle had to be shipped empty, we were told, and all of our possessions taken out. We convinced the agent to allow the unused tent and camping gear to remain in our jetbox on top of the car, and then we set about disposing of everything we could. This time, we gave our travelling items to the staff in our hotel.

We had been told the payment could be on credit card, but the agent informed us that a certain portion of the shipping charge had to be paid in cash and that I had to sign a statutory declaration to the effect that I was the owner of the car. In India, these seemingly minor tasks were lengthy and time-consuming procedures. A mountain of customs papers had to be completed, including a full list of the camping gear remaining in the car.

Despite the frustration and difficulties, we put it down to the experience of India. And we made friends. The female representative of the shipping agent invited us to lunch at a restaurant by the sea. Over a delicious meal, she asked about teaching opportunities in Australia, as her mother hoped to teach there. Drawing on her long career in the teaching field, Beth was able to provide help and advice.

Organising our plane tickets was a snap, compared to the shipping. With Qantas now flying twice weekly to Sydney, there was no problem getting onto a flight. Months ago, we had booked a tentative date. It was simple to change this, and we were given assistance with our excess baggage, the fruits of Beth's many shopping expeditions, which we had wrongly assumed could be shipped home in the Beetle.

In between the administrative tasks, we still had time to wander around the city. Photos were taken of the Beetle, Beth and I at the Gateway of India, a stone arch facing out over the sea. A man offered Beth a set of postcards, 'Ecstasy in Indian Temples', showing murals and statues in fascinating sexual positions. Laughing, she turned him down, but it reminded us that there was so much more we wanted to see. We had read of a town three days from Bombay that was famous for its temples and exotic, erotic sculptures.

Palm trees lined the sandy beach near the Gateway, behind which the chaos of the city began. The crowded streets were filled with Ambassadors, which was the regular Indian car. There were high-rise blocks everywhere, and multi-storeyed colonial houses with balconies. Everywhere, too, boys played cricket. I joined a game in a lane, the boys cheering at every ball I missed, pleased to encounter a worse player than themselves.

In the very early hours of Monday 25 November, 1996, we departed from Bombay airport. We had left the Beetle parked in the street, the key in the hands of the shipping representative. This time it was a sixteen-hour flight via Singapore, instead of a six-week voyage. The world had become smaller.

No-one was there to greet us at Sydney airport. Bleary-eyed and wearing the last of our good clothes, we watched Indian families reuniting with love and happiness. Suddenly, a familiar figure came running in through the automatic doors. 'You're early!' Britta cried, and then, 'Where's Keris and Liza? They should be here.' Eventually the other two girls arrived, showering us in hugs, kisses and apologies. The excitement of his grandparents' return wasn't enough to keep young Tahni awake. In the middle of the commotion, he stirred, glared at us with half-opened eyes and then fell asleep again. I empathised; after the plane trip, I was also looking forward to a good rest in my own bed.

'Your car broke down, Dad,' Keris explained. 'It just died in the Harbour Tunnel. Luckily Liza and Rob were driving past, so they stopped. I jumped in with Liza, and we left Rob stuck in the tunnel with a dead car full of flowers and balloons.'

We had to laugh. Our 1960 Gulf Blue Beetle sedan had made it eleven thousand miles from London to Bombay, while our new Mercedes couldn't make it to the airport.

For Love and a Beetle

Friends were made and remembered on both trips, although some couldn't be found and others didn't want to. When we passed through Austria in 1996, I contacted Felix, with whom we had travelled in Kashmir thirty-five years before. Surprised by my call, he was unwilling to reminisce. He and Maxine had broken up many years before, and the holiday in India was a lifetime ago.

In Sydney, we contacted Audrey and Mary, the Australians we'd met in Europe. We caught up with them once or twice before losing contact altogether. Often, we thought about the people we had met in 1961, particularly the Landrover crew (Dick, Pat, Sally and June) and our Indian flatmates, Jim and Aina; we wondered where their lives had led. And Jimmy in Calcutta—had he ever paid off the dowry and started to earn money for himself?

For me, part of the joy of the journey was the people: the locals, the travellers, the customs officials. Marc, the French motorcyclist, had been infected by the travel bug. We received regular postcards from him and his wife; they were in Spain or Italy or back in India. Once he started travelling, he just couldn't stop. The Dutch couple, Nannike and Geert, sent us a note with the news that they had finally returned to Nepal and were working as volunteers with the Himalayan Dog Rescue Squad. Our friends in Delhi, Annemieke and John, stayed in touch with letters about their life in India.

The year after our trip, we met up again with the PR team from Volkswagen in Germany. We had stayed in contact with Sabina and, while we were in London, she invited us over to Wolfsburg for our story to be filmed by German television. The New Concept Beetle hadn't yet been launched, but we were hearing more and more about it. Once again I suggested that as old, experienced Beetle fans, we could take the new one on a world tour, driving it wherever they liked.

Sabina and her new colleague, Emanuela, took us out to lunch. We discussed the footage of our two Beetle trips, and then Sabina announced they had a surprise for Beth and me. At 2pm exactly, she led us down to the test track. There were cars parked on the track, hidden underneath weatherproof covers. Beth and I glanced at each other expectantly, hoping our hunch was correct. A few minutes later, we were asked to sign a secrecy agreement in German. And then, two New Concept Beetles were unveiled.

Beth and I appraised the sleek, black machines before clambering in to be raced around the speed track. We were overwhelmed. Our excitement shifted into an even higher gear when the test drivers asked if we wanted a turn. Both Beth and I jumped at the chance to have the steering wheel in our hands. I undertook every manoeuvre with the utmost care, determined not to damage the prototype. As soon as we had stepped out of the cars, Sabina and Emanuela leapt into the seats, and we realised that it was also their first opportunity to drive the new Beetle.

While nothing could ever match the original Beetle, I was impressed with the New Concept, although they had moved the engine to the front, taking away one of the quirks of the original. Beth liked the little flower vase on the dashboard; there would be no problems of where to put the roses I gave her.

'What do you think?' Sabina asked.

'I want three—no, four,' I replied. 'One for each of my daughters and one for us.'

It was unlikely we'd even get one. Despite the fact that the affordability of the 'people's car' had been replaced by a luxury price tag, orders came flowing in as soon as the New Concept Beetle was launched in America in 1998. Customers were put on a waiting list, and it was likely to be another year before a left-hand-drive version was produced. But we were keeping an eye on the new Beetle, hoping for another chance to drive the car when it reached Australia.

In the meantime, our old Beetle had found a new home, arriving from Bombay onto Australian soil for the first time in its thirty-five year history. The year after the trip, we resigned ourselves to short distances in the Beetle, four kilometres from our house to the office. Various clubs asked me to speak on my Beetle travels at their functions. One day, I was amused to find myself chatting about our little Beetle to a group of Rolls Royce owners.

People often wrote to me to ask advice on planning long car journeys. I had an interesting email from a fellow in Zaire, Denis Le Jeune. He had my name from Paul Buckett, the PR officer in the UK, and wanted some tips on finding mechanical help for his Beetle when driving through southern Europe and the Middle East. His trip was part of the London-to-Cape Town Rally for classic cars. When I responded to his email, we discovered that we had much in common, including the fact that we'd both spent our honeymoons travelling by Beetle and then sold the cars to our mothers!

Dear Ivan,

Strange parallels in our lives! I'm also in insurance, having started in Cape Town, but spent the bulk of my career in Belgium and Belgian Congo/Zaire. My Beetle was given to me as a wedding present by my father, and I drove from Congo to Cape Town to get married, the honeymoon being spent doing the same trip in reverse. In 1960 we planned to drive the Beetle to Europe via Ethiopia and the Middle East, but the country blew up at Independence, and I sold the car to my mother. She trundled round Lubumbashi in it until her 80th birthday!

We then drove it down to Cape Town as a Silver Wedding 'outing', so when we first heard of the London–Cape Town Rally, taking place in the year of our ruby wedding, we just had to enter ourselves!

The 'Classic Reliability Trial' leaves London October 25th, arriving Cape Town December 4th, 1998, and after the countries mentioned in my first email, to Egypt, then an airlift (to avoid Sudan/Ethiopia and north Kenya roads ruined by 'El Nino') to Entebbe, across to Kenya, Tanzania, Malawi, Zimbabwe, Zambia, Namibia and south Africa. Thirty-nine Classics are entered, mine being the only Beetle, and also the second smallest.

I'm making the whole thing a bit more of a challenge by trying to raise $200,000 for charity (Orphanage in Kinshasa and White Rhino game reserve in north East Congo), mainly by using the Rotary International network (I've been a lifelong member); I worked out that the route we are taking goes through about 500 Rotary Clubs, with maybe 20,000 members.

Hope you can come along! All the best, Denis

Beth and I didn't make it to the Classic Reliability Trial and we never learnt the outcome of Denis' trip, but we did manage our next Beetle jaunt at about the same time. It was only in the one country, no visas or customs checks involved, just a long drive across the world's biggest island. A cousin was to be married in Perth, so we forsook the usual five-hour flight for a leisurely two weeks of driving the Beetle.

Sydney to Perth via Adelaide reinforced the beauty of our own country: the Blue Mountains, dry plains, outback towns, sand dunes in the desert, carpets of wildflowers, long beaches and dramatic cliffs looking out over the Southern Ocean.

We suffered the same fate as in 1961—breaking down in the desert (a fuse seemed to be the problem), and running out of petrol amongst the stunning wildflowers. Both times, we were rescued quickly by friendly locals. Instead of driving back home again, we introduced the Beetle to yet another form of transport, the Indian Pacific train, which took three nights to bring us back to Sydney.

Now that the Beetle has done its duty at Britta's wedding, chauffeuring the pageboy, young Tahni, to the church, Beth and I are looking forward to planning our next journey: South America or Canada or, my greatest dream, Burma. Thirty-five years on from our first trip, the political situation in Burma was still unstable and, once again, it had been impossible for us to cross the country. While the world had advanced in so many ways, the same conflicts remained.

We're not sure where our next trip will take us, the sights we will see or the characters we will meet. But I do know that it will be yet another long drive and the chance to experience different lives—all for love and a Beetle.